It Took
H EROES
Volume II

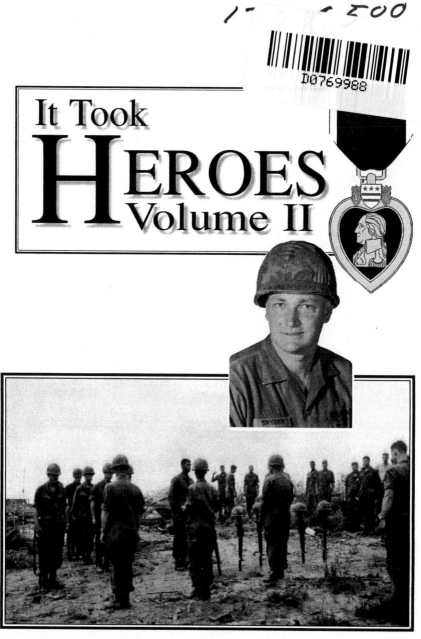

**Continuing the Story and Tribute
To Those Who Endured the
Darkest Days of Vietnam**

It Took

H EROES
Volume II

**Continuing the Story and Tribute
To Those Who Endured the
Darkest Days of Vietnam**

CLAUDE D. NEWBY

Copyright © 2000 by Claude D. Newby
All rights reserved.

About a half dozen names have been changed. The situations and events surounding these individuals, however, are real.

Published by: Tribute Enterprises
                  Bountiful, Utah
     Contact: (801) 299-1621
       email: cdnewby@deseretonline.com

Production by: SunRise Publishing, Orem, UT
                  www. SunriseBooks.com

ISBN: 09678431-1-1
Library of Congress Catalog Number: 00-190365

Table of Contents

Preface

Initially, this work was part two of a much larger book. Part One was published under the title, *It Took Heroes: One Chaplain's Tribute to Vietnam Veterans and Those Who Waited for Them.* It was my first publisher's idea, not mine, to divide the original manuscript into two separate books.

This second book, like the first one began as part of my autobiography. Sometime before 1995, I listed several good reasons for writing my life story, a wish to pay tribute and give due credit to key people for their influence in my life, to leave something for my posterity, and. Deeper down inside me, though, something gnawed at me, some motivation that my stated reasons failed to satisfy.

In the words of General H. Norman Schwarzkopf, "It doesn't take a hero to order men into battle. It takes a hero to be one of those men who goes into battle." That it took heroes was true early in the Vietnam War, as recounted in It Took Heroes, Part One. It was also true later at the height of the combat, perhaps even more so in some ways. While those who served earlier enjoyed a semblance of public support for their service in Vietnam, those who served later did so in the face of increasingly negative stereotyping and hostility toward the war and the warrior. The longer the war dragged on, the greater and more vocal was the opposition toward everything and everybody connected with it. And the louder and more vulgar the protests and opposition, the more they seemed acceptable to that very society that sent its young men into the terrible jaws of war in Southeast Asia. "Your friends and neighbors have selected you," began the draft notices that older Americans sent to so many of their sons in the 1960s and early 70s.

In November 1972 a military man wrote me: "The Vietnam War is over, and it's time to forget it. Please quit telling war stories, and let's leave the war behind us." These well-intended words pained me deeply, for remembering was a daily, mostly involuntary occurrence. The gnawing inside me increased. *If even military people want to bury and forget the faithful sacrifices rendered in Vietnam, does anyone care? Can we forget the event and still remember those who served and sacrificed so much?* There was a connection between Vietnam and the gnawing inside me, but I was still missing it.

In 1969 President Richard M. Nixon began pulling combat forces out of Vietnam. By 1973 the process was complete except for a few advisors. "Peace with honor" was declared. We Army Chaplains in Europe where I then served were ordered to celebrate the peace with special religious services. *No!* I declared. Rather, I would conduct a final memorial service for the soldiers and civilians on both sides who yet would die in Vietnam, and for their grieving loved ones. So in a special memorial service and in countless other speaking engagements over the years I shared my memories of many of the heroes who went into battle in Vietnam. As I shared these memories the gnawing inside me eased.

Finally, in 1995, I recognized the connection. My serendipitous awakening occurred the day I finished the first draft of the chronicle of my tours in Vietnam. Suddenly, a great weight lifted from me, a mental, emotional, spiritual burden of near tangible proportions. That's when I first realized the gnawing had been there all along because I needed to preserve "the rest of the story" in writing.

Thus, with my war memories on paper and in the computer, the gnawing almost ceased for a while. For the first time in more than a quarter of a century, I was free of a vague melancholy. It was as if I'd been properly relieved from some lonely guard post, of some awesome burden, which burden I never fully appreciated until it lifted off me. *I don't have to remember anymore. Now, whatever happens to me, the story is preserved.*

My strong feelings toward American involvement in the Vietnam War, should they show through, are incidental. This book is about heroes, about whole life spans compressed into months, day, hours. It is a tribute—tied together by my first-person experiences and observations—to those who fought and those who supported them up close and personal. As a chaplain in Vietnam, I served no war, just or unjust. I served soldiers, heroes—faithful souls who stepped forward when called upon by their country, while others received accolades for dodging their duty. Yes, it took a special kind of hero to answer the call in the sixties and early seventies. And I owe those special heroes for much more than memories. I literally owe them my life.

The reader will find no composite characters or events, no use of journalistic or poetic license for dramatic effect. And painful as it is to include some details, events and behaviors, I've striven to include everything, so far as that is possible to do without inflicting on the reader the very boredom a soldier often endures between the battles. I did not select material to enhance or damage unit esprit, to make a personal statement, to build up or tear down individual or collective images, or in any way to tell anything but the truth, difficult as the truth can sometimes be to pin down.

This book is not about tenets of religion or points of religious doctrine. However, considering its source, a former Army chaplains, it is occasionally necessary to refer to my own religious affiliation and to that of other chaplains and soldiers. It is impossible to do otherwise and remain true to the facts and context of the events and people described. A *prime directive* of each of America's military chaplains is that the he or she will not attempt to win soldiers from other religious denominations to his or her own. While retirement released me from this *rule of engagement,* I adhere to it in the pages of this book because my purposes are quite non-denominational. By the way, adherence by chaplains to this prime directive is not a sellout of their beliefs. Their commission is to provide or coordinate spiritual and religious support to soldiers and their families without regard to religious affiliation or lack thereof. In other words, the role of the chaplain, in most respects, is an institutional one rather than ecclesiastical. Of course, each chaplain must be endorsed to serve by a particular church or group of religious bodies, and he or she must be ordained in whatever way the church or body of churches describes. A chaplain is not required to violate the tenets of his religious vows or faith to support the soldier. However, he is expected to do all in his power to bring to bear those resources that are necessary to meet those spiritual needs of the soldier that he cannot personally provide. In this way, I was as responsible for the Baptist and the atheist as I was for those of my own faith.

The chronology of this memoir rests firmly on my personal journal, which provides the framework and chronology for the vivid memories. I augmented these by interviewing fellow soldiers and by personal and official journals and other sources. Not to brag, but my memory is verifiably exceptional, especially for directions, lay-of-the-land, and chronology. I've validated this capability through research and revisits to places of long ago. Almost always, my recollections of sites and events are accurate as to geographic orientation. And usually sites and layouts are the way I remembered them—schools, houses, farms, streams, roads; dates and sequences, too. I had this knack even as a toddler, before I knew of compass directions. Apparently, this talent is inborn in me, perhaps a psychological need to know where (and when) I am. Whatever its source, my gift served me well in combat and in writing *It Took Heroes, Parts 1 and 2*.

In the preface to *It Took Heroes, Part 1* I wrote: "The hardest thing about writing this book has been stopping, because every action and story has as many facets and perspectives as there were individuals involved in it." Yes, I stopped writing too soon, which became quite obvious as long-lost veterans reported in upon reading my first book. And yes, those who contacted me so far have forgiven me even as they provided rich perspective and detail for future editions of *It Took Heroes Part 1*. They gave me more than that. They provided me with insights and contacts to help me give a better account in *It Took Heroes Part 2*.

Again, I hope I didn't stop writing too soon, for I've continued faithful to my memories and journal and striven to verify and validate every detail and name whenever I could do so." But somewhere the gathering and writing has to stop and the publishing begin. So I trust my grunts (regular infantrymen), medics, LRRP rangers, scouts, artillerymen, aviators and former leaders will forgive me when my memories, notes and perspective differ from theirs.

Now a brief explanation about chapter notes. In no case are chapter notes necessary to the text. Rather, they are for the benefit of veterans as they seek to place their own experiences in context, and for them and their families as they seek each other. They are also intended to help veterans and families in their dealings with the Veterans Administration and other bureaucracies.

Most of the chapter notes are transcribed verbatim from official reports just as they were written at the time, jargon and all. For the reader who is familiar with, or willing to become familiar with the military jargon, these notes provide enlightening glimpses at combat and support down at the platoon, company and battalion. They reveal how official records fall far short of describing the reality of what the fighting men endured, as they reduce combat engagements to a few lines of acronyms and grid numbers and occasional names—lives blow away, limbs blown off. Consequently, the chapter notes are recommended, albeit unnecessary, reading.

If you have any information on the unidentified individuals in pictures or on individuals involved in any of the actions in this book, please contact the author.

Finally, the uninitiated reader will do well to refer to the Glossary beginning on page 303 for help with military terms and jargon associated with the Vietnam war.

Foreword

Claude Newby's personal story provides the framework, the tapestry, that ties together the unsung stories and heroics of many great young Americans. His own story should be understood by generations of Americans for whom the explanation of our being in Vietnam has never been made clear: we were there as a nation to help a beleaguered people that could not help themselves. We went hoping to prevent from happening precisely what has happened, since we—as a nation—did not succeed in our objective.

But this report is not an effort to make a full explanation of the circumstances that galvanized the bitterness, anger, and opposition felt by many across the land. It is an on-scene observation of one young husband and father of the terrible cost of that undertaking.

I met Claude Newby during his service in Vietnam as a chaplain in the United States Army. In several visits during his two tours of duty in that tormented land, I came to better understand the depth and breadth of the contributions of this remarkable chaplain, among comparably worthy others.

Chaplain Newby was awarded several medals for valor, and three Purple Hearts for wounds received in battle. He also received the Combat Infantry Badge, an almost unheard of honor for a chaplain. On many occasions, a cry for "Medic" was responded to not only by the medical specialists trained to help the wounded, but also by this chaplain who deliberately went into harm's way to assist the medics and to administer comfort and encouragement in his special calling. Not infrequently as I heard of Chaplain Newby's quiet, courageous, voluntary responses in moments of crisis, I recalled the words of A. E. Houseman spoken for other unselfish young heroes after another war, long past:

Here dead lie we, because we did not choose
To live and shame the land from which we sprung.
Life, to be sure, is nothing much to lose,
But young men think it is, and we were young.

But the powerful tribute of a seasoned commander under whose direction Claude Newby served seems to me to represent ultimate praise to a modest man of God who ministered to his valorous associates in lulls between military action, and then accompanied medics to give them needed succor in their sufferings. In an efficiency report he wrote:

"CPT. Newby is without peer both as a chaplain and leader of men. His numerous displays of personal courage and his sincere concern for the welfare of the men in this battalion have earned him the respect of soldiers of all ranks. He is unquestionably one of the mainstays of this combat battalion. In all my years of commissioned service I have never met an officer as uniquely qualified and professionally competent as Chaplain Newby. This officer has unlimited potential in the U.S. Army and should be favorably considered for promotion ahead of his contemporaries. To do less would be a tragic oversight on the part of the Army."

(Signed by Ronald R. Rasmussen)

To this high tribute to Claude Newby, I add my own, to him and to those honorable, faithful sons of America living and dead, whose sacrifices he chronicles, and whom he served and loved.

—Marion D. Hanks
World War II veteran,
Internationally noted life scouter,
speaker, author, and ecclesiastical authority
(emeritus), The Church of Jesus Christ of Latter-day Saints

Claude Newby writes compelling history and *Vagaries of War* is by far THE best book I have read on the Viet Nam War. It is well documented and researched, fast-paced and moving. It is one that I will have on my bookshelf and treasure for its scope, its honesty, and style.

— Kregg P. J. Jorgenson
Former ranger, and author of
Acceptable Loss, MIA Rescue and other books.

I am honored to again give my endorsement for Claude Newby's book, this time for *It Took Heroes, Part II*. I have know Claude for thirty years, and he has been a hero/son to me.

I have known him professionally in his role as a distinguished military chaplain during these years. The book, *It Took Heroes II*, and its predecessor, *It Took Heroes* is written with absolute truth, honor and integrity. It will give every reader a lump in his throat, a tear in his eye and a pride in his heart for the thousands of brave young men who served and gave their lives for all of us. "No greater love hath any man than this."

It Took Heroes dead and alive to make these books possible. Their voices are heard as if coming from the dust. We need to place both these books in an honored place among the treasures we accrue for our posterity.

—Lucile Johnson
Family therapist, speaker and author,
Recipient of the Bob Hope Five Star Civilian
Award in miniature for service to her country

Interlude

BETWEEN TOURS

I'm lying in a prone shelter. Suddenly, a Chicom hand grenade—a potato-masher—hurtles from the darkness and lands against my left thigh.

Frantically, I grab the grenade in my left hand and attempt to fling it across my body to the right. A bloodcurdling scream shatters my nightmare.

Shocked instantly from nightmare-haunted sleep into reality, I see my poor wife above me and half out of the bed; her frantic eyes pleading to know why I have a death grip on her hair and why I seem to be trying to hurl her through the window.

Chapter One

UNEASY PEACE

At Cam Ranh Bay, Vietnam that September day in 1967, I searched in vain for a familiar face among those waiting with me to return to the states. Then I boarded a civilian charter flight and headed home, leaving behind the dangers and faces of war, I thought. In my baggage were military orders assigning me to Fort Bragg, North Carolina and a written promise from the Office of the Chief of Army Chaplains that an airborne assignment waited there for me. But first things first—my wife Helga and our five children. Our children then were James, 12; Jeannie, 11; John, 8; Laura, 5; and Brenda Lynette, 3.

Helga, the children and I were a universe of our own for about two weeks as we got reacquainted and tried to make up for a year of lost sharing. Helga and I spent every moment together that we could. I played with the children a lot. We even played a home-devised game we called ambush, which awakened in me the simmering war memories and sensations. Of necessity, we attended to "normal" demands, and arranged for shipment of our household goods from Utah to North Carolina, visited friends, and such.

We delayed our departure for Fort Bragg long enough to attend a church-wide conference the first weekend in October. I attended a conference session, adorned for the first time in more than a year in my dress-green uniform, accompanied by my eldest son James. After the session in the world-famous Mormon Tabernacle, we visited briefly backstage with Elder Marion D. Hanks, an ecclesiastical leader and friend. He looked over my uniform and asked, "What is your rank?"

"Captain," I answered, pointing to my left shoulder where the silver double bars of a captain should have been clearly visible. After a year in the jungles, I'd become rusty at this dress uniform business, but to forget the insignia of rank? Elder Hanks smiled in good humor at my discomfort.

During one session of Conference, Elder Gordon B. Hinckley, Elder Hanks' senior ecclesiastical companion and leader, began a portion his remarks. "In the congregation is Chaplain Claude Newby, who just returned from Vietnam." With that opening, he shared with the conference a spiritual anecdote from my life as an enlisted man back in 1958. I felt quite honored.

In anticipation of earning paratrooper pay to replace the combat pay I no longer drew, we deemed it proper to report to Fort Bragg, North Carolina in a new car, rather than in the well-used Ford we owned. So we bought a 1967 Rambler Ambassador station wagon and shipped our household goods. We headed east, with stops in Idaho to visit Dallas and Joan Murdoch; and in Louisiana, Tennessee and Georgia to visit family.

Two disappointments awaited us at Fort Bragg. First, there would be a long wait for on-post housing. Second, despite a written commitment by the Office of the Chief of Chaplains, I'd not receive the airborne assignment I wanted.

Colonel Jim Skelton, the XVIII Corps and Post Chaplain said, "I need chaplains in the training center more than in airborne units. I manage my assets, despite what Washington might have promised you." So it was back to a basic training center, this time under the technical supervision of Chaplain (Major) Virgil Wood, a Baptist as I recall, and an easy man to work for.

Chaplain Wood assigned me religious support responsibility for a training battalion in a brigade commanded by Colonel John P. Barker. Barker and his Executive Officer, Lieutenant Colonel O'Brien, would soon play opposing parts in an effort to end my chaplaincy career. It was about to become clear that not all things dangerous had been left in Vietnam.

Chaplain Blanke (assigned alias), the Training Center Chaplain gave me a week to in-process and find civilian housing. Meanwhile, the family was assigned temporary accommodations in an unhealthy, dismal, coal smoke-choked barracks. After a futile week of house hunting, Chaplain Blanke warned, "find a place right away, or else." So we looked farther afield and rented a barely affordable house, a nice home on ten acres near the village of Cameron, North Carolina, seventeen miles north of Fort Bragg.

The property included a stable and corral. Farms bordered it on three sides and a commercial pine forest was across the dirt road to the south. The stable and corral would come in handy when Bishop Abe, a Hawaiian of Japanese descent, asked us to board two Shetland ponies. We took the ponies to be good neighbors, no charge, of course! I had grown up with horses and even served with a horse unit in the Army. The ponies would provide great fun and experience for my children.

There on the farm, I strove to atone for the time we had lost while I was in Vietnam.

The children and I got in lots of shooting practice with shotgun, rifle, and BB guns. Almost everyone who visited us was introduced to and became hooked on our homemade game of ambush.

One day the family was on the way to town when, from the back seat of the station wagon, Brenda Lynette suddenly threw her little arms around my neck and exclaimed, "My Daddy is as big as the sky!"

"What?" I asked, wondering fleetingly if she referred to my weight. "I mean my Daddy is as strong as the sky," she clarified, quickly tightening her little arms about my neck for emphasis. Not everyone felt so positively toward me.

While Chaplain Wood received me well, Chaplain Blanke's reception was something else. Blanke informed me during our first meeting that he had had trouble with the LDS chaplain who preceded me at Fort Bragg and added: "Nothing personal, but I don't understand how your church can have the audacity to place you men in the chaplaincy to compete with professional clergy."

With that "welcome" he advised me to move the on-post LDS meetings into his sphere of responsibility so he could "be sure the

Mormons are treated properly." By way of compromise, I promised to conduct weekly LDS services in the training center, to accommodate trainees during their quarantine period.

Chaplain Wood, on the other hand, appeared glad to have me in his brigade. He and several other chaplains were attending a class on "Offbeat Religions in America," presented by Duke University. Hill, like the other students, was assigned to prepare a written and oral report on one of the religious groups the professor considered offbeat. Wood chose the Mormons, intent on taking advantage of me as a resource. I agreed to help, with ecclesiastical approval, on condition that I be permitted to limit my participation to a presentation followed by questions and answers, free of argument over points of doctrine.

At the appointed time Wood introduced me to the theology class: "I resent Chaplain Newby. When God was giving out vices, Baptists, who came alphabetically before the Mormons, chose coffee. The Mormons came along and chose plural wives." The class members approved Wood's humor. I accepted it in good nature.

Besides my primary support for two training battalions, I took a turn one evening each week counseling trainees on a first-come basis, without regard to each trainee's unit. Each night, fifteen to twenty-five or more trainees lined up to see the chaplain. The trainees came seeking intervention over perceived unfair treatment, for personal and family concerns, for guidance on personnel actions such as becoming a conscientious objector, and seeking relief from some fearful aspect of training, like crawling beneath streams of live machine-gun fire on the infiltration course. They came to discuss the "advantages" of going AWOL, and for help to get out of the Army. Occasionally a trainee came seeking spiritual or moral guidance.

Because of heavy counseling demands, it was hard to find time to visit the trainees and cadre in billets, work and training areas. Consequently, I implemented the operational concept I'd developed at Fort Ord in 1966, making certain I was on hand during those times of greatest stress on the trainees and the cadre. This modus operandi saved my career, as events would show.

Immediately after arriving at Fort Bragg I recommenced training for the airborne assignment I hoped for, and for which I regularly pestered the Post Chaplain. But something was wrong. No matter how I tried, it took me almost three minutes longer to run the mile than it had in 1966. At Fort Ord I had found that I could easily run a seven-minute mile wearing combat boots. Now, I barely made a mile in ten minutes, wearing running shoes. I discounted the hip injury I had sustained in early 1967, for the pain had subsided and eventually disappeared, leaving only a numb big toe. Though I could jog slowly for hours, I feared I'd be unable to pass the airborne physical when my chance came.

Airborne units had a mockup of an aircraft, built from part of the fuselage of a C-47 airplane. I often watched paratroopers and hopefuls, like me, make practice jumps from the mockup. After several months of watching, I had a night dream:

I'm standing in full paratrooper gear in the open door of a C-47 aircraft, in flight. On the signal I leap out into space, but my main chute doesn't open! With the jumpmaster glaring disapproval at me as I fall, I pull the D-ring to deploy my reserve chute. It fails me too. As I plunge toward the ground, the jumpmaster, yells, "Don't worry, Chaplain. It counts!" My imminent death would not prevent me from becoming jump-qualified.

I awoke before "hitting the ground" and lay awake pondering the dream and my motives for going airborne. Never again did I pester Chaplain Skelton for an airborne assignment.

Chapter Two

RELIEVE HIM FOR CAUSE

Early in December 1967, I answered my office telephone and heard, "Claude, this is Chaplain Blanke. Mrs. Blanke and I are planning a Christmas party for the chaplains and wives in the training center. How will 1300 to 1700 hours Sunday, the nineteenth work for you?"

"That conflicts with my worship services at 1300 and 1500 hours and with another speaking assignment at 1700," I explained.

"It is seldom possible to find a time that fits everyone, but this time fits the other chaplains, so that is settled. You and Helga come by if you can, even if only for a few minutes between services, and we will appreciate it and understand," said Blanke, cheerfully.

On the day of the party, assuming Chaplain Blanke had been up front with us, Helga and I stopped in at his home for a few minutes. All seemed gracious and in good order. And things seemed to be going nicely at home and work. But unknown to me, Chaplain Blanke was building a case to rid the chaplaincy of me.

The plot thickened and came to a boil at the same time I became aware it existed, late in January. Earlier, I had gotten permission to take the LDS trainees to a meeting in Raleigh. On the Sunday of this event, I arranged for another chaplain to conduct my regular worship services, and posted notices of the change in the schedule for LDS services on the chapel doors and in the Daily Bulletin, required reading for all leaders.

Then came the ice storm. Cold rain commenced Thursday just as I started home from work and quickly changed to sleet. The roads had become ribbons of glare ice by the time I slid, literally, into our driveway about 6:30 p.m. We lost electricity and telephone service early in the evening. With the loss of electricity we also lost indoor cooking capability, heating, and culinary water, which all relied on an electric compressor and pump. By midnight the indoor temperature had plunged below freezing, where it remained for forty-eight hours.

Fortunately, our battery-powered radio worked well, and over it we heard orders, in the name of the commanding general: "Because of extremely hazardous conditions, all personnel will remain where you are, whether at home or at work...until further notice."

Bundled in sleeping bags and doubled up in our beds, we were reasonably warm through the night. Friday morning we awakened to clear skies and a white, crystal-like winter wonderland scene, a sparkling world of ice-encrusted, frigid beauty. The pine trees across the road bowed their tops to the ground like followers of Islam in prayer, without breaking off. Every wire, branch, and twig sported a coat of ice diamonds. The general's "stay put" order was still in effect, and just as well in my case. An ice-coated main power line drooped across the road just a few inches above the road surface, blocking our exit. I wasn't about to see if the wire was live.

For two days we melted ice for drinking and sanitation and cooked soup over an outside fire. Saturday morning the ice glaze remained, but was showing signs of melting. The "stay put" order was still in effect. By mid-afternoon the ice had dropped off the power line and it had sprung up, opening our way to the outside world. We headed for town, but thought better of it when the approaching headlights of a car suddenly switched sides with each other. We came very close to crashing into the upside-down car. Black ice, or glare ice, coated the hardtop rural highway. The unhurt driver of the overturned car slithered out on his back through the driver's window.

Back home a few minutes later our telephone rang—it had still been out of order when we'd ventured out. Chaplain Bobby Moore, standing in for Wood, was on the line. He informed me Chaplain Blanke had written to Colonel Barker and recommended that I be relieved from duty "for cause."

Blanke accused me of gross dereliction of my duties. Specifically, he charged me with: (1) neglecting the trainees during the stressful period of the ice storm; (2) failing in my social obligations, to wit, coming late to his Christmas party and departing early; (3) neglecting my responsibilities to LDS soldiers; and two allegations that I no longer recall.

Reportedly, Colonel Barker reacted angrily to Blanke's charges and ordered me, through Moore, to report to him at 0800 hours Monday. Moore opined Barker would relieve me from duty and my career would be destroyed. Next day I went about my Sunday duties with a heavy heart.

Early Monday morning, I waited in my office for the moment of doom, with good reason to suspect this was the end of my career, though I believed myself to be innocent of any wrongdoing. Colonel Barker was notorious for relieving officers first and asking questions later, thus ending careers, so the rumors went.

While I waited for the appointed hour of judgment, there entered my mind Christ's admonition and promise to his apostles, applicable when they would be brought before the law for *righteousness sake*: "take no thought what you shall say...for the words will be given...what ye shall say." Perhaps this promise applied in my case. I prayed fervently for divine intervention, that my "calling" might be spared.

Lieutenant Colonel O'Brien, the Brigade Executive Officer, called just before 8:00 a.m. "I've convinced Colonel Barker to listen to your side regarding Chaplain Blanke's allegations. So instead of reporting to Colonel Barker, be in my office at 0900 hours," he instructed. This reprieve totally surprised me, especially because O'Brien was an enigma to the chaplains, so the consensus was that he disliked them.

Yet another surprise came while I waited anxiously for 0900 hours to arrive. The surprise arrived in the form of a letter from the Office of the Army Chief of Chaplains. Normally the mail came after lunch. The letter said:

> *Dear Chaplain Newby:*
> *"We have just received the efficiency report...for the period of 1 August to 10 September 1967. Although the report covered a very short period...it is a testimony to your dedication to your Calling, to your courage and capacity for work. It is an outstanding report....Please accept our congratulations...prayers...."*

(Signed by G. W. Hyatt, 5 January 1968)

Feeling much better, I knocked on O'Brien's office door promptly at 0900 hours, entered on command, saluted sharply, and reported myself "present as ordered." O'Brien put me at ease (a semi- relaxed, half-at-attention standing position), read the allegations against me, and asked me what I had to say for myself.

In my defense, I first explained how I had but obeyed the commanding general's orders by remaining home during the ice-storm crisis. "Besides," I explained, "I really had no choice in the matter because a power line blocked my way."

Second, I related my conversation with Chaplain Blanke concerning the scheduling of his Christmas party. Third, I outlined the background and justification for all my actions related to the LDS services and trainees, and explained why I had declined to place all LDS services under my accuser's supervision. After responding to the remaining two allegations, which I no longer recall, I described Blanke's negative reception when I first arrived at the training center. Finally, I proffered the letter from the Office of the Chief of Chaplains. "This letter, which I received this morning, belies most of the things of which I stand accused," I said.

Lieutenant Colonel O'Brien studied the letter for a moment in silence and returned it: "I wish my branch would write letters like that. Go back to work. I'll handle Colonel Barker." O'Brien called an hour later: "Everything is fine with Colonel Barker. However, he wants you to move into on-post quarters as soon as you can. He'll use command influence to help you get housing."

Henceforth, no one at Fort Bragg openly challenged my credentials or my duty performance. To the contrary, once Colonel Barker ordered other chaplains to emulate me, by name. Another day he singled me out for praise in the midst of a chewing out that he was administering to the Training Center Chaplain and my colleagues. Though the attempt to get me "fired" worked in my favor for the most part, I was marked down on my next efficiency report in the sociability category. Probably, the lower sociability rating was justified. Following Vietnam, I found it very difficult to be at ease amid the chatter and clatter of social gatherings while the war raged in vivid color on the nightly news.

As mentioned earlier, I tried always to be with the units in the field during times of highest tensions. Consequently, I was present and frequently took part when my trainees went through (crawled) the infiltration course under live machine-gun fire.

On the infiltration course the trainees, armed with M-14 rifles, entered a deep trench that was reminiscent of the trenches of World War I. Then, on a signal, the trainees scampered from the trench and belly-crawled or slid on their backs across a course crisscrossed with barbed wire and pocked with sandbagged pits. In several places, strands of the barbed wire were stretched tight and crisscrossed between stakes, just high enough to allow a man to slither beneath them on his back, using his weapon to hold the barbs up to keep them from snagging his uniform. From behind the objective or finish line, several machine guns fired bursts across the course. The guns were locked into position so they couldn't fire lower than 30 or 36 inches at the highest point of the course. But they were still dangerous. And those sandbagged pits offered no protection. Rather, each pit contained explosive charges sufficiently large to blow off an arm or leg, or even to kill a man. These charges were set off among the trainees to simulate exploding mortar rounds.

Occasionally, I crawled the infiltration course for fun or to provide emotional support to trainees. For example, a first sergeant sent a trainee to me who was petrified by fear and had refused to leave the trench for the first of two daylight crawls. The trainee agreed to attempt the night course (his last chance), provided I accompany him. I did, we made it, and he was graduated on time. Immediately following that crawl, I stood beneath a floodlight in my mud-spattered splendor, visiting with some members of the cadre. Colonel Barker appeared, glared at me for a moment, and walked off without saying a word. *He's perturbed by my appearance and wishes he'd relieved me when he started to,* I suspected.

Putting concerns about Colonel Barker aside, I turned my thoughts to what I saw around me. I reflected on the fear the trainee had demonstrated earlier. An idea flashed into my mind. *From now on, I'll hold a worship service right here for the trainees, just before they crawl the infiltration course. I'll have the trainees' full attention here! It will be great for them. Perhaps I can get the service added to the training schedule.*

For effect, I would conduct these unique services with the trainees seated in the bleachers and looking over my shoulders at the dreaded infiltration course, a great visual aid.

These special, simple services were an instant success. I began each service with us singing *The Battle Hymn of the Republic*, followed by prayer and a sermon by me, then another song and a closing prayer. In my "infiltration-course sermon" I compared the infiltration course to life and the drill sergeants' instructions to scripture—the sergeants liked the comparison. Birth I compared to leaving the trench, to leaving comparative security behind and going forth to face obstacles, uncertainty and danger. "In life, as with the infiltration course," I said, "there is—or should be—a clear objective, the reaching of which places one beyond the danger. Just as in life one has the scriptures to give him spiritual guidance, so on the infiltration course one has his drill sergeants telling him how to proceed. If one heeds his sergeants' instructions and keeps going, he will get past the obstacles and explosions and pass unharmed beneath the cracking bullets, reaching safe haven. And in life, one who heeds God's commandments and keeps going will be protected from the 'fiery darts' in life and will return back to God, from whence he came, through Christ." Almost all trainees attended these services voluntarily, as did most of the cadres.

Unknown to me, Colonel Barker observed one of these services. The next day he issued a written order: "Every chaplain in this brigade will conduct worship services at the infiltration course, and will include *The Battle Hymn of the Republic* in these services." Colonel Barker had no authority to dictate the contents of chaplains' worship services, but how could I object!

Some weeks after I began these special services, a trainee in another battalion was shot in the arm while crawling the night infiltration course (I suspected he stuck his arm up and got it shot on purpose to avoid going to Vietnam).

By coincidence, the next day all the Training Center chaplains, about ten of us, gathered in a headquarters building at Chaplain Blanke's call. We met Colonel Barker coming in as we were leaving the building. His face was livid and his teeth clenched, probably because he'd just come from trying to explain the shooting mishap to his own boss. Anyhow, Barker got in Chaplain Blanke's face and roared, "And where were you chaplains last night when my man was shot?" Then glancing at me, he said softly, "I don't mean you Chaplain Newby. You're always there." After aiming a few more harsh words at Blanke, Barker stormed away without waiting for any response.

As previously mentioned, I tried to always be on the range when a company of trainees fired the rifle for record. These were high-stress occasions for the cadre, whose efficiency reports, even their careers, were on the line. Out of the blue one day a company commander challenged me to a shooting match. He was feeling great because his men had just fired for record and done very well. I accepted the challenge, though I'd never fired an M-14 rifle. The M1 Garand and M-1 and M-2 Carbine rifles had been the standard weapons back when I was infantry.

The company commander and I each loaded a 20-round magazine and took a shooting position. He knelt and rested his weapon on a sandbag. I stood to fire freehand, without a rest for the rifle. Our impromptu rules were simply to knock down a line of about twenty silhouette targets at maximum range, 300 yards as I recall, beginning with the target on our right and working left. We were free to fire when the pop-up line of targets appeared.

Feeling very relaxed; I took a left-handed stance and aimed where I expected the first target to appear. The target appeared. I fired instantly and shifted left as the target fell. Six times in rapid succession I dropped targets before the captain could get off a shot using his by-the-book method. Finally, he fired and hit his target, but he had to skip ahead to do so, in violation of the "rules of engagement." Quickly, I knocked down the targets the captain had skipped and passed him again. The referee, a sergeant, declared me the winner—a brave act, as he worked for the captain.

To ease the captain's embarrassment at being "bested" by a chaplain, I confessed my prior infantry experience, and how I'd grown up with weapons and shot competitively. The captain took defeat well and I didn't gloat.

Chapter Three

BELOW THE ZONE

It was about 9:00 p.m., October 1968. The children were preparing for bed. Helga and I were just beginning to relax when the telephone rang. "Hello Claude. Virgil here."

"Virgil. Virgil who?" I asked.

"Virgil Wood—Chaplain Wood, Claude." He caught me off guard, for while he usually called me by my first name, I had the impression Wood expected me to address him as "Chaplain" or "sir." I did that naturally because he was my superior officer.

Wood continued "Claude, do you know you made the majors' list?" I didn't even know such a list existed. He explained he'd accidentally found my name on a list for promotion to major from "below the zone.' Below the zone, he explained, meant I was selected for promotion ahead of my contemporaries, from among the top 10 percent of captains in the Army. This was quite a change from eight months earlier when it looked like my career was destroyed.

Normally, an officer was notified of selection for promotion by his chain of command when the promotion list was released, or sooner. But everyone in both chaplain and command channels had missed my name, and I hadn't known to check.

In late summer 1968, author Daniel Lang of *The New Yorker* magazine called me. He wanted my version of the story about the Mao incident in Vietnam in 1966. This incident is recounted in detail in my earlier book, *It Took Heroes, Part 1;* in a piece titled "Casualties of

War" in the September 1969 issue of *The New Yorker* ; and in a movie by the same title starring Michael J. Fox.

Lang had learned my identity and about my connection with the Mao incident during interviews with Sven (alias for one of the parties involved) at the latter's home in the Midwest. I told Lang what I knew, with the approval of the Fort Bragg Information Officer, of course. My account, Lang said, agreed in every important detail with Sven's. He promised me a copy of the article when it got published.

After January 1968, with Chaplain Blanke's attack behind me, life was quite good, except for the children's schooling. Our recent move to on-post housing had forced the children to change school again, their fourth change of the school year.

Beginning with Jeannie's birthday on April 13, we made frequent overnight trips to the beaches about 110 miles east of Fort Bragg. Wayne Boring, who had followed me here from Vietnam, usually accompanied us on these fun trips, where we had great times playing ambush amid the sand dunes, surfing—body and air mattress—and "gigging" for flounder in the coastal tide pools.

We planned an April trip for Helga to visit her mother Martha Raasch in Berlin, Germany. To contain costs, we booked her flights in and out of the John F. Kennedy International Airport in New York, where I'd drive her and pick her up. The Borings agreed to stay with us so Carmen Boring could tend the children while I worked. The murder of Martin Luther King Jr. in Memphis, Tennessee significantly affected these plans, coming as it did a few days before Helga was scheduled to depart for Berlin.

That this trip would be different immediately became obvious. We knew Army and National Guard units were out in-force, but I expected they would be deployed in actual riot areas. Not so. As we passed in the dark through Raleigh, North Carolina, armed troops were visible on almost every corner and combined patrols of policemen and National Guardsmen were everywhere. At several checkpoints, we had to "prove" our peaceful intentions to suspicious military and civilian officers. Several times we were advised, but never ordered, to turn back for our own safety. An eerie, familiar feeling, a heightened state of awareness and wariness, accompanied me through riot-torn cities. I felt as though I was in the jungles of Vietnam.

We felt better between Baltimore and Long Island, New York, because we saw no evidence of riots or troops on the freeways and turnpikes. Though New York City had experienced heavy rioting, we got to JFK, and I got out too, without interference from either rioters or the military or civilian police.

The boys and I took a canoe trip in July 1968, thanks to the willingness of a lieutenant to take a chance on us. He was the recreational officer at Pope Air Force Base. Our trip was down the Little River, which was in a flood stage.

For the occasion I wore jungle fatigues, with pockets buttoned down. Helga delivered us to the river and we pushed off into the current just outside Fort Bragg, with me in the stern, James in front and John in the middle.

We made good time all morning, slipping easily between and around the snags and sunken logs that created few obstacles in the high water. About noon, we tied up near a bridge and purchased the fixings for lunch at a country store. That is when I forgot to button my pocket after returning my wallet to it.

An hour later, we hit a particularly rough stretch of water that was too muddy to be called white water, and the current pushed us into a sunken tree near the south bank. We would have made it, but John stood to dodge a limb and tipped the canoe. James easily pulled himself to the bank while I secured the canoe to a snag and turned to rescue John, who was being carried away by the current. Swimming hard, I caught John and pulled him to safety; life vests made the difference between rescue and tragedy.

A few minutes later with the boys safe on the bank, I got the water out of the canoe and we were on the way again, refreshed by the dip and exhilarated by the adventure.

About two hours later, we arrived ahead of schedule at he place where Helga was to pick us up. Storm clouds were threatening. After pulling the canoe up a steep bank to the roadside, I left the boys with it and went to call Helga from a farmhouse a quarter mile down the road.

Hard rain hit as I approached the farmhouse. The call completed, thanks to a friendly farm family, I waited on the porch for the rain to let up—it came down in sheets, like the heavy monsoon rains in Asia. Lightning flashed almost without letup, the strikes coming seconds apart and striking all around.

James and John were safe from the lightning beneath the concrete bridge, I thought. Then dimly through the driving rain, I saw two shapes dragging a canoe through a hail of lightning that hit like a heavy mortar barrage.

"Leave the canoe! Run!" I yelled, as I raced to meet the boys. A moment later, back safely on the porch, we watched the area where we'd abandoned the canoe. We could hardly see the road, much less the canoe in the driving rain. The lightning passed on after half an hour. We hurried through the slackening rain to retrieve the canoe, but some-one—a pickup had passed during the storm—had stolen it.

While I waited for Helga to come for us, I reported the theft of the canoe to the county sheriff. That's when I discovered I'd lost my wallet with all my identification cards and meager funds; it had floated out of my unbuttoned pocket. And the worst was still ahead. I had to explain this to my Air Force lieutenant friend who had bent the rules to rent to Army personnel. Eventually a formal military procedure called a *report of survey* absolved me of responsibility for the loss of the canoe. I hope the incident didn't hurt my Air Force friend's career.

Sundays were very busy. Usually I conducted general services in the morning and an LDS service for trainees in the early afternoon, then participated in a service for singles in the late afternoon and attended civilian meetings in Fayetteville with the family in the evening.

The civilians at church seldom saw me out of uniform. One evening, I dressed in "civvies" and proudly accompanied Jeannie to a daddy-daughter dinner date. We arrived at the chapel a few minutes early and took seats to wait for the program to start. A lady sitting behind us whispered to another woman, "Chaplain Newby looks funny with clothes on." Presumably, she referred to civilian clothes as opposed to my usual uniform.

In September 1968, thinking back to occasions when I had arranged for soldiers in the field to attend conferences in Vietnam, I got the bright idea of doing the same thing for soldiers at Fort Bragg, North Carolina. If it could be arranged, I'd take a group two thousand miles to attend a stateside religious conference. My superiors in the chaplain line gave their blessings to the idea along with their collective opinion that it couldn't be done. Well, I did it anyhow.

By carefully coordinating with various Army and Air Force commanders and staffs, I got permission to take as many trainees and soldiers to Salt Lake City as a C-130 cargo aircraft would carry. A line colonel in the chain of command included with his endorsement of the plan his off-the-record warning that the operation could ruin my career. "You can't expect to turn loose an airplane load of soldiers and trust them to stay out of trouble and all show for the return flight." But I trusted that these soldiers would not let me down.

Well, we went to Salt Lake City, and every soldier stayed out of trouble from Friday to Sunday. Each one of them showed up at the appointed time for the return flight, to my great relief.

During the conference, something else happened to bring the Vietnam War close to home again. It was Sunday afternoon, as I recall, and Helga and I were strolling around Temple Square. I was in uniform. A man and woman approached us, and the lady tentatively asked, "Are you in the Army?"

"Yes Ma'am, I am."

"We wonder if you can tell us how to get information about our son. He was killed in Vietnam."

"Gladly. What is your son's name, his unit in Vietnam, and when did he die?" I asked, after expressing condolences.

"Our son was PFC Danny Hyde," said Melba (Denney) Palmer. Her companion was Marlow G. Palmer, Danny Hyde's stepfather.

It wasn't hard to tell them about their son, and it required no research. I'd been intimately involved with him from the time he was wounded in October 1967 until his death eleven days later. What was hard was controlling a flood of emotions at the mention of Danny Hyde's name and the realization that Danny's parents stood before me. I shared with the couple all I knew of their son's last days, and how he'd declared his intention to his buddy David Lillywhite to quit smoking and get his life in order. I told of my futile attempt to visit Danny earlier on the day that he was wounded. I related his last words as I'd heard them from his buddies and the medics. Finally, I shared the details of my visits to Danny in the hospital, holding back only the gruesome details about his wounds, and how I finally commended their son to God's will.

Author's family, that he left behind to serve in Vietnam:
L-R Jeannie, Laura, Helga, John, Brenda, James.
Ogden, Utah, Fall of 1967

Daniel was born after the author
returned from Vietnam for the
last time.
A constant reminder of the
blessings of survival.

Chaplain Claude D. Newby and Helga M.A. (Raasch)
Tacoma, Washington 1987.

Helga is one of the true heroes who waited for her husband through two tours of Vietnam duty with five children, enduring the death of a sixth child. Her experience in waiting was magnified by her own experiences during World War II. As a child, allied bombing forced her and her family to retreat for shelter in bunkers and cellars. Bombing became so intense that they eventually had to flee war-torn Berlin. Near the end of four dark and terrile years the advancing Russians forced them to return to their devastated home city.

(Used with permission, Ensign, June 1987.)

Chapter Four

HASTE TO THE BATTLE

—From the Hymn, "We Are All Enlisted"—

Try as I might, I adjusted poorly to the business-as-usual attitudes in the stateside military and civilian communities and to the relegating of Vietnam to the nightly news. I doubted the nation was doing nearly enough to support the sons and daughters it sent into combat in an increasingly unpopular war. My disdain grew rapidly for those antiwar demonstrators, reporters, and politicians who blamed the soldiers in the field for the war and for the failings of civilian leadership. These feelings influenced what I did next, as did the fear that I might receive orders to Korea. If I must be away from my family for another year, it had to be Vietnam. I couldn't bear the thought of another year away otherwise. Thus reasoning, I volunteered for a second combat tour.

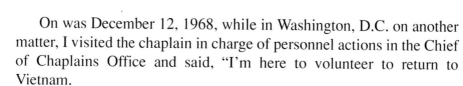

On was December 12, 1968, while in Washington, D.C. on another matter, I visited the chaplain in charge of personnel actions in the Chief of Chaplains Office and said, "I'm here to volunteer to return to Vietnam.

The chaplain eagerly accepted my offer. Then to my chagrin he informed me that I would be assigned to a battalion of Reserve or National Guard engineers that had recently been activated in Idaho, the members of which were 95 percent LDS. This would mean a rear-area assignment. It was too late to say no, but I "belonged" in the 1st Air Cavalry Division, or at least in another infantry unit. Sure, the idea of serving with a modern-day "Mormon Battalion" had its appeal. But I believed with all my heart that I was needed in the field.

Helga was in the hospital recovering from pneumonia when I returned to Fort Bragg from Washington. No doubt I slowed her healing by informing her that I was returning to Vietnam. She had a surprise for me, too.

"I'm pregnant," she said. Words can't begin to describe the guilt that swept over me.

Orders to Vietnam arrived before Christmas. We would depart from Fort Bragg for Utah in January and take thirty days of leave there. Jim Skelton, the XVIII Airborne Corps Chaplain, upon learning I had volunteered to return to Vietnam, offered, "If you will let me get your orders canceled, I will give you an airborne assignment next Spring." I declined his offer.

Christmas 1968 was hectic, a period of checking children out of school, shipping household goods, clearing post, and attending to personal affairs—wills, insurance and so forth—and saying goodbye to very good friends, colleagues, and leaders.

Before departing from Fort Bragg, I made the rounds and bade farewell to selected soldiers, sergeants, and officers, mostly those with whom I'd served in Vietnam. When I called on Dowd, my former brigade chaplain, at Post Headquarters, he took me to see the Post Sergeant Major who had been our Brigade Sergeant Major in Vietnam. The Sergeant Major took me to the Corps and Post Chief of Staff who had been in our brigade in Vietnam. The Chief of Staff took me to the Commanding General, John Tolson, as I recall, who had commanded the 1st Cav alry Division during part of my tour in Vietnam. Without any coaxing or hint on my part, the general asked, "Chaplain Newby, do you want to go back to the 1st Cav ?"

"Yes, sir, very much, sir," I responded with more enthusiasm than he expected.

Turning to the Chief of Staff, the general said something like, "Bob, call Jim at USARV and ask him to be sure Chaplain Newby is assigned back to the Cav.

I left Fort Bragg somewhat more hopeful of another infantry assignment, but at the same time doubtful it would come about. After all, the "Mormon Battalion" waited in Vietnam and I happened to be a *Mormon* Chaplain. And promises made didn't necessarily mean promises kept. Still, I hoped; this promise came from a three-star general and former commander of the 1st Cav.

On the last morning of a stopover in Chattanooga, we awakened to about seven inches of snow on the ground. The tires of our car never touched a road surface that was clear of ice and snow until many miles and a few days later, when we drove into the Murdoch family garage in Grace, Idaho.

We visited the Murdoch family, rested for a couple of days and attended church on Sunday. Then, leaving the children there, Helga and I went south for a day and rented a home in Ogden. We returned to Idaho to visit and to squeeze in all the play we could before I left again.

Most memorable about our visit in Grace was the deep snow and hours spent pulling the children on a car-hood sled behind a snowmobile. These antics took place on white fields and over and through massive snowdrifts in the Murdochs' front yard—they had few close neighbors then.

On another day during our stay in Idaho, Dallas, Joan, Helga, and I took a daylong snowmobile trek far back into the wilderness somewhere north of Soda Springs, Idaho. During the snowmobile trip, I discovered the true meaning of "white out" in blizzard country. We were standing beside an isolated dirt road. A snow-filled field that appeared to be on level with the road stretched to the south. I started to step onto the field, but Dallas grabbed my arm. Then he dropped a stick or rock onto the seemingly solid snow. The object fell straight down for at least fifteen feet, destroying the illusion of a flat, level field at my feet. But for Dallas' greater experience, I might have broken my neck on the boulders below.

All too soon the fun and games were over. It was time to put our children in school in Ogden, get our household goods delivered, set up a new home, and for me to be on my way to Vietnam.

A day or two before I left for Vietnam, Daniel Lang of *The New Yorker* magazine called for a final interview about the Mao incident that occurred during my first tour.

That last night home, I dreamed of dying in combat (more in the next chapter). This was one dread that I withheld from Helga for a year. Holding back the dream from her was something of an infraction of our covenant to share everything. I justified my actions to myself because it was only a dream and would worry her, perhaps unnecessarily—though the dream seemed very real. Helga was quite familiar with some of my night dreams, like one that I had in Cameron.

The dream came to me about November 1967, about a month after we settled into our farm home in Cameron, North Carolina. We were sleeping in our bed with me on my back on the right side of the bed. *I'm lying in a prone shelter. Suddenly, a Chicom hand grenade—a potato- masher—hurtles from the darkness and lands against my left thigh. A bloodcurdling scream shatters my nightmare.* I awaken to find poor Helga half above me and half out of the bed, her frantic eyes pleading to know why I have a death grip on a large cylindrical hair curler atop her head, and why I seem to be trying to hurl her out the window.

The dream I had the night I left to return to Vietnam seemed even more real and is indelibly imprinted in memory.

The landscape is all in shades of black and gray in the pale moon-light. Bushes stand out from the ground in darker shadow. The damp earth presses against my chest and elbows. A patch of gray distinguishes a clearing from the surrounding bushes.

The clearing is roughly circular and about twenty-five feet across. On the other side of the clearing lies an enemy soldier, Vietcong (VC) or North Vietnamese, who is drawing a bead on me with his AK-47 assault rifle. Frantically, I try to push up with my arms and fling myself to the right. But I'm too late. I'm just beginning to push when the AK-47 muzzle flashes and a sledgehammer-like blow slams into my forehead. Suddenly, I feel myself being thrown upward and back. Then, in an instant, I'm in the air about three feet above the ground and to the left of my body, watching it tumble and fall to the right, face upward, dead eyes staring blankly. I awoke then, wondering, *am I only dreaming or is it a vision, an omen, or something else?*

Since I placed little stock in omens and didn't credit myself with frightful imaginations, I was left with something else. The dream was from a spiritual source, I concluded, and was intended to reassure and comfort me, that I might comfort others during the year ahead. I drew comfort from the dream because it reassured me that change from death to spiritual existence—from mortal awareness to spiritual awareness—is quick and sure. The experience left me with neither a foreboding of impending death nor any reassurance that I would return safely. Simply, it comforted me.

Chapter Five

"QUICK TO THE FIELD"

—From the Hymn, "We Are All Enlisted"—

March 1 was a bittersweet day of extreme emotions. I finished packing, which wasn't all that difficult because I would deploy laden much more lightly than in 1966. The family accompanied me to the airport, just like last time. I was grateful to be leaving everyone generally well, except for Helga's expectant condition and for Laura, who faced surgery to correct a "wandering eye." Too bad I wouldn't be there to soothe her fears

At the airport, after sharing final hugs and kisses, I marched onto the plane with feigned courage, wondering how I could do this to my family and to myself again. I almost turned around and stayed home, but a sense of duty or mission, not fear of the consequences, kept me going.

This moment confirmed stronger than ever that war is harder on family members than on soldiers, mentally, emotionally, and spiritually. A feeling in the form of words seeped into my soul: "Your family is not alone. I will be with them." And it was so. Take Laura's eye surgery for example. She was operated on at Hill Air Force Base soon after I departed. Afterward, Helga stayed with her every moment in the recovery room.

"Where is the nice man who was holding me?" Laura asked upon awakening.

"No one was holding you, dear. I've been here beside you the whole time," said Helga.

"But, Mommy, I was so scared, and a nice man came and held me in his arms, and I wasn't scared anymore," Laura said, adding that she had felt overwhelming love and comfort in her "visitor's" arms. Laura recalls those wonderful feelings vividly. Helga and I believed this was confirmation that I wasn't leaving my family alone; He was with them.

At the top of the Salt Lake Airport boarding ramp, I turned for a last sight of and wave to my dear family. I didn't think I could bear it, and I wondered irrationally if it were possible for Helga and the children to hurt as much as I did.

During the flight to San Francisco I swallowed my woes and recalled why I had volunteered to return to Vietnam and to our much-maligned soldiers who were serving faithfully there. A few hours later, at Travis Air Force Base near Fairfield, California, I was booked on a flight scheduled to depart early the next morning. It was delayed until the following evening. I used the delay to attend church meetings, and accepted a dinner invitation to the home of Lewis and Karen Madsen. Over dinner I discovered that Lewis and Karen were good friends of Dallas and Joan Murdoch from their dental school days. In addition to feeding a homesick and Vietnam-bound soldier and stranger, the Madsen s also treated me to a telephone visit with Helga and the children.

My assigned seat on the commercial charter flight to Vietnam was on the aisle about halfway back on the right. In the center seat next to me was Lieutenant Colonel Richnak, the same who had been my platoon leader in the 287th Military Police Company, Horse Platoon, in Berlin in 1954-56. I quickly confirmed recognition of Richnak with a glance at his name tag. Richnak seemed even more surprised than I that we were on the same flight in adjoining, assigned seats. We reminisced during much of the flight. Richnak seemed nothing like the Spartan, reserved, aristocratic young lieutenant that had commanded the horse platoon fifteen years earlier.

Our flight, having departed America the evening of March 2, arrived at Bien Hoa Air Base in Vietnam the afternoon of March 4. We had skipped a day as we crossed the international time zone somewhere west of Hawaii.

Surprisingly, Vietnam was not nearly as hot as I remembered and expected it to be, coming as I did almost directly from deep winter in the Rocky Mountains.

We replacements were hustled off to in-process at Camp Bravo, 90th Replacement Battalion, Long Binh. Then, in company with the handful of chaplains who arrived on the same flight, I went to the USARV Chaplain's Office to receive my assignment. This was a very anxious moment. Would I get my first wish, the 1st Air Cav? If not, then my second wish, another infantry division?

At USARV Headquarters, on Long Binh post, the Deputy USARV Chaplain welcomed us, gave us a pep talk and, finally, told us our assignments: "We've had several calls and written requests from the USARV Commander's office and the Chief of Staff of the 1st Cav. The Cav wants you back and that's where you're going. But it is not what we had in mind for you. You shouldn't have tied our hands by politicking for a specific assignment."

"There was no politicking," I assured the deputy. "I simply responded honestly to a three-star general when he asked me if I wanted to return to the Cav." I thought it unnecessary to mention my petitions to God, as I didn't consider praying the same as politicking. Nor did I describe how enthusiastically I responded to General Tolson's query about my wishes.

On March 6, at Camp Radcliff, An Khe, I began in processing to the 1st Cav. Why, I wondered, did replacements for the division still come through Camp Radcliff? Radcliff had been turned over to the 173rd Airborne Brigade (or was it the 101st Airborne Division?) after the 1st Cav moved north to participate in the 1968 Tet Offensive battle at Hue and other locations. Now the 1st Cav was operating in its new AO to the north and northwest of Saigon in III Corps, well south of Camp Radcliff and the Central Highlands.

The commandant of the orientation school gave me the option of attending or skipping a three-day combat orientation the 1st Cav provided for new troopers, because I was a "sandwich." Soldiers like me who returned to Vietnam for a second or a subsequent combat tour with the 1st Cavalry Division were called sandwiches because we were authorized to wear the big yellow and black Cav patch on each shoulder. By Army regulations, a soldier ever after is authorized to wear on his right shoulder the identifying patch of any unit with which he or she served in combat, while wearing the unit patch of his current assignment on the left shoulder. Thus, after a combat tour with the 1st Cav, during subsequent assignments with the 1st Cav one could wear the distinctive, "horse blanket" shoulder patches—like slices of bread— one on each shoulder. I opted for the orientation period because it would give me time to begin acclimating to the heat and humidity and to explore old haunts.

Camp Radcliff had the lonely, ghost town-like feel of a schoolhouse during vacation. The camp had bustled day and night when the 1st Cav was here. Now much of the camp was abandoned and some of it seemed on the verge of being reclaimed by the jungle.

I wandered around the camp between rappelling practices and booby trap demonstrations. First I visited what had been the 15th Medical Battalion area on the east-southeast end of the main flight line. The hooch I'd built in 1966 still stood, but no one occupied it. The old 2nd Battalion, 8th Cavalry area was vacant and overgrown. The PX no longer existed at the site where I once faced down a sergeant who tried to deny access to my troopers and me. Pleasing to the eye was the continued presence of the gigantic 1st Cav patch in yellow and black on the side of Hon Cong Mountain. A fellow replacement, LTC Ivan Boon, was pulled out early from the orientation course to replace LTC Peter Gorvad of Oakland, California. I'd soon become better acquainted with Lieutenant Colonel Boon and LZ Grant. Gorvad, whom Boon replaced, had been killed the previous night when an enemy 122mm rocket with a delayed fuse exploded in his tactical operations center (TOC). This death occurred during an NVA assault on the 2nd Battalion, 12th Cavalry (2-12 Cav) firebase at an old abandoned French fortress that we called LZ Grant. More than 250 NVA died in the attack.

Alan Syndergaard of Mount Pleasant, Utah, and a door gunner on a LOH (pronounced loach) for Apache Troop, 1-9th Cav, said that after daylight following the attack, he counted 287 NVA bodies—some still showing signs of life—scattered outside the wire around LZ Grant (from *Headhunters,* Edited by Matthew Brennan, Presidio Press).

From other sources, I heard that an American listening post (LP) was caught among the NVA outside LZ Grant that night. Shortly after first light, a "grunt," the only surviving member of the LP, attempted to walk into the perimeter. (Grunt was an honored designation for the infantryman—the equivalent of "Dog Face" in World War II.). One source said the grunt was small and badly burned, and had been mistaken for an NVA soldier by one or more grunts on the perimeter. A hail of automatic fire cut him down and snuffed out his life as he drew near, after all he'd just gone through. Alan Syndergaard said that a soldier had waved to his LOH from a hole near where all the dead NVA were. The LOH radioed LZ Grant that an American was coming in. However when the guy reached the wire, "shots rang out and he collapsed to the ground. Two guys ran out and pulled open his shirt. He was wearing a crucifix."

On March 9, I reached 1st Cav Headquarters at its latest and last base camp in Phuoc Vinh, about thirty-five miles north of Saigon. There I got the word. "You are going to an infantry battalion, the First Battalion, Fifth Cavalry (1-5 Cav)."

The Division Chaplain received me well, but the Deputy Chaplain, Lieutenant Colonel Frank (assigned alias) reiterated the USARV Deputy Chaplain's accusation that I politicked to return to the Cav. "You will regret returning to the Cav," Chaplain Frank promised me.

The 1-5 Cav battalion would have two chaplains for about a month because Captain Henry Lamar Hunt, Assemblies of God, was staying on until his imminent promotion to major. Combat action was light in the 1st Cav area of operations (AO), insisted the personnel in the Division Chaplain's Office.

It being Sunday, and not having any pressing duties, I located the LDS Group Leader, Captain John Thomas Kalunki, who was the Assistant Division Information Officer (DIO). I attended a service with him, at which I spoke by invitation. Colonel McPhie, an Air Force combat pilot and the ecclesiastical head of the LDS organizations in the Southern Military District of South Vietnam, was present at the services. Also in attendance was a Sergeant Kapule, recently of the elite Army parachute team, the *Golden Knights,* and currently with the 101st Airborne Division.

I spent the night of March 9 with my nephew PFC Earl Dyer, my sister Billie June Ramage's eldest son. The next day I reported to the 1-5 Cav field trains in the big 25th Infantry Division base camp at Tay N inh. Upon arriving, I drew essential field equipment and spent a night under intermittent rocket attacks. Over the next year rockets or mortars exploded on the Tay Ninh B ase every time I was there, some quite close to me.

On March 11, I arrived at the 1-5 Cav combat trains on LZ Dolly. Dolly was situated atop a north-south razorback ridge that rose above the Michelin Rubber Plantation on the east and southeast, and jungle on the north and west. From the ridge one could see the Nui Bau Din or Black Virgin Mountain, about twenty-five kilometers to the west. The Black Virgin and razorback were the only prominent elevation features in the western sector of the 1st Cav AO.

When I arrived at LZ Dolly, Bravo 1-5 was fighting down below in the Michelin Rubber. The company was so near we could have seen the action, but for the foliage. At 1435 hours, the second platoon of Bravo 1-5 attacked a bunker complex where it had pinned down three or four NVA.

Between 1618 and 1627 hours, Bravo 1-5 was mortared while it attempted to medevac its casualties. Three minutes later and for the next twenty-seven minutes, the Bravo 1-5 forward operating base (FOB) took heavy fire from three sides, resulting in two friendly WIAs, George Densely and Gary Jolliff.

While Bravo 1-5 fought on, I met Chaplain Hunt, then reported to the battalion operations officer and requested permission to join Bravo Company.

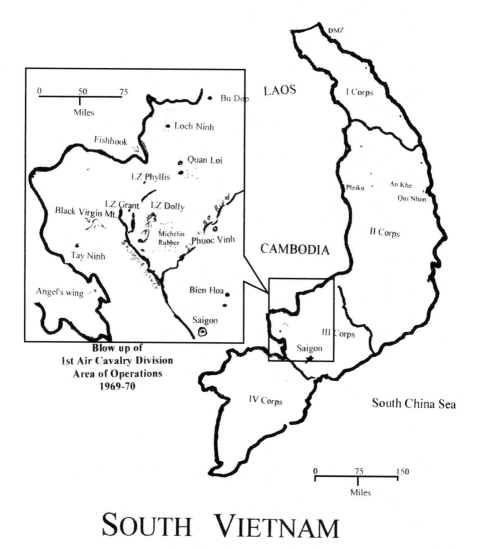

*Map of South Vietnam with blowup of 1st Cavalry Area of Operations
in 1969 and 1970*

"Not until you meet Colonel Peterson," he insisted. LTC Robert J. Peterson and his executive officer (XO) were in the air over the battle, so I'd have to wait.

By mid-evening Bravo 1-5 had broken contact with the NVA and settled in for the night—a quiet one, the battalion operations officer expected.

About 2000 hours, Lieutenant Colonel Peterson received me cordially. "You know what to do. Get to work. To receive a max OR [Officer Efficiency Report], all you have to do is walk on water," Peterson said, tapping the 1st Cav combat patch on my right shoulder.

Well, it was too late to get to work, so Chaplain Hunt and I got acquainted. He briefed me on his arrangement for area support that he had with Chaplain Hugh Black of the 2-12 Cav. The Army applies the principle of area support to distribute assets across unit lines. Area support is applied most often because some requirements, legal support for instance, are so specialized that the cost of placing such assets in small units would be prohibitive. The same is true of denominational (Catholic, Jewish, Baptist, etc.) religious support. Chaplains provide essential religious support, but each chaplain is an ordained clergy member of a particular religious denomination. Baptists can't conduct Catholic Mass, nor can Catholics conduct Protestant communion services. Consequently, most chaplains support one another across unit lines.

In accordance with this principle, Hunt provided Protestant support for the 2-12 Cav and Black provided Catholic support for the 1-5 Cav in return. I liked this cross-pollinating arrangement and opted to continue it, though I called my support "General Christian support" rather than Protestant. Black and I would usually pass back and forth at will between our two battalions, which usually worked quite well for both of us. Some chaplains preferred to coordinate more closely and even travel together.

The next day, March 12, Chaplain Hunt suggested I go to Bravo Company. "I don't think B Company is going to have contact today,"

he opined. He would go to Charlie Company, which he thought was much more likely to see action. Again, I accepted Hunt's suggestion, but dismissed his estimation of the situation; my senses were humming. I could almost feel the sensations of close combat.

At 1410 hours, I hopped a chopper to return to the infantry on the field of battle, eighteen months after leaving Bravo 2-8 Cav on the Bong Son Plain. My arrival in the field had been delayed much of the day because Bravo 1-5 had returned to the area of some of the fighting that had occurred the day before; intense enemy fire promptly pinned down the first and second platoons. Two soldiers died and four were wounded before the platoons could disengage.

When I reached Bravo 1-5 about 1440 hours, the company was in its FOB among the rubber trees, and preparing to return to where it had fought that morning. From the open chopper door as we swept down past the treetops, I studied the squad of sky troopers who were securing the temporary LZ. Each of their young faces appeared exhausted, wary and old, and each set of eyes appeared to stare a thousand meters beyond us.

My feet hit the ground the moment the skids of the chopper did. Quickly, I moved off in the direction one of the grunts pointed. Two rows of rubber trees later, I passed a line of log- and sandbag-covered foxholes, each with a couple of troopers sitting nearby. Drawing nearer, I noted their uniforms were black-streaked and soaked with sweat. Obviously, the troopers had recently fought in a burned-over area. Fifty feet farther, at the command post (CP), I easily picked out the company commander.

Approaching Captain Bailey, I began to introduce myself. We were still shaking hands when an excited message blared over a nearby PRC-25 field radio. The message came from a 1-9 Cav scout ship that was flying nearby, part of a two-ship team that consisted of a Low-level Observation Helicopter (LOH) and a Cobra gunship (or Snake)—a pink team. "Gooks* on the bunkers. They're sunbathing," radioed Apache 28, the light observation helicopter (LOH) pilot. "We're taking fire!"

"Our LOH is down at [map coordinates]!" radioed another voice, the pilot of the Cobra. The LOH and its three-man scout crew were down less than a klick from our position. Time: 1445 hours. I'd been back in the war on the ground for less than five minutes.

Immediately, Captain Bailey ordered two platoons of troopers to move out to rescue the scout crew. I joined the rescue and we moved out to the south without our rucksacks. The grunts moved through the rubber plantation on-line (side-by-side) toward the crash site, with Bailey, the platoon leaders and me in a second line about ten to fifteen feet behind them. Here we were heading almost certainly into a fight, and other than Captain Bailey, I didn't know a name or face. We moved out less than eight minutes after I jumped off the chopper.

Meanwhile, at 1505 hours, Lieutenant Colonel Peterson radioed that he had spotted the wreckage of the LOH from his Charlie-Charlie (Command and Control, or C&C) helicopter, with the crew nearby and apparently unhurt.

We quickly covered about half a kilometer, moving easily and at a steady pace through sparse undergrowth beneath the rubber trees—the trees were evenly spaced in rows about twenty feet apart.

About 1519 hours, in company with the leaders, I stepped onto an east-west running dirt road and had made it about halfway across the road when the troopers on-line stepped warily past the first row of trees on the south side. Ahead, two rows of trees deeper in, the ground was obscured by fallen, leaf-covered tree branches, as though the branches had been knocked off the trees during earlier fighting, *or intentionally knocked down to conceal something*. My combat senses were tingling. Surely, hell would break loose at any moment.

Hurrying on across the road, I reached the first of the downed branches. That's when the NVA opened fire at us.

The first burst of AK-47 rounds cracked past me on both sides as I, on the way to the ground, glimpsed muzzle flashes directly ahead. By the time I reached the ground, several other AK-47s had opened up, joined a moment later by two enemy 30-caliber machine guns.

Right behind the incoming machine-gun fire, NVA snipers opened up on us from the trees. The sniper fire was quite distinct. It came in single shots and was harder on the nerves. It seemed more personal than the automatic fire because I knew each shot was probably aimed at a specific target. Fortunately for us, the snipers were too far back to have much effect.

Notwithstanding combat experience and already anticipating what to expect, for a moment the ambush almost overwhelmed my sense of purpose, coming so suddenly as it did about twenty minutes into a year-long combat tour.

SP4 John Bezdan Jr., whose name I learned later, returned M-16 automatic fire at the most immediate threat to the two of us, the automatic weapon that had fired the first burst of the engagement. From twenty feet in front of me, Bezdan fired straight ahead at a concealed fighting position two rows of trees to his front. As I watched from my prone position, Bezdan fired around the trunk of a small rubber tree. Quickly, he emptied a twenty-round magazine in two or three bursts. Then he shifted to his left side to better extract another magazine from a pouch on his right side. His weapon reloaded, Bezdan raised onto his left knee, apparently in an attempt to get a better shot at the NVA in front of him. Quickly, he swung the barrel of his M-16 around the right side of the tree and tracked toward the enemy bunker. A shade faster, the NVA fired. Bezdan's body was flung backwards and to the left, with a fist-size chunk of muscle and other tissues torn from his inner right thigh area.

Indescribable shock accompanied the instant realization that I was nearest to Bezdan and he needed help fast, and that rendering that help would probably cost me my life, for he lay wounded in clear sight of the gunner that cut him down. I hadn't been back in combat long enough to be prepared for this.

"Why me," best describes my first impulses. Still, after a moment of hesitation, I began low- crawling toward Bezdan, and promptly got my pistol belt snagged on a root or twig. Awkwardly, taking care not to rise too high, I unhooked and wiggled out of my load-bearing suspenders and belt. While I got unstuck, SP4 Henglier -, the platoon medic, slithered past on my right (he moved on his stomach fast enough to shame a Tennessee blue racer snake). "I've got him,

Chaplain!" Henglier called as he scooted past. Word of the new chaplain's presence was spreading.

Henglier, still on his stomach, was examining Bezdan's wounds when I reached their position. Off to the left front I saw SP4 Robert Lewis, a Kentuckian, low-crawling toward the NVA position. From about halfway between us and the NVA position and a little to the left, he threw a grenade at the machine gun and followed it with a long burst of M-16 bullets. While Lewis suppressed the NVA, Henglier and I each grabbed one of Bezdan's shoulders and began dragging him back toward the road. At the edge of the road, we bandaged his wound as best we could before pulling him across it.

All this activity with Bezdan was accompanied by the continuous din of heavy volumes of American and NVA small-arms and machine-gun fire, punctuated by the distinct chatter of at least one body-shredding NVA 51-caliber. Distinct over all this noise was the dreaded thump of enemy mortar shells leaving the tubes. Luckily for us, the first barrage of mortar shells exploded harmlessly near the company CP rather than in our exposed position. The second barrage, though aimed at us, fell short and caused us no grief.

North of the road, we set about solving the problem of how to quickly retreat with a trooper too badly wounded for a shoulder-carry. Scrounging around on his stomach, a trooper found a single stout pole about ten feet long. The medic and troopers were stumped for a moment; in their experience, a makeshift stretcher required two poles and a poncho or two jungle-fatigue blouses.

The Army belt buckle by chance or design was useful for more than holding up a soldier's pants. So turning on my right side, amid warnings to "Keep down, Chaplain," I removed my standard brass-buckled Army issue belt. Then, after borrowing another belt from a nearby trooper, I laid the pole long ways over Bezdan's body. Then, with the two belts hooked together, I bound Bezdan's chest to the pole. Catching on fast, the troopers used all the belts necessary to secure Bezdan to the pole, from head to foot.

With Bezdan secured to the pole, we were ready to withdraw, but we'd never survive running upright unless the intense enemy fire was suppressed. To keep the enemy off of us, Air Force jet fighters attacked. One after the other, the jets screamed across our front at tree-top level from west to east and strafed the NVA with what sounded like mini-gun and cannon fire. Concurrently, artillery pounded the NVA positions farther back. The fighter planes at one hundred feet away roared so loudly that it was hard to distinguish bursting artillery and the ripping blasts of mini-guns and aerial cannon fire.

At 1650 hours, we reached the company FOB without taking more casualties. A lot of thanks for this goes to the danger-close fire support provided by the Air Force fighters, the gunships of Apache 1-9 Cav and ARA (aerial rocket artillery), and tube artillery. This time I arrived soaked in sweat and covered in black soot, just like the soldiers I'd studied two hours earlier. At 1720 hours, we loaded Bezdan and SP4 James T. Freeman onto a waiting, idling Medevac chopper. Bezdan was going home, alive if not quite whole.

Introductions within Bravo 1-5 seemed anti-climatic after what we'd just been through, but Bailey and I completed them anyhow. Then he introduced me to his CP members and lieutenants.

Lieutenant Colonel Peterson, who had landed for a face-to-face conference with Captain Bailey, looked me over and nodded his head approvingly. "All right, my new chaplain walks on water," his eyes seemed to say.

But I was feeling anything but elated. Yes, I was glad to be with the infantry and I felt accepted already, and thankful I had been of some assistance with Bezdan's rescue and care. But I wondered: *How can the grunts keep up with this? How can I? I've had it after two hours, but they've been in action and taking casualties continually for three or four days.* Bravo 1-5 had already sustained two killed and eight wounded this day. SP4 Robert E. Spires of Tewksbury, Massachusetts had died of gunshot wounds to the head and stomach, and PFC James A. Gazze of Chicago, Illinois had died of gunshot wounds to the head.

For their actions in the fight, I recommended Henglier for the Silver Star and Lewis for the Bronze Star with "V" for Valor. They each got their awards. Henglier was Catholic and a conscientious objector, willing to serve, but not to bear arms. He really deserved the Silver Star. He and I would visit often over the next months.

About a month later Lewis became one of only two troopers who were, to my personal knowledge, bitten by a poisonous snake in the reptile-infested jungles of Vietnam. We had found a bamboo viper hanging over the entrance to an NVA bunker. A trooper cut off the snake's head. Lewis picked up the head and it bit him. He lived.

One of the heroes that first day (name withheld) was part of Secretary of Defense Robert McNamara's "Project 100,000." This project was a plan—or special ploy—that made it possible to meet draft quotas by allowing many mentally "below par" Americans to fight and die for their country while others enjoyed student deferments from the draft because of their good grades in college.

Instantly, I respected, admired and loved these troopers in the 1-5 Cav. I'd known these men in the 2-8 Cav, only the names and faces were new.

In most other ways, though, things were different. The society we served had changed; the support we received was different. The enemy was different. Even 1st Cav tactics and equipment had changed. Not all equipment changes were for the better. Notable improvements included the LOH chopper as replacement for those fire-prone death traps called H-13 helicopters, and the modified M-16 rifle, which was less prone to jam and had a muzzle flash suppressor that was less prone to get tangled in vegetation.

For a while this first day, I wondered if I could endure another year, especially if the first hour was any indication of what the year held. That first night I found peace of mind and spirit by reminding myself anew that I was here precisely because everything was different, and because it was worse. I was in the right place to serve these troopers, God's beloved sons, sons so much condemned, neglected and maligned by much of America. But they were obedient sons, all the same, and each one of them laid his life on the altar of sacrifice for a nation that had turned its back on him, from most appearances.

Renewed determination welled up in me as I remembered why I was here, and that the safest place for me was where I was most needed. *To keep going, I must remember why I am here.*

Anyhow, the events of the first two hours certainly cut short the period of "feeling one another out" between my new men and me. Already, the officers, sergeants and troopers appeared to accept me as completely as I'd ever before been accepted.

By the way, we rescued the helicopter crew. The three-man crew of the scout bird simply followed the sound of shooting and linked up with our right flank, without being shot by us in the process.

A minor casualty of the day was my new hunting knife. I'd returned to Vietnam with an expensive Buck knife, only to lose it in the first hour. It was on the load-bearing equipment (LBE) I wiggled out of during Bezdan's rescue. Perhaps my Buck knife brought joy to some NVA soldier.

At 1945 hours, the second platoon, which had just set an ambush 150 meters from the FOB, detected heavy movement and spotted several NVA on every side except the one nearest the FOB. The platoon pulled back and artillery pounded the area. Nearby at the same time Delta 1-5 Cav reported rockets being fired from near its position toward the town and base camp at Dau Tieng. Charlie 1-5 received five 82mm mortar rounds at 2110 hours, and five minutes later about fifteen NVA approached one of its Second Platoon ambushes. Two of the approaching NVA soldiers spotted a claymore mine that the troopers had put out. One of the NVA picked up the mine and the two were examining it when a Charlie 1-5 trooper squeezed the detonator, or klacker as the men called it. There was little left above the chest of either of the two NVA.

The next day, March 13, about 0825 hours, two Bravo 1-5 platoons and the CP moved south. The plan was to go south a short distance, turn east and then north to reenter the area of one of the firefights that had occurred the day before, the area where the two troopers were killed. I moved with the company CP group.

Fifteen minutes later we came onto a freshly buried NVA soldier. After ascertaining what the grave contained, we moved a little farther south-southwest and turned due east.

As we moved, two NVA soldiers paced us from the front, keeping about two hundred meters between them and us. The troopers fired sporadically at the NVA, who simply jumped behind a rubber tree each time until the shooting stopped. These were definitely not the sly, elusive VC and NVA of the 1966-67 days. *We'll not be sneaking up on the enemy today*, I thought.

We turned north after moving eastward a few hundred meters. That's when American artillery began bursting ahead of us. Bravo 1-5's artillery FO walked the exploding shells ahead of us as we advanced northward on a wide front. He kept the rounds bursting near enough to us that shrapnel rained on and around us, but far enough away to avoid cutting us down with shrapnel flying directly out from the bursting shells. In this way we hoped to catch the NVA while they were still in shock from being on the receiving end of heavy artillery. The strategy might have worked, as we reached our objective without receiving enemy fire.

We came to an east-west road, probably the same one I'd become so intimate with the day before. In the middle of the road lay the rucksacks where troopers had dropped them during one of the earlier fights the previous day. Though it didn't seem logical to assume that the NVA had withdrawn, many troopers sighed with relief at the sight of the apparently undisturbed rucksacks.

Captain Bailey established his CP beside a bomb crater, one that had taken out the north side of the road. The Second Platoon spread out east of the bomb crater and settled down along the north side of the road to await orders.

Things were not as they appeared. I suspected the NVA had left the GI rucksacks alone to lull us into a false sense of security, to get us to drop our guard; a successful ploy as it turned out, intentional or otherwise.

Something else bothered me. It seemed the ground north of the road was almost obscured by downed tree branches, presumably freshly blown off the rubber trees during the earlier artillery barrage. But the ground south of the road was almost bare of freshly fallen branches. I suspected that branches might have been moved from the south to camouflage something to the north. If Bailey took my concerns seriously, he didn't show it.

The guys in the CP were too bunched up, so to put some distance between the CP and all those antennas, I walked east along the road, greeting resting troopers as I went. SP4 Eiker was among the troopers I met and greeted. About twenty-five yards from the Company CP, I stopped and visited with Sergeant Fognoi, the platoon sergeant.

Orders cut short my visit with Fognoi at 1118 hours. Bailey ordered Fognoi to sweep his platoon on-line straight north from the road. Without hesitation, the men moved out as ordered. Fognoi and I moved about five feet from the road and stopped when SP4 Eiker -, fifteen feet in from the road and twenty feet to our left, signaled us to hold up. He had almost stepped on a well-camouflaged bunker. Eiker - pulled the pin from a CS tear-gas grenade, cocked his right hand low and backwards and leaned forward out of sight. *He's throwing the grenade into a firing slit of a bunker*, I correctly deduced. Eiker - never finished the toss.

A burst of 30-caliber machine-gun fire nearly cut off one of Eiker's legs at mid-thigh. He fell, terribly wounded and pinned down just inches beneath the flaming muzzle of the machine gun. The NVA machine gunner must have fired a sweeping burst because his first volley also shattered a medic's shoulder and wounded another trooper. The medic ran wildly back past the bomb crater in which the CP was already taking cover, and thus avoided being pinned down. The second wounded trooper fell beside Eiker -, as did two unwounded troopers. A split second later enemy fire opened up all along the road.

Sergeant Fognoi and I reacted instantly and reflexively, but slightly differently to that first burst of machine-gun fire. Fognoi dropped flat where he stood, while I dived forward amid cracking AK-47 rounds to take advantage of the meager protection and concealment offered by a small rubber tree.

It was instantly obvious that my reaction served me poorly, for while it gained me meager concealment and protection, it also halved the distance between the enemy soldier and me. The dive also put a small clearing between the road and me, and machine-gun fire was raking that clearing.

From the other side of the clearing, Sergeant Fognoi took stock of my predicament. "Here, Chaplain," he said, tossing a CS grenade next to my left hand. Then, unknown to me, he belly-crawled with most of his platoon to the south side of the road, leaving me behind.

Very carefully and as quickly as I could, I brought the smoke grenade near my face, pulled the pin with my right hand, and lowered the grenade to my leg to prepare to toss it. As I tossed the grenade, an AK-47 fired a burst from about ten feet in front of me and three rounds cracked past my left ear. I saw the muzzle flashes of the AK-47, but not the NVA soldier behind them.

Seconds later, partially concealed by a CS gas cloud, I scurried backward to the road on my stomach, feet-first. I made it unhurt, despite the NVA fire that continually swept the clear area I had to cross.

Once into the roadbed, I spun around and, crawling headfirst, quickly caught up with Fognoi and his platoon on the south side of the road. He and his troopers were hugging the ground behind the fence post-size rubber trees and an occasional termite dome. Except for those pinned down with Eiker, - and the CP, which was pinned down in the crater, I was the last one on the right flank to withdraw across the road. Enemy machine-gun fire continually raked the rim of the bomb crater into which the whole CP group had disappeared when the shooting began.

At 1206 hours, 82mm mortar rounds started thumping from tubes several hundred meters to our south and east. At the sound of the tubes, Fognoi and his men leaped to their feet and ran westward parallel to and about two rows of trees south of the road. Running like that made no sense to me, for the mortars could just as easily be targeted on the troopers' destination as on where the troopers had been. Still, not about to be left behind, I brought up the rear again.

Though I ran as fast as I could, something much faster pursued me. Over my right shoulder I saw a line of dirt geysers overtaking me; I had an NVA machine gunner's undivided attention.

I knew that hitting the ground probably wouldn't save me, for the machine-gun rounds were striking low. Looking frantically ahead, I spotted a small hump of earth, a termite hill, between two trees. Increasing my speed, I dived, twisting my body in the air as I did so to offer the machine gunner a smaller target. Almost as if in slow motion, I watched the approaching geysers, doubting I would reach cover before hot bullets tore into me. But I made it, barely.

As I sailed and dropped behind the eighteen-inch-high mound, I saw plugs of wood burst first from the tree on my right and then from the tree on my left, as bullets tore through them and stitched across the face of the mound which protected me.

Meanwhile, that first barrage of enemy mortar rounds, the one which panicked the troopers I was with, landed near the company FOB. Four shells also burst near us, but caused no casualties.

Pinned down but unhurt, I at first thought the mound I was behind offered the only protection from the machine gun for at least twenty yards in any direction. Soon, though, I discovered I could move in the depression between the rows of trees, provided I stayed on my stomach.

Across the road, beneath the hot barrel of the machine gun that had fired at me as I ran, Eiker's unwounded buddies struggled to administer first aid and to keep him and the other wounded trooper alive. A few meters from them in the bomb crater, Captain Bailey and the CP group tried to follow and get control of events via PRC-25 radios. Enemy machine-gun fire had quickly dissuaded most of the CP group of any ideas about eyeballing the scene or evacuating the bomb crater. Fortunately for the CP, Army of the Republic of Vietnam (ARVN) Sergeant Van Nie was not dissuaded.

The following details I learned later. Sergeant Van Nie, in the bomb crater with the CP, repeatedly risked instant death by popping his head up to check the area around the bomb crater. Following one such "peek," Van Nie gestured wildly to the northwest and yelled, "Beau coup GI! Beau coup GI!"

Captain Bailey and the artillery forward observer (FO) at first thought Van Nie was trying to give their position away—after all, we were the GIs. "But the Gooks already know where we are," Bailey told himself, and ventured a quick look, just in time.

Seemingly from nowhere, twenty-five NVA infantrymen were advancing on the CP in the crater. Van Nie opened fire first and an NVA fell. The FO dropped another, and the NVA retreated, the element of surprise having been lost.

Help arrived quickly. ARA choppers and gunships came on-station and began taking some of the pressure off us by pounding the NVA with 40mm grenades, rockets, and mini-gun fire. Artillery commenced pounding the area farther to the north. Air Force fighters arrived ready to help. However, we couldn't bring all these supporting fires near enough to be immediately effective because Eiker and his buddies provided an unwilling shield for the closest NVA.

Meanwhile, the First Platoon remained north of the road and west of the CP group during the fight, sustaining friendly WIAs in its efforts to rescue Eiker and his buddies and protect the CP.

My hands were quite full helping with the wounded, so I missed some of the details of Eiker's eventual rescue. It went like this: At great calculated risk to itself and the grunts with Eiker -, an ARA chopper hovered in "danger close" and placed a rocket just behind and almost on top of the NVA machine-gun position/bunker. Then, while the troopers of the First Platoon concentrated fire on that bunker and others that were more exposed because much of the concealing foliage was blown away, one of Eiker's buddies pulled the pin from a fragmentation grenade. Carefully he released the handle to activate the time-delay detonator, counted off the seconds, and then slipped the grenade through the firing slit. The grenade exploded before the NVA could throw it back out. The machine gun was silent after that.

With the enemy machine gun out of commission, the First Platoon pulled back, dragging Eiker and his buddies with them, protected somewhat by an umbrella of aerial rocket and mini-gun fire. Right behind the last of the First Platoon, the CP group escaped from the crater. A rocket exploded on the north rim of the crater just as the last CP member went over the south rim. That's how close we were bringing in the suppressive fire.

Eiker and the other wounded troopers were brought to my location. We stabilized Eiker's flapping leg and attended to the other troopers' wounds. A Medevac chopper arrived above the trees to hoist Eiker -

out, but withering NVA gunfire thwarted the attempt. So Peterson braved the bullets to hover over us in his command and control chopper (Charlie-Charlie) long enough for the door gunner and crew chief to kick out stretchers, some of which hung out of reach in the trees. Thus, with our wounded, we withdrew and left the NVA to the pounding of artillery and air attacks.

It is hard to estimate how long the fight lasted. It seemed like hours. According to official records, the shooting started within seconds of 1118 hours. The CP was still pinned in the crater an hour and thirty-seven minutes later, at 1255 hours. Probably the engagement ended after about two hours. Amazingly, we sustained no friendly KIAs, but easily could have, as events proved.

According to a report I read a few days later, a company of 25th Infantry Division Armor killed some 120 NVA in a tunnel, the exit of which was at the spot where Van Nie first saw the twenty-five NVA soldiers who attacked the Bravo 1-5 CP in the crater.

Subsequent intelligence revealed that Bravo 1-5 had for two or three days repeatedly bumped into the weaker points of an NVA regimental position. The NVA position was horseshoe-shaped, with the open end of the horseshoe to the west, and defenses around both the inside and outside of the horseshoe. The stronger defenses were presumably on the outside.

Bravo 1-5 maneuvers the day before had taken the company north-to-south past the tip of the north prong of the horseshoe, and into the soft inside of the southern tip. The next day, we'd again maneuvered south past the northern prong of the horseshoe-shaped position, turned east between the prongs and then north into the jaws of a trap.

One can easily imagine our fate had we hit the harder outside of the NVA position, or if Eiker hadn't prompted the NVA machine gun to open fire before the Second Platoon passed the first line of enemy bunkers and fighting positions. Had we gotten farther in among the NVA, the tunnel exit would have been between the rest of the company and us, which would have allowed overwhelming numbers of NVA forces to engage us at such close quarters that outside help would have been impossible.

My instincts had been reliable. Surely, the NVA had left the GI rucksacks in place to lure us in, and had gathered the downed tree branches south of the road to conceal their positions, clearing fields of fire south of the road in the process.

About mid-afternoon, back at the company FOB, it occurred to me I'd been back in combat less than twenty-four hours. A lifetime.

Following a quiet night, Bravo 1-5 moved out to the northwest the next morning, March 14. In the order of march, I was just ahead of the CP group in the lead platoon. We were leaving the Michelin Rubber Plantation, and good riddance. Along the way, we passed a dead NVA soldier. He was about twenty feet off to the left of the path. One of the troopers said Bravo 1-5 had killed the NVA three days earlier. It was amazing how much the NVA soldier's remains had decomposed in so short a time. His torso appeared to be melting and blending into the ground.

A few hours later and a few kilometers farther, the rubber trees abruptly gave way to jungle. Ahead, the trail continued in a northwest-erly direction, intersecting a path that went south and disappeared into a draw. The lead platoon turned south along the new path. Suddenly, three bicycle-mounted NVA soldiers came zipping along from the northwest, just as I reached the intersecting path and started to turn south.

The NVA reacted almost too quickly to follow. With practiced moves, they leaped from the bikes while drawing AK-47 rifles from scabbards on the bikes, and sprayed us with bullets. Just as quickly the three abandoned their bikes and disappeared into the brush.

I hastily backtracked toward the CP as troopers moved forward and blasted the vicinity where the NVA had disappeared. Moments later after the CP moved to the south and against a line of trees on its west, a trooper next to me fired an M-79 high explosive (HE) round. He intended to fire over the tree line and at least harass the evading NVA. His aim was slightly off. The grenade exploded against a tree limb almost directly above the CP Group. A radioman (RTO) caught a piece of shrapnel through the muscle between the thumb and forefinger of his right hand.

After confiscating the NVA bicycles, we moved a hundred feet to the south and set up a FOB. There, beneath heavy foliage I conducted my first worship service since returning to Vietnam. It was my first service with an element of the 1-5 Cav.

Late that afternoon I caught a chopper back to LZ Dolly, where a very apologetic Chaplain Hunt waited. Actually, he'd seen action, too. Earlier in the day the NVA had attacked while he conducted a worship service. The enemy quickly broke off the attack because it had mistakenly assaulted the Charlie and Delta Companies of the 1-5 Cav in their two-company position, thinking they were attacking a CIDG (Vietnamese home guard) unit—this according to the confessions of an enemy prisoner of war (EPW or POW).

Hunt continued with the worship service following the aborted attack. Unlike Hunt's experience that day, I never in two years of combat had a worship service interrupted by an enemy attack.

The next day, March 15, I began making rounds to become acquainted with the other units of my new battalion. About noon Chaplain Hunt and I flew from LZ Dolly down into the rubber trees where Charlie and Delta Companies were co-located on a FOB. The companies were preparing to begin air assaults, each onto a different company objective in the jungle. Chaplain Hunt introduced me first to the Delta 1-5 commander, then to Captain Jim Cain of Charlie 1-5, after which I stayed with Charlie 1-5 for the air assault while Hunt returned to LZ Dolly.

Charlie 1-5 air assaulted into a small clearing in the jungle about two kilometers northeast of LZ Dolly. We came in behind an impressive barrage of tube and aerial artillery. The LZ was green, meaning we received no unfriendly fire. Within minutes of being inserted, the men of Charlie 1-5, all unfamiliar faces to me, had formed up and pushed north and deeper into the jungle. Almost immediately, we found ourselves in a massive, recently-vacated bunker complex.

Captain Cain called in a report on the bunkers and the company pressed on, leaving the complex for others to investigate and destroy. We had contact about 1630 hours when our point man met the point man of an NVA and they blasted away at each other. We sustained no casualties and saw no sign of NVA casualties.

We stopped an hour later to dig in for the night and I began my foxhole at a spot about five meters or so from where the radiomen were digging in—digging my own hole reinforced my credentials with these men. The FO, Lieutenant Bill Haines, approached me as I dug in. He introduced himself and offered to share a two-man hole with me.

I noted that these troops, like the ones in Bravo 1-5, dug in differently now than had those in 1966 and 1967. First, Cain selected the site of the FOB, a different and more difficult process in the trackless jungle than it usually had been in the more populated areas around Bong Son —areas where land features, rice paddies and villages offered points of reference.

With the FOB site chosen, the platoon leaders promptly sent out cloverleaf patrols to sweep a hundred meters or so in front of their respective sectors of the perimeter. Each cloverleaf patrol went forward a specified distance. Then each patrol turned in the same direction, right or left, and looped back to the perimeter; by this means the patrols usually, but not always, avoided running into one another.

With patrols under way and OPs going into position, it was time to dig foxholes. Every trooper switched back and forth between guarding the perimeter and digging. Each NCO and officer that was not otherwise occupied with vital duties took his turns at pick and shovel. Enough holes had to be quickly dug to permit every man a place under cover from which to stand and fight, if necessary. After the foxholes were dug in relative silence, the men filled sandbags—each trooper carried a few empty bags in his rucksack for this daily protective routine. At each foxhole, once the sandbags were filled with dirt from the excavations, the men stacked a few bags at each corner of the foxhole and put the remainder aside for later use. Then with holes dug and sandbags filled, noise discipline was relaxed enough to permit the troopers to chop down small trees (my favorite digging-in task) for overhead cover. Next, short wooden crossbeams were laid across the stacked bags at each end of the hole and four to six long poles were laid across these. Finally, the remaining sandbags were laid across the logs. Thus, in an hour or so almost every day, we dug five-foot-deep fighting positions and constructed overhead cover for protection from mortar, artillery and rocket bursts, including overhead bursts in the trees. After dark, ambushes were set and listening posts (LPs) replaced observation posts (OPs). The dissimilarities between how we now dug in 1969 and how we had dug in 1966-67 reflected the differences in the war itself. We were definitely in a different kind of war on this, the fifteenth day of March, nineteen hundred and sixty-nine.

Chapter Notes:

2 March 1969, 1-5 Battalion Journal: A Co WIAs 1LT Cecil Harrison, SP4's David Witte, Richard D. McCoy, Ralph L. Froehner, Thomas N. Schenvert and D. Knox."

8 March 1969, 1-5 Battalion Journal: 10, B Co WIA Sp4 Jack S. Keyes, c/a. 1315 B Co WIAs Pfc Wilbert Ford and Pfc Roy Hudson, claymore.

9 March 1969, 15 Battalion Journal: A Co WIA Aniline, eye. C Co, Appendicitis—Allen Niedwell.

11 March 1969, 1-5 Battalion Journal B Co WIAs George Desley or Dealey RA52338083 and Gary Tolliss.

12 Mar. '69, 1-5 Battalion Journal, item 36 cont'd: "[B Co] proceeded into yesterday's contact area...26 element was into area 50 meters before being pinned down...16 element came in from north and pinned down after 100 meters...02 US KIA and 04 US WIA." 1505: B Co at 1445 hrs, reports Apache 28 finding bunkers with enemy in area...Apache 28 reports low bird has been shot down...GM-6 spotted downed bird...crew seems all right because GM-6 sees strobe light 30 meters from downed bird. B Co is moving into area of downed bird." 1520: "B Co taken under fire from flank and front" 1525: "B Co at 1520 hrs are now pinned down...enemy on both flanks, firing from bunkers and fighting positions." 1535: "B Co still receiving fire...flanks and front...B Co maneuvering to link up with crew of downed bird." 1650: "B Co has linked with down bird crew at 1540...[crew] neg injuries." 1650: "B Co has broken contact at this time and is headed for their FOB." 1650: "B Co request medevac for 02 EM at 1650 hrs." 1730: "B Co reports knocked out machine-gun bunker...their 35 did it, he [Lewis] crawled within fifteen feet of bunker and threw frags...confirmed 02 NVA KIA." 1945: "B Co 26 element was moving from FOB to ambush loc, when spotted 4 to 5 indiv and heavy movement on both flanks, 150 meters from FOB." Casualties today: B Co KIAs - Pfc James Gazze and Sp4 Robert Spires; WIAs Pfc's Jan Bingel, GSW back; John Bezdan Jr., GSW

leg and testicles. Sp4's WIA were James Woodall, GSW side and arm; and James Goggins, GSW foot. Charlie 1-5's WIA were Sp4 Harold Curtis, frag arm, and Pfc Jool P. O'Kula frag to leg. Delta 1-5's WIA were James Sargent, frag head; and Samuel Hunter, frag head, and James Freeman, frag eye shown also in B Co with Sp4 David Bowers, frag. wd. leg]. 12 Mar. '69, 1-5 Battalion Journal, item 51, 1730-1800: B Co. reports knocked out machine gun bunker, 35 did it. He crawled within 15 feet of bunker and threw frags in...confirmed 02 NVA KIA as a result.

13 March 1969, 1-5 Battalion Journal: 0840: "B Co has dug up grave...will move into yesterday's contact area."

0846: "spotted 04 NVA 75 meters to the south...two carrying 50 cal. B Co has one squad maneuver and rest laying low."

0930: "B Co...spotted 2 more individuals, 150 meters to S.E....area is full of bunkers...two contact areas are all one bunker complex." 1005: "B Co is in contact area...thinks this is large complex." 1120: "B Co is in contact...02 US WIAs. B Co will pull back for arty...then proceed to objective: 1145: "B Co 26 element is pinned down by 30 cal. fire from bunkers 20 meters [actually 20 feet] to their front...others flanking 26 element on left. 26 is trying to pull wounded out. B Co is completely surrounded & awaiting arrival of ARA. 1206: "B Co FOB is receiving mortars." 1210: "B Co is receiving mortars in contact area. 1215: "B Co is being flanked to the N.E. Believe they killed 2 or 3."

14 Mar. '69, 1-5 Cav Battalion Journal: 1013 "B Co is in contact with 03 individuals 45 meters away, running, 3rds returned fire, riding 03 bicycles...fork, bamboo on bicycles to carry weapons...B Co, as most of its people assembled in bomb crater with one element on west side of road. One WIA, hand, no name."

March 1969 2-12 Cav Operational Report: On the morning of 8 March Company D's PO/LP's around LZ Grant picked up heavy movement. Shortly after that LZ Grant received a heavy rocket, mortar and recoilless rocket attack, followed by a heavy ground attack. During the mortar attack a 120mm mortar hit the TOC, killing the Bn. Co., LTC Gorvad, the Assistant Operations NCO, the LNO, and one RTO. The round also wounded the Intelligence Sergeant, the Operations NCO and one other RTO...Operations Officer, Major Brown - assumed command...[105 and 155 batteries on Grant] fired 1400 rounds...both direct and indirect fire...mortar sections of C and D Companies fired over 1000 rounds of 81mm mortar. Spooky and Blue Max provided additional support. Contact broke at 0530 hrs....150 NVA KIA, 2 NVA/WIA/PW...Friendly losses were 15 US/KIA and 31 US/WIA.

March 1969 1-5 Cav Operational Report: 15 Mar C Company captured P.O.W. w/AK-47. When the company's 2nd Platoon blew its ambush, killing one or two of his companions, the P.O.W. ran toward company's F.O.B, and was tackled. He was a medic with the 7th NVA Battalion, 29th Regiment.

12 April, 0900, 1-5 Battalion Journal: "B Co requests medevac for Sp4 Robert Lewis, snake bite."

Chapter Six

BEST COMBAT SOLDIER
I EVER SAW

—Robert W. (Bill) Snyder—

Captain Cain and I got better acquainted while we dug in. He, upon learning I was LDS, pointed to a large, sweating trooper who was digging a machine-gun position on the eastern side of the perimeter. "See that man? He's a Mormon, Bill Snyder, and the best combat soldier I ever saw," Cain said.

Casually, I approached PFC Robert William Snyder and his machine-gun team, all of whom were shirtless, except Snyder. His fatigue shirt was off, but he wore what appeared to be two green tee shirts. Knowing Snyder was LDS, I applied my keen intellect and I deduced the "tee shirt" next to his skin was actually a religious garment, covered reverently by a regular tee shirt, despite the added heat and discomfort that prompted others to shed every item of clothing they could.

"Hello. I'm your new battalion chaplain," I greeted Snyder and his buddies, revealing no specific interest in Snyder. We went through the usual pleasantries—names, hometowns, days left on short-timer calendars. When Snyder, in turn, said he was from Springville, Utah, I responded,

"Mormon country. Are you a Mormon?"

"Yes, I am," responded Snyder, with that combination of confidence and absence of sanctimoniousness of voice and demeanor that I'd hoped for.

"Are you a good Mormon?"

"I try to be," Snyder answered.

"Fine! I'm LDS too," I declared as I again reached out my hand.

"Great!" he said, his countenance beaming like a lighted Christmas tree, "Now I can write my folks and tell them something good. Now I can receive the Sacrament."

Bill Snyder had been in combat for several months and was the only man of his faith in Charlie Company so far as he knew. After promising Snyder that we'd share a two-man sacrament service the next day, I returned to finish my foxhole. It was too near nightfall to have the service then. Little did I anticipate how hard it would be to keep my promise to Bill Snyder, nor the impact his life would have on mine.

A 1-9 Cav scout LOH reconnoitered around our position while we dug in. Soon the LOH pilot alerted us to large stacks of ammunition boxes and probably a bunker complex about 150 meters to our south-west. Exploitation of the information would have to wait for another day, as Cain did not want our patrols to go out that far so late in the day.

It was 2300 hours and the night was pitch-black beneath the triple-canopy jungle. I slept on my partially inflated air mattress beside my foxhole with my head toward the hole. In an instant, I awakened standing upright in my foxhole. My reflexes had carried me faster than my mind could register what had awakened me. The blast of a claymore mine had shattered the night. The chatter of Snyder's M-60 machine gun and of several M-16 and AK-47 rifles shattered whatever was left of sleep. Green tracers snapped across the FOB and exploding hand grenades punctuated the din the automatic weapons were raising.

Men on an ambush out beyond Snyder's position had pressed the detonator, blowing a claymore mine on about ten NVA soldiers. The NVA had stumbled onto the ambush about a hundred feet from me, and some fifty feet beyond Snyder's position. The NVA soldiers' reflexive return of fire showed combat experience and discipline, especially con-sidering that they were walking wounded, as we learned later.

The shooting stopped as quickly as it had begun and someone yelled from Snyder's three-man foxhole, "Gook in the perimeter!" Two

NVA soldiers, probably in considerable confusion, had charged straight at Snyder's machine gun. One fell dead in front of the machine gun, and the other one ran past Snyder into the perimeter and threw himself to the ground near Platoon Sergeant Raymond Clark. I heard Clark whisper, "Who's there?"

Silence....

Clark, sensing a presence in the pitch-black darkness, lunged with both hands at where he thought the presence was. One hand clamped onto a head and the other to an AK-47 rifle. "I've got him! Help! I've got him!" Clark yelled. The bewildered NVA soldier surrendered without a fight. Clark and a trooper soon had him searched and tied up, ready for interrogation and evacuation, come the dawn.

The POW said he was part of a group of walking wounded, all dazed survivors of an American bomb strike, and that they had been en route to an NVA field hospital when they stumbled onto our position. We had unintentionally dug in for the night on the eastern edge of an NVA bunker complex that combined a hospital with an ammunition cache.

On March 16, dawn arrived with more shooting, and another NVA dead and two enemy prisoners of war in hand. Sergeant Thomas Eugene Hoover of Dayton, Ohio was either on an LP, not likely considering his rank, or on dawn patrol when he and two other troopers engaged two NVA soldiers about twenty meters outside the northwest perimeter. I arrived on the scene moments later and found one dead NVA soldier and the troopers standing over a seriously wounded one on which a medic worked to staunch arterial bleeding from a mangled thigh. I stopped the bleeding with a combination pressure bandage-tourniquet, using the NVA soldier's own belt.

From their expressions, the troopers disliked my choice of wound bindings—NVA belt buckles made prized war trophies. Later, before the wounded NVA was evacuated, I noticed someone had replaced the belt with a bandanna. No Americans had been hurt in the brief engagement.

Soon, a chopper arrived and took the two POWs off our hands. We quickly broke camp and moved a few meters to investigate the ammo boxes and bunker complex that the crew of the 1-9 LOH had reported the evening before.

Immediately, the troopers discovered hundreds of mortar and rocket rounds, all in boxes above ground, and all bearing Chinese markings. For the rest of the day the troopers hauled in munitions from all over the area. Army engineers and the press arrived, the engineers to blow the enemy munitions in place and the press to follow the story of the day.

By late afternoon the troopers had finished collecting and stacking scores of boxes of munitions. The finished stack was roughly squared, thirty feet on each side and as high as a one-story building. After the grunts stacked the munitions, the engineers laced C-4 explosives all through the stack and connected the charges to each other with detonating cord. Finally, the engineers ran the det-cord a thousand meters westward into another section of the NVA bunker complex.

While the stacking and lacing were going on, we searched the bunkers closer at hand, which included a forty-bunker hospital complex, side-by-side with munitions bunkers. From one bunker I collected my only trophy of the war, a *Bic* pen, which prize I justified taking because it was made in America. Later during the tour I would reluctantly comply with a personal request by a friend to bring him an NVA pith helmet.

In one of the hospital bunkers I saw rare examples of NVA personal taste—fresh-cut flowers on a table and a calendar on the wall that had the current date scratched off.

With the munitions pile ready to blow, I followed the detonating cord along a freshly beaten path toward the bunkers where we would take shelter from the anticipated explosion. An engineer was in the lead and an infantry lieutenant was behind me. We passed a trooper, as skinny and bedraggled as any soldier I ever saw. He stood in deep grass at a point where the detonating cord made a slight turn to the left. As the engineer approached, the skinny, slouching trooper said, "Don't step on the det-cord."

The engineer responded, "That's all right, troop. You won't hurt the det-cord."

"Makes no difference, Sad Sack. You keep doing what I told you. Keep people off the det- cord," ordered the Lieutenant from behind me.

Dutifully, the trooper advised me to not step on the det-cord. I stopped before him and extended my hand with, "Hi, I'm Chaplain Newby, your new chaplain. What's your name?"

"Sad Sack," he said in a voice every bit as beaten as its owner appeared to be.

Surprisingly the image of the trooper's sagging body being held upright only by the grime in his uniform, I said, "I'll not call you Sad Sack. What is your true name?"

"Private Rodriguez." Was it my imagination, or did Rodriguez's shoulders straighten just a bit at the use of his own name?

"What's your first name?"

"Ronaldo," the trooper said, though the record reads Ronald.

"I'll call you Ron, for short. Is that all right with you?"

"Yes, sir," Ron answered with a slight smile.

I continued along the route marked by the det-cord toward the NVA bunker. Once out of earshot of Ron, I asked the lieutenant why he had the trooper performing an unnecessary task. "Because," he answered in effect, "we can't rely on Sad Sack to do anything important. So we look for stuff for him to do, things that won't get others hurt."

Later in the day, after what I considered adequate time for reflection and tactfulness, I challenged a couple of leaders to see what would happen if they started addressing Rodriguez either as Ron, by his last name, or by his rank and last name. "Besides, Ron sees through busy work. I wish you would stop giving it to him," I said.

One of the leaders reacted defensively at first, then agreed to call "Sad Sack " by his name or rank. Perhaps it was my imagination, but Ron looked better, more soldierly, whenever a leader called him by his true name, during the few months he had left.

A few minutes later in an NVA bunker, I placed my helmet on the head of a newswoman, moments before an engineer hit the detonator.

The resulting explosion was nothing like the fantastic bang we anticipated. Rather, the placed charges detonated with just enough force to
scatter the stacked munitions and render them more dangerous for the
grunts to re-collect, which they of course had to do. The Charlie 1-5
troops used the remaining daylight to re-stack enemy munitions.
Meanwhile, another day had passed without Snyder and me getting
together as I promised.

It rained hard in the late afternoon, which was rare for the season
and made for a wet, uncomfortable night in the same FOB we'd used
the previous night. I again shared a foxhole with 1LT Bill Haines, the
son of Navy Admiral Haines, Commander of all the American Forces
in the Pacific, including us in Vietnam. Bill Haines and I got along
quite well during the short few months we were together off and on.
His parents invited Helga and me to use their guesthouse in Hawaii for
R&R, but the timing didn't work out.

On March 17 I moved on, leaving the troopers of Charlie 1-5 to finish re-collecting and stacking the enemy munitions. Though I was elsewhere when it happened, the engineers did the munitions demolition
job right this time, so I was told.

Though I wanted to remain with Charlie 1-5 and have that service
with Snyder, I felt I had to move on because there remained first visits
and worship services for three other companies in my battalion plus all
the companies in the 2-12 Cav. Fortunately, Chaplain Hunt had held
services for Charlie 1-5 five days earlier. The troopers were so busy
and scattered that I couldn't even locate Snyder to explain the delay in
having a sacrament service.

During the period of March 16-26 I visited the rest of the companies in both battalions and got reacquainted with Lieutenant Colonel
Boon of the 2-12 Cav. I was almost constantly on the move and was
with units during a couple of fights. My closest call during this ten-day

period was probably an incident that occurred in the battalion field trains (rear) area at Tay Ninh. Shouting awakened me there late one night. An intoxicated trooper, one I'd met several days earlier in the field, was waving a loaded M-16 and threatening to kill anyone who messed with him. As I was the only officer on the scene, I approached the trooper very slowly and calmly said, in essence, "Look, I'm your chaplain and I don't want to hurt you, but I can't let you hurt anyone else either."

He blustered for a moment, then handed his weapon to me. I passed the weapon to the sergeants, who put the trooper to bed under watch. I don't think anything else ever came of the incident.

On March 20, we got an impressive demonstration of armor against infantry. The engagement began as an operation to rescue a long-range patrol (LRRP) team. The LRRPs (H Company, 75th Rangers) were pinned down and hard-pressed by a very large NVA force in the jungle near the northeast edge of the Michelin Rubber Plantation.

In preparation for the rescue operation, half of Alpha 1-5 air assaulted in and linked up with a mechanized company of the 11th Armored Cavalry Regiment. While Captain Cecil Harrison placed Charlie 1-5 in a skirmish line between the armored personnel carriers (APCs) and tanks, facing west, one of the five M-60 tanks in the force quickly cleared a field of fire by knocking down a swath of trees around the contact area. Then with the men on-line between them, the five M-60 tanks and eight armored personnel carriers charged ahead to rescue the rangers.

Unfortunately, the tankers demonstrated little appreciation of the difficulties that the downed trees presented for infantry on foot. Soon, the tanks were well out in front of the struggling foot soldiers—a big mistake.

The NVA made their presence known just moments later, at 1300 hours, after the tanks had charged beyond the LRRP team. Concealed in bunkers and spider holes, the individual NVA soldiers had let the tanks pass over them. Then, before our guys could catch up, the NVA popped up and fired rocket-propelled grenades (RPG) into the soft rear grills of the tanks. Farther back, other NVA took the grunts under fire from behind. Sergeant Mario Grisanti of Tyler, Texas describes part of what happened next. "We were assaulting a bunker complex on-line. This was the only time I ever worked with an ARVN unit. The ARVN soldiers were interspersed between Americans as we attacked on-line. Ahead of us the tanks were also attacking on-line. An ARVN soldier on my right pointed ahead at an NVA soldier behind a tree and said something in Vietnamese. At that point it became one of those slow-motions deals. I remember slowly bringing up my weapon, firing on full automatic. Even the recoil was in slow motion. I hit the NVA in the chest and watched him throw a Chicom grenade as he fell. Then I watched the grenade slowly as, trailing smoke, it arched up and down, bounced, and rolled right between my feet, where it exploded," said Grisanti.

"I wasn't unconscious very long, but when I woke up I was completely paralyzed. And I was aware that my legs were all wet—I thought they were shattered. Someone pulled me behind a tree and a medic came and I could feel his hands when he cut my pants' legs off using a sapper knife that I'd taken off a dead sapper. I kept asking the medic how my legs were and he kept shaking his head and saying something that I could not hear. I interpreted his shaking head to mean my legs were gone. Finally, he…lifted my head and made me look at my legs," said Grisanti.

"I never had a scratch. My legs were wet because the shrapnel had hit the American on my right and blown apart his canteen, splashing water all over my legs. I thought my ears were bleeding. They weren't. After about fifteen or twenty minutes, feeling started coming back. The next day, hearing started to return."

Meanwhile, the tanks and their crews were generally less fortunate than Grisanti. Within minutes of beginning the attack, four of the five tanks were burning, total losses, and the fifth tank had a track blown off. A burning tank swung about and attempted to withdraw, running headlong into a bomb crater in the process. The tank came to rest with the barrel of its cannon resting across the rear rim of the crater, the way a soldier on guard might rest his weapon on the berm of his foxhole.

The LRRPs were rescued alive. Alpha 1-5 sustained one killed and nine wounded. An NVA soldier shot Sergeant Victor D. Kahla Jr. of Texas while he, John Gayman, and some others were checking bunkers and fighting positions that had been bypassed by the armor. Kahla was shot from inside the bunker when he leaned down to toss in a hand grenade. The NVA who shot him died quickly at the hands of Kahla's angry buddies. Kahla was alive when he was evacuated from the field, but died later in the day. The mechanized unit sustained eight killed men and thirty wounded, in addition to losing four of their five M-60 tanks. The withdrawing NVA unit left the bodies of seventy-two NVA. Several NVA soldiers were captured.

While half of Alpha 1-5 was engaged in the action described above, the other half was in action with tanks elsewhere. Of the other action, Tom Holcombe said, "Kimbrough and I dug some NVA soldiers out of caved-in bunkers and took them prisoner. This we did after Rex Storey had seen them behind us after we had passed them....Rex Storey pulled several NVA soldiers out of a bunker and took them prisoner."

"This was the easiest clearing of bunkers we ever did. The tanks would drive on top of a bunker and pivot back and forth until the bunker was collapsed. Then we would literally dig the enemy out with our shovels," wrote Platoon Leader Lieutenant Steven A. Holtzman of Agoura Hills, California.

Trooper David J. De Leon of Alpha 1-5 became a "delayed" casualty during the night after the fighting ended. His platoon was in position on-line about fifty feet from the barrel of the tank cannon, the one that fell into the bomb crater. Sometime after midnight, a flechette round cooked off in the breech of the cannon on the burning tank. De Leon, who was lying barely exposed on his side or stomach, caught one of the steel flechettes (arrows) in one of his lower cheeks.

From the air the next morning, I saw a freshly-beaten trail along the edge of a bomb crater to the north. It looked like hundreds of pairs of feet, many wearing BF Goodrich sandals, had beaten a retreat from the area during the previous night.

About an hour after I joined with Alpha 1-5, we climbed atop the APCs and one remaining tank for a very unpleasant ride out of the rubber trees to the southeast. This ride took us into an area where Rome Plows (giant Army road graders) had cleared away several acres of jungle. These jungle-clearing operations were executed to deny enemy forces the concealment they had to have in order to stockpile war supplies and to assemble in preparation for attacks against us and other lucrative targets like Saigon.

On the way to the clearing we passed through an area that had been seeded with persistent CS (tear) gas powder. The tank and APC treads stirred the CS powder into billowing clouds of tearful misery for us. Crying silently, we survived the best we could.

Once out of the gassed area, I got a bright idea. By rolling down my sleeves one turn at a time, I uncovered consecutive strips of gas-free cloth with which to wipe some of the gas-impregnated dust from my face and eyes. Pretty soon the other troopers were following my example.

Pleasant relief waited ahead. A cool, swift, deep stream ran northeast to southwest through jungle near the north edge of the clearing. The men of Alpha 1-5 went swimming, led into the water by their company commander. They were taking advantage of the security provided by the 11th Armored Cavalry Regiment (ACR). After his swim, an officer went about his duties for an hour or so wearing only his jungle boots, steel helmet, and holstered pistol on a web belt—not an impressive picture.

Sergeant Elvin Jackson of Fremont, Utah, whom I'd just met, wanted a bath as much as anyone else, but he and I held back until most of the troopers finished with theirs. Then we went upstream a hundred feet or so and found for ourselves a pool that promised at least the illusion of privacy. After looking around to be sure we had no unwelcome company, I stood guard with Jackson's M-16 while he bathed and washed out his religious clothing. Then we switched roles.

Following the baths, we gathered the company and held a memorial service for Kahla. I'd already decided to hold memorial services in the field, at company level, as soon as practicable after a soldier fell, rather than to wait for larger services in the rear, as had been the common practice in 1966-67. This policy turned out to be wise because during this tour there were no opportunities for larger-unit services in the rear.

The company commander spoke at his own request during the service and by a poor choice of words he seriously damaged his credibility with the troops. He said something like, "We're sorry Kahla was killed, but we made the SOBs pay for it with seventy-two of their own."

When the captain said this, I sensed an almost tangible wave of anger sweeping through the assembled troopers. Eyes turned cold and faces hard. SP4 Rodney J. Linn, machine gunner, interrupted his captain. "No way does seventy-two Gooks 'pay' for one grunt, for Kahla," he declared. Later he said, "After the memorial service you came to us, Chaplain, and calmed us down. 'Don't do what you guys are thinking,' you advised us."

The general feelings were that *the old man doesn't care about our lives.* That was too bad. The captain probably meant well, intending only to console the men and perhaps boost their spirits. After all, a ratio of 72 to 9 was impressive as body count comparisons go. And this time the enemy never got away unhurt, as so often seemed the case; usually we fought at times and at places of the enemy's choosing, and seldom knew how badly the enemy was hurt. But what the troopers heard the captain say was, "Your lives mean nothing to me."

Perhaps with time the captain might have gained the hearts and loyalties of the men in Alpha Troop, but judging from officer and enlisted comments thirty years later, it never happened. Phil Gioia replaced Harrison as Company Commander of Alpha 1-5 soon after I arrived. One of Captain Harrison's very sensible moves had been to create an unofficial position in his company of "pace man." Without reference points, it was very difficult to know one's exact location in the featureless jungle. This made it very difficult to call immediate and accurate artillery and air support early during a contact with the enemy. The lack of exact map coordinates always multiplied the risk of friendly-fire casualties. Consequently, Captain Gioia designated Terrence M. Brain of Pasco, Washington as his pace man. Brain, standing well over six feet tall and always smiling and friendly, literally counted steps as the

CP moved through the trackless jungle from a known to an unknown point. He also served as an ex-officio bodyguard to his commander.

Brain came to his duties as pace man via a very hazardous route. He explained it this way: "I was a fairly new guy and walking point for the first or second time with Smoky [Herb West, according to Rod Linn] behind me teaching me what to do. We were taking a break when I spotted three NVA coming along the trail. They hadn't seen me. I alerted Smoky and he said, 'On my signal, you rise up and fire twenty and dive left. I'll stay low, fire twenty and dive right.'

"Smokey gave the signal, a tap on the shoulder, and we executed the plan perfectly. A fraction of a second later, the NVA answered us with a hail of bullets straight down the trail between Smoky and me.

"Calls from the rear, 'What's going on?' Some guys hurried forward to help without being asked. CO sent patrols forward, about twenty meters to the left and right of the trail. [The patrols] went forward, crisscrossed the trail and back down the opposite side...reported lots of blood ahead.

"CO asked if we wanted to continue in the lead to check out the contact area. 'We spotted them, so we'll lead,' Smoky and I agreed.

"As we moved forward beside the trail, he whispered from ten feet behind me, 'Don't look at the ground. Look straight ahead and left and right. Use peripheral to check the ground. If you see something on the ground that way, then feel for it with your hand and bring it up to your eyes, but keep your eyes up and moving.'

"That way, I spotted...tracer and regular rounds and while looking ahead brought them up and whispered to Smoky what I had [found]....Handed them behind me to Smoky without taking my eyes off the front and flanks....

"Again, from about ten feet behind me, Smoky cautioned, 'Keep your eyes up. Be careful, Terry. We're getting close.'

"A moment later, something, like a voice, said to *dive for that tree*! I pulled the trigger and dove just as a hail of fire swept the spot I'd just vacated. Slow motion. Hit the ground hard. Awful pain in my stomach area....Thought I was hit four times in stomach. Became aware of massive fire from my left...caught in cross fire. One moment the sixty-pound pack on my back was knocked to the left by a bullet and the next it was knocked to the right. That was one of two times that I had my pack shot to pieces on my back.

"I kept firing magazine after magazine, figuring if I was firing the NVA would not shoot at me. Two machine guns came forward [Rod Linn and Darrell Thompson] and laid down fire on both sides of me, leaving me a lane about three feet wide to pull back. Pretty sure Rod Linn was one of the machine gunners.

"Someone called, 'Brain, are you hit?'

"'Yes!'

"'Check yourself out and see how bad it is.' I felt my chest and stomach. Nothing. Sure thought I'd been hit bad, though.

"By rising to a squat, I made a 180 [degree turn] and pulled back under cover of the machine guns. Smoky wasn't hit either. Don't know how he survived.

"After all that had happened, I was told I could stay in the FOB while my squad went on ambush. I borrowed a poncho liner (mine had been destroyed along with everything else in my pack) and went on ambush about where I'd been ambushed earlier—the company had moved forward of the ambush site before it stopped for the night."

Brain would be wounded at least twice, once before becoming pace man and again months later. "By order of the CO, I took a squad and linked up with a mechanized unit of the 11th ACR. I'm riding the lead APC with my RTO and the rest of the squad is spread out on other tracks. We'd been told how far to go along this road, and when we passed that point, I told the armor master sergeant— track commander—that we'd gone far enough. He said, 'There is lots of daylight. We'll go a little farther.'

"Right after that, I pointed out to the sergeant that smoke rounds were popping on the road behind us. That's when they hit us with mortars, machine guns, AK-47s, and B-40 rockets. The APC driver swung the track off the left side of the road, spun it around and brought the front end back onto the road, at which point in place and time it took a B-40 rocket to the front. The blast took off the track commander's fingers.

"About the same time, a mortar round exploded nearby and knocked me and my RTO off the track. On the ground, and me unarmed, we huddled next to the long horizontal piece of rubber that runs outside the top of the APC track. Again I got one of those premonitions, warning to get lower. I'd just gotten flat and pulled the RTO down beside me when a machine gun stitched that rubber mudguard from end to end. Obviously, the NVA were all around us.

"A crewmember dropped the rear gate on the APC long enough for the RTO and I to scramble inside—didn't like being inside, but had little choice.

"A tremendous volume of NVA fire was coming in. Could hear rounds hitting all over the APC and expected a B-40 to explode inside any moment. Decided to get my M-16 off the top of the vehicle. I reached up through the open hatch and felt around, then raised up until my helmet and eyes were barely out of the track [hatch]. I got hold of the M-16 and, with the barrel point straight up, started to withdraw into the vehicle. That's when I felt and heard a loud explosion or bang and felt a tremendous shock to my head and face. A bullet had hit my helmet right on the rim, next to my right eye. The bullet deflected upward and tore a gash in my helmet and helmet liner. I remember being in the APC after that, but I don't remember getting out of it or anything else until later in the day at the 15th Med. They kept me on the firebase for about five days because I blacked out every time I moved or stood up quickly.

"Soon after that, when we were on LZ Dolly, Clemens— just remembered that name—said the CO wanted to see me. Captain Davidson - wanted me to be his pace man—to keep track of his position in the trackless jungle, so we could get close artillery and air support quickly when we needed it, without getting it on our own heads. Davidson - was a wonderful commander. I loved him. He wanted me to attend the University of Missouri and play football...promised to pull strings to get me on the team....I got wounded and that ended that," concluded Terry Brain.

Rod Linn, by the way, didn't seem to be a troublemaker, despite his angry remarks during the memorial service for Kahla. Rather, he seems to have been one who felt very close to his buddies. Thirty years after Vietnam, Linn retains an exceptional memory for names and details. At least two of his leaders describe Linn as the best machine gunner they ever saw. Linn has the same high praise for a fellow machine gunner, Darrell Thompson, who does not appear in the journals or company roster in my possession. Linn said, "Darrell was wounded up north about July 1969 by mortar fragments in the shoulder."

Darrell Thompson had a close encounter of the odd kind with Lieutenant Steve Holtzman during the latter's first fight with the enemy, sometime before the action on March 20 with the tanks. Holtzman describes what he thought happened. "I was 3-6 [platoon leader] and we had the point. Three Gooks ambushed us....I dropped my ruck[sack] and hid behind it for a while until I realized it would not protect me at all. I then moved...behind a tree for cover. Inside my ruck I carried a framed 5x7 picture of my wife, an air mattress...etc....the picture had a line of holes across it and the mattress was destroyed. Thirty years later he learned what really happened while attending a 5th Cavalry reunion. At a motel in Peoria, Illinois, "Rod Linn asked me if I recognized some guy he was talking to—neither of us recognized each other. It was Daryl [Darrell?] Thompson, the other M-60 gunner from Third Platoon. He doesn't remember much—sort of like I was ten months ago. Thompson asked me, 'Remember when I shot your pack up?'"

"Why didn't you tell me?" Holtzman asked.

"You don't tell your lieutenant that you almost shot him unless you're very stupid," Thompson replied.

"It seems the ruck was lying next to a log that Daryl tripped over and as he stumbled, he squeezed the trigger," said Holtzman.

Meanwhile, at 1140 hours on March 24, Alpha 1-5 got into a fight and sustained three KIAs and nine WIAs. Though Rod Linn names Johnny Ray Parker of Idabel, Oklahoma as one of the KIAs, he also says, "The KIAs were machine gunner Monty Gilbert Lackas of Columbus, Nebraska; his assistant machine gunner Corporal Joseph Schimpf of Philadelphia, Pennsylvania; and Ken Richie of Sandusky, Ohio, as I recall."

Earlier in the day, Charlie 1-5 sustained nine WIAs and Delta 1-5 sustained one. Later in the day, Delta 1-5 had three more troopers wounded when the NVA mortared its FOB.

The next day I found Bill Snyder on LZ Dolly. His company was pulling firebase security for a week. Firebase security duty was usually safer than being in the field, especially up on the razorback ridge where LZ Dolly was. While the duty was usually safer, it wasn't always easier, for the grunts spent most of their days patrolling, filling sandbags and hardening defenses; and their nights on perimeter guard, LP duty and ambush. Well, Snyder and I decided to have the sacrament meeting we'd been trying to hold, only to postpone it until the next morning because we could not find an LDS trooper named West who also wanted to share the sacrament. The delay seemed reasonable and practical. After all, we expected Snyder to be relatively safe and available for the next few days—LZ Dolly had never been attacked by ground forces and seldom received rocket or mortar shells, probably because of the difficulty involved in targeting the LZ there on the razorback ridge. I flew out to conduct services and spend the night with Bravo 1-5, intent on returning the next morning for the service on LZ Dolly.

Sounds of explosions and heavy volumes of small-arms fire shocked me awake at 0410 hours on March 26. Bill Snyder wasn't so "relatively safe" after all.

The NVA launched a B-40 rocket attack on LZ Dolly in preparation for a sapper attack. The sappers (demolition engineers) prepared for quick penetration of the perimeter by sneaking in close, taking advantage of soldiers' natural tendency to be lethargic at that hour of the morning—especially in "secure" areas—and by securing defensive trip flares with rubber bands to keep them from igniting. With the flares secured, the sappers snipped concertina wire, then crawled through and waited for the rocket barrage. Simultaneous with the rocket barrage, the sappers tossed satchel charges over the perimeter bunkers, proba-bly intending to cause the men on guard to take cover inside the bunkers by making them think that mortars had zeroed in on them.

The next five satchel charges went into perimeter bunkers, includ-ing the one where Snyder slept. Meanwhile, two sappers charged toward the battalion TOC through their own hail of B-40 rockets. About the same time, other NVA soldiers captured a live, dazed trooper on the perimeter and tried to pull him out through the wire.

Snyder had been sleeping in the back of a perimeter bunker when the attack began, with some of his buddies lying between him and the entrance to the bunker. His buddies, including his assistant gunner Donald Forest—who had been wounded a few days earlier—died in the blast and collapse of the bunker.

Elsewhere on the perimeter, battle-hardened troopers quickly recovered from their initial shock and killed the sappers, including those assaulting the TOC. They also rescued the trooper that was being dragged through the wire, and killed his would-be captors in the process.

With all the NVA inside the perimeter dead, Captain Cain hurried to the perimeter to assess the damage. There he found Bill Snyder sur-rounded by dead buddies in the midst of a collapsed bunker. Snyder, face toward the jungle with a weapon in hand, was straining to hear any sound from outside the perimeter. He appeared to be blind.

Heroics had been in abundance during the attack. Chaplain Hugh Black from the 2-12 Cav received the Silver Star for his actions there during the attack. He was there to provide Catholic support to my troopers.

A chopper plucked me out of the Bravo 1-5 position shortly after first light. Captain Cain was waiting for me. "Claude, Bill Snyder *got it* last night. He's blind. They medevaced him to Tay Ninh.

Most of the wounded had been evacuated to the hospital in Tay Ninh by the time I reached Dolly, so I went to where the dead were laid out. There I prayed, meditated and said goodbye to our dead, including one we thought dead who wasn't. Then I went looking for Lieutenant Colonel Peterson.

"Sir," I recommended, "it would help the wounded and the men here, too, if you visited the hospital ASAP." Peterson was hard pressed, I knew, but I had to reach the wounded, especially Snyder, for I was feeling very guilty that we'd postponed that sacrament service until today. And Charlie 1-5 really needed a strong, visible demonstration of command concern. So we flew immediately to Tay Ninh on a very tight time schedule.

Snyder wasn't blind after all. He had only appeared to be blind because of all the dust and debris that had been blown into his eyes by the satchel charge that killed his buddies. He expected to return to duty in a day or two. Snyder and I were unable to have a sacrament service during this visit because he was being treated and Peterson couldn't tarry longer at the hospital.

What to do? I was torn by conflicting calls of duty, whether to stay with Snyder or to return to the shell-shocked "non-casualties" of Charlie 1-5. Perhaps my decision was too much affected by my professional determination to not allow service to LDS members to cause me to neglect others. So once again, Snyder and I put off our sacrament service.

Eight troopers gave their lives in the attack on LZ Dolly and twenty-three were wounded. One of those pronounced KIA at the scene by the battalion surgeon was found to be alive later at the morgue, Naturally, the doctor suffered a severe case of self-doubt over his mistake. One of the wounded troopers died later in the day.

Stranger things than live soldiers in the morgue happen in war. During war, in my experience, anything one can imagine happening probably will happen. Often even the unimaginable happens. For example, a trooper in one of the companies was killed sometime before I joined the 1-5 Cav. The unit carried the dead trooper "present for duty" for a month or two, until his dog-tagged skeleton was found by another unit operating in the area where he had been killed. That the body might be "lost" in the night and aftermath of intense battle was understandable, as the trooper's body had been placed behind a bush, he being but one of several KIAs and WIAs being evacuated. How, though, could he be counted present for duty for a month or so, considering all the personnel accounting checks and balances we had?

In addition to several failed attempts to share the sacrament with Snyder, while covering two battalions, and despite frequent battles and firefights, I tried to minister to LDS beyond the 1-5 and 2-12 battalions and to be liaison between Army and Church.

Sometime in March I attended at least one LDS meeting in Saigon, during which I was called to a leadership position, on the usual condition that it would not be allowed to cause me to neglect my battalions. Besides the general services, I conducted several LDS services in the field and attended meetings at Tay Ninh and Phuoc Vinh, taking my nephew Earl Dyer with me to one in Phuoc Vinh.

A month had passed from the time I left my family. Amid all this carnage, Helga and the children seemed a vivid but distant memory. Well, at least I'd gotten past the period of almost unbearable homesickness. Except for passing the one month in-country point, my journals and memory provide scant details about the first five days of April 1969, except that they were busy days and full of fright.

At 1100 hours on April 2, Alpha 1-5 got in a firefight and sustained six WIAs. SP4 Tom Holcombe explained, "Alpha 1-5 was walking [in columns] in company strength. Dennis Knoch was walking...point for the left column. We walked into a linear ambush....a guy in our squad, Caldwell, took a round through the knee, and...J. J. Johnson was hit in the eye by a round that bounced off his M-16. Lieutenant Dave Neff was wounded in the upper torso by a round that hit a frag on his pistol belt, breaking off the blasting cap inside the grenade, but it did not detonate."

Lieutenant Steve Holtzman said of this action, "My Second Platoon was the trail platoon on the right column, parallel to the Captain Harrison's CP that was in the left column. When the NVA sprung their ambush, they focused most of their fire on the command post. To a man, my entire Second Platoon flanked left and attacked on line, passing through the CP and other platoon, without any commands from Platoon Sergeant Nelson or myself.

"We pressed the attack through a bunker complex, one hole at a time. Nelson and I took out one bunker and got quite a surprise for our efforts. Keeping away from the firing slits, we got close to the bunker, then we each tossed a smoke grenade into the entrance, followed by frags. Then we moved away from the opening and lay up against the side of the bunker for protection from the frags, not expecting that the bunker contained a stash of explosives. The resulting blast lifted our bodies about three feet off the ground. Nelson and I lost our hearing for several days."

After the bunker-clearing operation, J. J. Johnson, Caldwell, and three or four others were medevaced out, and the rest of the company went on its way again.

"Later," said Holcombe, "we crossed a field and the CO decided we'd FOB there, to use the field for the LOG bird. Dennis, Bob Fussell, and I were assigned to the same foxhole. We had Dennis pull security while we dug our foxhole because he was beat from walking company point all day. Dennis put on his gear and went out about 10-15 meters in front of our position and we started digging. However, I was pulled away to pull security around the open field so LOG birds could bring in supplies.

"A guy with a PRC-25—who was placing the security detail— pointed me to a section of the wood line that was across the clearing that kind of paralleled the FOB. Right away, I found an unoccupied bunker and a well about twenty meters inside the tree line, and a trail that led deeper into the jungle. On the trail were little beads of water and footprints on the trail. I reported what I had seen to the guy with the radio and asked him to send me an M-60 machine gun, then I took a position by the well to watch the trail. A few minutes later two guys show up, one with an M-79 and the other with an M-16. No M-60....one may have been Bill "Big Daddy" Morris. A couple of minutes later an enemy probe came down the trail and veered off to our right when we opened up on them. Quickly, I shifted position to cover our flank, and discovered a trench. Beyond the trench the NVA were breaking brush as they tried to flank us. At that point the noise of breaking brush stopped and heavy shooting broke out back across the clearing around the FOB. I didn't know until I got off the security detail—only one chopper made it in, only to take off again with most of our supplies when the NVA opened up on it—but that was when Dennis Knoch was killed with a round through the heart.

"No way," Holcombe continued, "was Dennis caught napping. He was one of the most alert, if not the most alert, soldiers I ever knew. Dennis had kept the enemy from sneaking in close enough to open up on our guys digging in. And he had fired two or three magazines before he was hit. Dennis' death shook us. Bob Fussell was severely hurt by it, and later he visited the Knoch family in Ohio after he recovered from the wounds he would sustain on June 5, 1969."

Machine gunner Rod Linn of Marquette, Michigan, added, "When the shooting started, C. Brooks and I were about three or four inches into digging a foxhole for our M-60 position. We both tried to fit into that little depression when the firing started that killed Knoch. Word quickly passed from hole to hole that he had been killed and shortly someone, a sergeant or lieutenant, asked for volunteers to take an ambush out. Brooks and I declined. We'd stay in our M-60 machine gun position. I thought it was bad judgment to try and set an ambush when we were already in contact with the NVA (who were in bunkers nearby). As it turned out Aggie [SP4 James W. Agnew] volunteered to go. Brooks and I couldn't believe that he would go, being so short."

1LT Steve Holtzman said, "Captain Harrison wanted to send out an ambush patrol even as the guys on the LZ were in contact. Both Dave Neff and I argued against the idea. "When I want your opinion I'll ask for it," Harrison said. Harrison threatened to shoot or court-martial us when we refused to get up the patrol. I'm not sure who went around asking for volunteers. It wasn't Neff nor me." Brave young men recovered Knoch's body while the lieutenants faced Captain Harrison's wrath.

Captain Harrison got his volunteers. With the coming of the night seven troopers crept stealthily away from the relative security of the foxholes and perimeter and into the position that had been selected for the ambush. At 0145 hours, April 3, the NVA attacked viciously, not on the company but on the ambush site.

Holcombe described what happened. "Volunteers were sought for ambushes and James Agnew and Keith Welsh went on the one out in front of our foxhole. Way late that night we heard tubes (mortars), and jumped in the hole. But the rounds landed short of the FOB, tragically on the Welsh-Agnew ambush. ...Agnew was KIA. The rest were wounded....One lost a leg. The NVA followed the mortars with a ground attack. What was left of the ambush, mainly Keith, fought them off. Then the trip flares in front of our hole went off. The hole next to us blew a claymore thinking it was an attack. We yelled, 'Hold off, he's one of ours!' The guy who was trying to come in yelled, 'I can't see!' Another guy from my hole and I went out and brought him in. Soon after that Keith Welsh brought the rest of the wounded in—making more than one trip. One brave son of a gun.

"Rex Storey was beside himself. Someone out there kept calling, like *'oui, oui.'* Rex imagined Agnew was alive and calling 'Storey, Storey.' Welsh had assured us that Agnew was KIA, but Rex couldn't stand it. [Story] rounded up guys from the foxholes near ours to go out for Agnew —he got his volunteers, but the CO wouldn't allow it. The 'oui, oui' noises turned out to be a wounded enemy soldier," said Holcombe.

Though the enemy fire let up once the surviving members of the ambush got inside the perimeter, the grunts still had good reason for concern. Reports of heavy movement and Vietnamese voices were coming in rapidly. The NVA were pressing toward the perimeter on three sides. Lieutenant Holtzman said, "I remember that we got hit some time after dark....We could hear moaning all night. Both Neff and I asked Harrison to let us go bring the LP back in but he turned us down. He didn't want to risk any more people. We explained to Harrison that Foggy Day [Alpha Company] had never left wounded or dead in the field and we didn't want to leave anybody to become a POW either. Harrison flatly refused to let either of us go...[and] threatened courts marshal against us if we couldn't get all of the troops to stop mumbling about how dangerous he was....It was at this time that

I first started to hear troops talk about fragging him....prior to this...the term fragging was totally foreign to us."

Holcombe said, "I spent the night in my foxhole with Dennis's poncho-wrapped body beside me, a very sad and lonely night."

Early on April 3 a patrol sustained more WIAs at the same time that others were recovering Agnew' s remains and the destroyed radio. Cautiously, the patrol moved past's and Fussell's foxhole toward where the repeated mournful wails of *chieu hoi* were coming. "They hadn't gone far when a claymore mine went off and wounded several of them. The enemy had set up a claymore and used one of their own wounded as bait. Pretty ruthless I think. Soon after that we got into our holes for a napalm strike—real close. After that there was no more resistance. We carried the wounded enemy soldier all day, until we could send him out on a chopper. Holcombe added that I was the first other than himself to recall the *chieu hoi* aspect of that action.

Also in early April, I hitched a ride in a LOH from Bien Hoa to LZ Dolly. En route, I snapped a picture of the pilot. He was shot down the next day along the Saigon River, in the area we had flown over. Wild pigs partly consumed him before rescuers found and reached the crash site the day after he went down. I hope he was already dead.

Also in early April, I hitched a ride in a LOH from Bien Hoa to LZ Dolly. En route, I snapped a picture of the pilot. He was shot down the next day along the Saigon River, in the area we had flown over. Wild pigs partly consumed him before rescuers found and reached the crash site the day after he went down. I hope he was already dead.

For Easter services, April 6, the Second Brigade Commander dedicated a LOH for Chaplain Hugh Black and me to share so we could conduct both General Christian and Catholic Easter services for all the companies in the 1-5 and 2-12 battalions, an all-day operation. We began the operation by having the chopper drop Black at one 2-12 company and me at another. Next the chopper picked up Black, brought him to where I was, and took me to yet another 2-12 company. Thus, we leapfrogged through most of the 2-12 Cav. Later in the day, Black conducted masses for my 1-5 companies, where Henry Lamar Hunt was providing Protestant Easter services.

To deliver me so I could conduct a service for Alpha 2-12, the pilot of the LOH hovered over a small, cluttered clearing amid smoldering jungle while I jumped to the ground. The troopers were already gathering in an area on the west side of the clearing where the vegetation had already burned away. The line of still-smoldering vegetation was about thirty feet north of where we were and was burning away from us.

My part of setting up for the service consisted simply of removing song materials and scriptures from my pack and placing my helmet atop the pack with the insignia of a chaplain facing congregation. The Easter service for Ace High (Alpha 2-12's call sign) was underway within minutes of when I jumped from the LOH.

Almost every trooper who could get free from pressing duties was there to worship. We'd sung and prayed, and I was well into a sermon that focused on the significant linkage of Easter and Christmas, when I of necessity paused to wait out the noise of an H-model helicopter. The chopper slipped carefully between the trees to hover about five feet above a bomb crater. Simultaneously, the crew chief and door gunner kicked out supplies while grunts hustled on both sides of the chopper to get the supplies away from it and the crater.

Suddenly, the chopper engine stalled. Without a sputter it dropped like a rock toward the bomb crater and came to rest with the front end and tail rotor on opposite sides of the crater, and with the main rotor skimming at full speed toward the rear and on both sides.

We worshipers abandoned the service and dashed to the crash site, fearing troopers were being cut to pieces by the spinning main rotor. Amazingly no one was hurt. Even more amazing, about the time we made that happy discovery, a dud 105mm artillery round exploded in the burning vegetation, about a hundred feet behind where I'd stood to conduct the service. The falling chopper had drawn Easter worshipers from the "kill zone" just in time! Apparently, the burning vegetation set off the 105mm round, a dud left over from the earlier fighting.

The crashing chopper and exploding dud were the closest I came during two tours to having one of my worship services interrupted by combat.

That afternoon we had a service for another 2-12 company, commanded by Captain Shine. (I believe that was his name because I remember this captain's last name as Star, and Shine comes closest to that of any of the officers listed as commanders in the 2-12 Cav at that time. This CO asked for permission to address his troops during Easter service. Of course he was welcome to do so; it was his company. He began his remarks by identifying himself as a devout, born-again Christian, and said in essence, "I claim all your lives in the name of God. None of you will die while you are in my company."

I liked this captain. I admired him for his spirituality, and understood his desire. In my heart, though, I *knew* he couldn't keep his promise to the men, and I feared some would be spiritually worse off when his promise failed. I regretted letting him speak, and hoped the best—a futile hope as it turned out.

By late afternoon I had conducted three Easter services in the field and one on LZ Grant. I was aboard the LOH on the way to conduct a service for Bravo 2-12 when the pilot said, "Alpha [1-5] is in a fight and has sustained twenty casualties."

We changed course toward Alpha 1-5 in the jungle northeast of LZ Dolly. The company had disengaged from the enemy and pulled back about three hundred meters to set up a FOB and cut a PZ (pick-up zone) so the wounded could be evacuated. The last of the wounded were being placed aboard a Medevac chopper when I arrived. Among the wounded was Private Ernest K. Baller—Baller had taken a bullet through his helmet some months earlier, up near the DMZ.

Upon reaching Alpha 1-5 late Easter afternoon or early evening, I arranged for and conducted two small, low-key services. After the services, I visited one-on-one with small groups of men and tried to help restore individual and collective spiritual resources, part of the Army reconstitution process. The company definitely needed reconstituting, because it had been at about half strength going into the Easter fight.

Chapter Notes:

15 March 1969, 1-5 Cav Battalion Journal: 1906: "A Co, 2-6 WIA, serious leg wound."

16 Mar 1969, 1-5 Cav Battalion Journal: 1010: "'? Co received AK-47, B-40, MG from bunker...6 WIA.

18, 19 March 1969, 1-5 Battalion Journal: A Co WIAs Seikert, US 544452112 and N. RA55380871.

1308, D Co KIA's Sp4 Barry Jackson; WIAs Robert Vastu [?], US51983981, AK rd. hit claymore and M16 mag, frag stomach and side; Rosado RA67194464, heat stroke."

19 March 1969, 1-5 Battalion Journal: B Co Casualties, KIA, Sp4 Roy Womack and Pfc Peter McCallum

20 March 1969, 1-5 Battalion Journal: A Co KIA's Victor D. Kulla ; WIAs Holmes, Schraud [Schrauer]. [Douglas A.], Lightfoot, Wess and Hecke or Heikle, and Jones (1/77) [FO?]. "A Co, opcon 11th Cav, reports...04 tanks destroyed. 09 WIA from A Co, also about 30 US WIAs, 08 KIA from Armor...Name of A Co WIAs: Holmes, Savard, Lightfoot, Wess, Kulla, serious D.O.W, Chenvert, Heckle, DeLeon, Jones of B 1-77.

21 March 1969, 1-5 Cav Journal: 1850 "D Co taking incoming 82 mortars...resulting in two [?] WIA...Joseph A. Gatto, Arnold W. Wright and James A. Lukas."

22 March 1969, 1-5 Cav Battalion Journal: 1630, "A Co inserted 30 feet from tree line...received AK-47 fire Sp4 Moises Tapia [Los Angeles, California] is KIA and Clement is WIA."

23 March 1969, 1-5 Cav Battalion Journal: 1600: "D Co, WIA, Pfc Barry Overlee. 1927: "[company?] WIA, Rudy M. Blehm."

24 March 1969, 1-5 Cav Battalion Journal: 0945: "C Co 3 US WIA, Pfc Eddie Ellis, Sp4 Curtis Harold and Sp4 Rudy M. Reyes." "B Co, Joe L. Fergerson, appendicitis."

1125: "C Co, 3 WIA...Pfc Donald forest, Pfc Benny Gerrell and PSG Raymond Clark."

1150: "D Co Robert Karasturdy, WIA."

1330: "A Co 1 US KIA."

1345: "A Co 2 US KIA, 5 US WIA, KIA...additional KIA...[KIA were Sp4 Johnny Parker, Sp4 Monty Lackas and Pfc Joseph Schimpf. WIAs medevaced, Sp4s Eppy, Ruty and Harper, and SSG Dayton. WIAs stayed in field, Rash, Schmidt, Pierc and Anderson. Norman Brimm, no company given, medevaced with head cut." [Note: Terry Harper's arm was broken when the canister from an artillery marking round fell on him. He was previously wounded up near the DMZ in July 1968, at the same time as Baller, when a bullet penetrated Baller's helmet and cut a groove on his head, according to Rodney Linn.]

26 March 1969, 1-5 Battalion journal: "0410, LZ Dolly. Started receiving...B-40 rockets - also 67 sappers on NE side of perimeter...total number of WIA 21, 19 medevac & 08 KIAs." KIAs from Charlie 1-5 were Sp4 Patrick Benze [of O'Neill, Nebraska], Pfc Donald Forrest, Pfc Robert E. Green, Pfc Edward Lamoureux [of

Plainfield, Connecticut] and Sp4 Carlton Monroe of Portsmouth, VA]. Other KIAs were Sp4 Theodore Heinselman of HHC 1-5 [and Jacksonville, Florida], Sp4 Terry Moore of Bravo 1-5 [Washington, Illinois], and Greg Mills of 1-8 Cav [of Mendota, Illinois. WIAs from Charlie 1-5 were 1LT Stephen Grubb; Sp4's Jimmy Brown, Frank Marshall, Gary J. Walz and Eddie Melendez; Pfc's Steve Gonzales, Louis O. Kroh, Allan Jewell, Joseph LePoint Jr., Robert W. Snyder, Thomas Bieme and Thomas W. Kreuger. Bravo 1-5's WIAs were Sgt. Darrel R. Rutz and Sp4's Louis A. Bachus, Ireland G. Hassler, Richard G. Bergeron and Dickie L. Nelson. Also wounded were Sp4 James Adams of Echo 1-5, Maynes and Blanchero of 1-8 Cav, and 1LT Smith and Sp4 Young of 13th Signal-Division Relay.

15 March 1969, 1-5 Cav Operational Report: Early on 26 March, LZ Dolly came under attack by B-40 rockets and 6 or 7 sappers...received 9 KIA and 21 WIA before enemy fled.

27 March 1969, 1-5 Battalion Journal: "1150, D Co an individual stepped on a mine, butterfly type, 8 WIAs, Jeffry Gelden, Thomsas Robben, Everett Roberts, Angel Hosea Bonilla, Douglas Miller, Bartel Caklo, Thomas James and David Beeker.

28 March 1969, 1-5 Journal: "1505, B Co 3-6 element engaged...two WIA, Richard Barker and Samuel Usted.

30 March 1969, 1-5 Journal: "Beginning at 0006 to 1300, B Co...two KIA, Sp4 Roy Womack and Pfc Peter McCallum; WIAs, Sp4 Sergeant James, 1LT Chester Hargrewski, Sp4 LeRoy Hopes, Sgt Robert Dykstra and Pfc Charles Kritt."

2 April 1969, 1-5 Journal: "1100, A Co. (firefight)...6 WIAs, Sgt. Pedro Trevino, Donald Davis, Pfc Dale Carr, Pfc Dale Caldwell, Jackie, 1LT David Neff." "1815, A Co. hit by smf and 1 B40, 1 KIA, Sp4 Dennis Knoch [Ohio]."

3 April 1969, Battalion Journal, 0753-0815: "As A Co was policing area of last night's contact, heard someone yelling Chieu hoi...walked into a NVA ambush...02 US WIA." 1130, A Co KIAs Sp4 James W. Agnew; WIAs, Sp4's Tomie Parker, Kieth Welsh, Thomas Harris, Michael Maphis, Jazquez Cruz, Joseph Couie; Pfc Robert Davidson; Injured, non-hostile were Pfc John Hoffman, Sp4 Joseph Casonhr [?} and Sgt. Gerald Phiehl.

6 April 1969, Battalion Journal, 1215 hours: "A Co contact...received 13 WIA: Eugene Davis, Michaell Schroch, Donald Savlier, Stacy Holmes, Robert Hunder, Ernest Baller, Charles Truitt, Michael O'Connel, Jeus Jimenez, Thomas Rudy, Kenneth Deal, John Hoffman [again] and Ronald Tipton B/177 Arty."

1 April 1969, 2-12 Battalion, Operational Report/Lessons Learned. Friendly Casualty in March: KIAs, 23; WIAs 100; Non-hostile wounded, 1. Enemy casualties: KIAs 261, WIA/PW, 2, Chieu Hoi, 2."

Chapter Seven

No Greater Love

Before dawn on April 7, orders came for Charlie 1-5 to attack the objective that Alpha 1-5 had assaulted the previous day. At first light a log bird (lift ship) transported me from Alpha Company to Charlie 1-5. There I found Cain and his men breaking camp, emptying sandbags, collapsing fighting positions, destroying unwanted C-ration items like peanut butter and ham-and-eggs chopped, redistributing ammunition for the heavy weapons, and making a final check of weapons.

"Move out," Cain ordered a few minutes after I arrived. I joined Cain's CP group, which was with the second platoon, and fell in about five positions behind the point. A moment later we crossed the east perimeter of the FOB and came on Bill Snyder and his M-60 team. He would stay behind us during the fifteen thousand-meter hump (moving, patrolling by ground troops) to the objective, unless we hit the enemy on the way.

"Bill, we'll have a sacrament service today, no matter what," I promised. Snyder agreed. We would share the sacrament, even if we had no time for any other elements of the service. Snyder's sincere desire and eagerness to renew his covenants exceeded anything I witnessed in any other soldier. With God's help, I'd not let Snyder down again.

We moved out in three columns with a platoon and part of the weapons platoon in each column. The company CP group and I were in the middle column. To lighten some trooper's load and, consequently, be a less-inviting target myself, I carried a half-filled plastic water bottle in one hand and a pick or shovel in the other.

We'd moved more than half the distance to the objective when the point man for the left column ran into red ants. Everyone held in place while he, throwing caution to the wind, did a quick striptease, which anyone familiar with Vietnamese red ants will understand.

While we waited, Captain Cain crawled to me and, in violation of his own strict rule against nonessential talking in the jungle, said, "Claude, I want you to teach me about the Mormon religion."

"I'll be glad to, Jim," I answered, surprised, "but why now?"

"Because of Bill Snyder," he answered, and added, "Snyder is the most honest, trustworthy, cheerful and best infantryman I've ever known." It sounded like he was describing the perfect boy scout.

In fact, Snyder was an Eagle Scout, who had ridden horses at a gallop by age four, hunted and tamed wild horses as a youth, played the saxophone at school and church functions, and taken second place at State one year in high school wrestling. Three or four special young women in attendance at Snyder's funeral confided to his parents that they had expected to marry Bill when he returned from Vietnam.

"I want to know about a religion that makes a man like him," said Cain.

"I'll be glad to teach you about the Mormon religion," I assured Jim Cain. Of course the teaching had to wait. It was time to move on.

A little before noon we swept through a new, fancy bunker complex and held up in a north-south running ditch just beyond it. There we waited out an Air Force bombing attack that we hoped would soften up our objective.

New NVA fighting positions were spaced about every ten feet down the center of the ditch. The condition of the newly-dug soil suggested the NVA diggers had abandoned these positions barely ahead of our arrival. The fighting positions confirmed what we already knew. The NVA were ready for us, and they knew exactly where we were. I confess to hoping that our foes were waiting where we expected them to be, right where the bombs were raining down. The NVA were even nearer to us, as it turned out.

Snyder and his machine-gun team had moved forward of the ditch when we stopped to wait out the bombing strikes, as had Cpl. James

Derda of Albuquerque, New Mexico, with his 90mm recoilless rifle. Following the bomb runs, I went ahead of the CP and paused to speak with Bill Snyder and his buddies while I waited for the CP element to catch up. With Snyder were Cpl. Derda, Sergeant Thomas Hoover and others.

"Chaplain, don't look so serious. It hasn't rained, and maybe it won't rain bullets today," Snyder chided me.

We all chuckled, heartened by Snyder's attitude. A moment later I fell in with the CP element as it passed. I was about six men back from PFC William Allen Jr. of Cantonment, Florida, who had the point. Hoover, Derda and Snyder's machine-gun team fell in behind the CP. A trooper we called Gator was among those between Allen and the CP. Gator's nickname reflected his roots in the swamps of north Florida and South Georgia. The time was 1433 hours.

We moved forward with Second Platoon and the Company CP element in a column on a well-used path with the First and Third Platoons in columns on our left and right flanks. The platoon on the left faced tough but safer going through thick jungle with no trail to follow. The other platoon entered an open field after moving five meters from the ditch where we had waited out the air strikes.

An NVA machine gunner opened fire at 1435 hours from a well-concealed position about a hundred feet ahead, where the trail turned sharply to the left and where the open field on our right ended. Less than a minute had elapsed since I left Snyder and his buddies to move forward.

With his first burst, the machine gunner killed Allen instantly and drove everyone ahead of me to the ground. While I hit the ground slightly to the left with my feet still on the trail, Captain Cain and two radiomen dived behind a large termite mound to the right of the trail. Simultaneously, 1LT William (Bill) Haines, his RTO, and the company medic dove to cover behind a mound on the left side of the trail. The mound on the right, behind which Cain took cover, was closer to the enemy machine-gun position by about five feet.

Up ahead, Gator hit the ground behind the meager protection of a tree, unhurt. All the other troopers between the NVA machine gun and Cain's CP were wounded.

Several AK-47s joined the enemy machine gun almost immediately, firing on our front and left flank. Simultaneously, our platoon on the right flank moved into the tree line from the open field, unhurt— presumably the NVA hadn't covered the field because they couldn't imagine Americans approaching in the open.

While others scurried to cover, I lay where I fell, confused because a hearing handicap prevented me from pinpointing exactly where the fire was coming from. I knew I had to move, but *which way*? Carefully, I raised my helmet-covered head in an attempt to pinpoint the source of enemy machine-gun fire.

In an instant the NVA gunner answered my unasked question with bursts of machine-gun bullets. The first burst clipped off a half-inch-thick stem of a bush where it pressed against the left side of my neck. Reflexively, I dug my left cheek into the ground, a split second before the second burst filled my face with stinging gravel as the bullets dug into the ground and ricocheted past my face. I decided to play dead for the moment.

"Get the 90 [recoilless rifle] and machine gun up here!" yelled Captain Cain.

A moment later Snyder came into view with Hoover right behind him. In response to Cain's call for the machine gun, Snyder hurried forward at a crouch, keeping to the right of the trail for the little protection that Cain's termite hill offered. Hoover was right behind Snyder. Dropping to one knee as he drew even with me, Snyder looked directly into my eyes, a look that haunts me still. "Goodbye, Brother," his eyes seemed to say.

Then he leaped forward and threw himself onto the path slightly ahead of where Cain crouched behind the termite hill. Instantly, the machine gunner shifted his fire from me to Snyder. Almost simultaneously with Snyder's move, I rolled to the left behind the relative security of the termite hill on the north side of the trail, timing my move to coincide with the first burst of fire that at least now didn't crack right in my ears. That burst of fire was aimed at Snyder, who was trying to take the enemy machine gun under fire. From ten feet away Captain Cain watched helplessly as Snyder's head jerked backward from the impact of a bullet between and just above the eyes. Snyder died instantly.

Derda had arrived perhaps a moment behind Snyder, keeping left of the trail. Dashing to the left, Derda dropped to one knee and fired a flechette round, which he had already loaded, against the NVA forces that were assaulting our left front. The Third Platoon yet struggled through thick undergrowth, trying to get into position to protect our flank.

From behind Cain's termite hill, Hoover yelled, "Gator! Snyder's hit! Here!" With that he threw his heavier-hitting M-14 rifle to Gator and dived for Snyder's machine gun. Hoover died before he could pull the trigger.

"Hold this for me, Chaplain," Derda said, tossing me the strap he used to carry the heavy 90mm recoilless rifle. Then he too was gone around the termite hill into the line of fire. Perhaps the blast of the recoilless rifle had temporarily dampened enemy enthusiasm, for Derda made it to slight cover. But upon seeing that Snyder and Hoover were hit, Derda abandoned the recoilless rifle and dove behind Snyder's machine gun. He took a round in the head before he could fire, and joined Snyder and Hoover in instant death.

"Snyder is dead," Cain called to me, after watching helplessly as the sequence of death played out ten feet before his eyes. I had no doubt Cain knew what he was talking about.

Snyder's death shocked me more than all that had occurred before. Sorrow, remorse, even guilt almost immobilized me, but people were still being hurt. The enemy machine gun yet fired, and NVA soldiers were attacking our left front. For the moment the defense of the left flank was left to a medic, the FO, his RTO, and me. Our only cover was the termite hill behind which we had gathered a few wounded grunts.

Very quickly, the urgency of the situation snapped me into action. Leaving the wounded to the medic's care, I picked up an M-16 rifle that a wounded trooper had dropped and helped defend the left front flank long enough for the Third Platoon to get into position to take some of the pressure off us.

Meanwhile, Lieutenant Haines already had high-explosive shells pouring in as near to our front positions as he dared. But the artillery coming from several directions could do little more than suppress enemy maneuvering to the rear of the NVA fighting positions. We were too close to the enemy for anything better.

After the Third Platoon relieved the pressure on our left front, and with the wounded troopers within our reach attended to, I looked around. Suddenly, I felt very exposed, vulnerable. In a flash of insight, intuition or inspiration, I *knew* what was wrong. While our attention was focused forward, the NVA were about to hit us from another direction: *from across the field! The NVA are about to mortar us from there!*

I pulled on Bill Haines' leg to get his attention. "Better get some fire across the clearing to the south. They're going to mortar us from there," I advised. Haines, his hands already quite full, put me off for a moment—understandable, as he had only my word on a threat from any direction but the front and left flank. Finally, perhaps to humor me, Haines targeted a single barrage of artillery where I asked him to. "First rounds HE [high explosive]. Fire for effect," Haines radioed to a battery fire controller."

"On the way, wait," replied the fire control officer a moment later.

In the few seconds that the shells took to arrive, five enemy 82mm mortar rounds thumped from tubes located behind the tree line across the clearing. The NVA shells exploded harmlessly fifty feet or more out in the clearing, just outside our position. Our artillery shells exploded right on target before the NVA mortar men could adjust their fire. Enemy mortars stayed silent for the rest of the engagement. *How many NVA soldiers died there because of my insistence? How many Americans lived?*

Another "truth" flashed into my mind sometime after the mortars threat had been taken care of. *The NVA are moving into the fortified ditch behind us to cut off any withdrawal!*

Calling across to Cain, I recommended, "NVA are going to occupy the ditch to our rear. You'd best secure it." Reacting immediately, Cain ordered the First Platoon to secure the ditch, and just in time too. NVA soldiers were coming along the ditch from the north when our trooper arrived. The enemy pulled back without much of a fight.

After almost two terribly frustrating hours, Cain became fed up with the NVA machine gun which yet pinned down some of our troopers and kept us from recovering our dead. I had joined him behind the mound on the right, having crossed the machine gunner's sights unhurt.

A hard, grim look of resolve came over Jim Cain. Without a word, he laid his weapon down, withdrew two grenades from his webgear (pistol belt and suspenders—LBE) and pulled both pins. It dawned on me that Cain intended to take out the machine gun single-handedly, or die trying. "Wait," I said, as I picked up another M-16, checked the magazine, ejected a spent shell and simultaneously chambered a round, and moved the selector switch to semiautomatic. "Now!" I yelled.

Cain charged the machine-gun position, straight down the path past his dead troopers. Simultaneously, I laid a steady stream of well-aimed single-shot covering fire directly on the machine gun position. With only AK-47 rounds cracking about both of us, Cain charged to about twenty feet from his objective and dropped—rather than threw—the hand grenades into or very near to the enemy machine gun. He was halfway back to me when the grenades exploded. He returned unhurt to the protection of the termite hill.

The enemy machine gun stayed quiet during and following Cain's charge. Though I can't know for sure, I believe my support made the difference. And though several troopers had sprayed the area with automatic fire as Cain charged, no one else placed steady, aimed rounds straight into the machine-gun position.

Top: Crash of chopper in background drew worshippers away from Easter Services just in time to avoid being cut down by shrapnel from dud artillery round.

Left: "Best combat soldier I ever saw," is how Captain James Cain described this Charlie 1-5 trooper, Robert William Snyder. Soon after Cain said that, Snyder threw himself between the author and an enemy machine gun, giving his own life and saving the author's in the process. Picture taken prior to Snyder's deployment to Vietnam

Top Next Page: Field memorial service twelve 1-5 Cav soldiers, including Hoover, Snyder, Derda, and Allen, who gave their lives in service to each other and for their country. April, 1969

With the enemy machine gun finally silent, we soon succeeded in pulling our four dead and the wounded troopers back behind the termite hill on the left side of the trail.

After almost four hours in close contact, and with the enemy pressing as hard as ever, less the machine gun, we withdrew behind the fortified ditch with all our dead and wounded. To keep the NVA at a distance as we withdrew, we set a line of claymore mines across our front, then backed off a few meters and set another line. We blew the first line of claymores while backing away from the second line to set up yet a third line. Thus, we kept the NVA at bay while we withdrew behind the ditch, which, fortunately, we didn't have to fight our way across. At 1711 hours we arrived in an old FOB about 200 meters west of where we had fought all afternoon.

Sergeant Clark had been outstanding during the whole battle. He was everywhere, constantly risking his life to fill defensive gaps and maneuver his men. Without his valiant efforts the company CP group probably would have been flanked and possibly put out of action early in the fight. Clark had maneuvered his platoon to take the pressure off us as I fought beside a medic to hold the left front. Clark frequently exposed himself to enemy fire to help retrieve wounded troopers. I nicknamed him "Audie Murphy" after the most decorated American soldier during World War II.

After our withdrawal to the old FOB, Cain put a few men to work turning a small clearing into a PZ so Medevac and re-supply choppers could come in. He ordered the platoon leaders to get the men to work filling sandbags and digging out old, partially collapsed foxholes. I intended to stay with the wounded until they were picked up, but changed my mind when all around the perimeter as far as I could see, grunts sat immobile in a daze and stared blankly, silently into the partially collapsed foxholes or into space. None dug or filled sandbags.

Approaching a foxhole, I suggested we'd better dig in for the night. One or two troopers glanced in my direction. The others just stared glassy-eyed at nothing. None started digging.

I picked up a shovel, dropped into a hole and started throwing out dirt. After a minute or so, a trooper nudged me from the hole and took over the shovel.

Going from hole to hole, I dug until someone nudged me aside. Gradually the effect began spreading ahead of me as troopers in adjacent holes began digging before I reached them. Soon, everyone who had nothing else to do was either digging, filling sandbags or collecting logs for overhead cover.

In the telling of this, I don't wish to give the false impression that I was tougher than those troopers were. Sure, I'd had some rough moments today, but nothing like what these young men had endured. And I'd had advantages that most of those guys lacked. I had a termite hill to hide behind and had been close enough to the commander to have some concept of the whole picture. It is amazing how it helps one to have some idea of what is going on in the chaos and confusion of a battle.

By the way, while I'd been close enough to the CP to have some idea what was happening, a lot more occurred than what I perceived. For example, several times during the fight, I had urged Haines to get us more artillery support, only to discover later that more than fifteen thousand rounds of friendly artillery had been expended during the fight. And the artillery barrages continued after the fight, off and on all through the night, as it seemed likely we would be attacked in the FOB before dawn.

For me, personally, the night was tumultuous, not because the NVA attacked, but in consequence of my internal struggle with remorse, guilt, self-recrimination and even shame, tempered with amazement that I was alive. Over and over, I relived the events of the day.

Repeatedly, I considered everything from every angle. I replayed in my mind each contact I'd had with Bill Snyder. These thoughts gave me little solace, for I felt I had let Snyder down. Rationally, in the light of circumstances and conflicting demands, each delay in sharing the sacrament with Snyder seemed logical and reasonable, given the limitations of human foreknowledge.

All night long, following the deaths of Snyder, Hoover, Derda and Allen I wrestled with very strong emotions and feelings. And I reflected anew about how amid all the chaotic sounds and furies of close combat, for me the worst combat noise of all is the profane use of God's name and of motherhood by young men in the face of imminent death. Cursing under fire hadn't changed since 1967, except perhaps for the worst. Men continued to employ the most sacred of names and titles during the vilest, most frightful moments of war.

Profanity and obscenity during battle were reflexive, I thought, and reflected habits formed during individual struggles for peer acceptance during youth. Some of the cursing was probably intended as "tokens of bravery" or "manliness." This most disturbing of battle noises bothered me because, as I had cautioned Sergeant Wade back in '67, "God will not hold him guiltless who taketh His name in vain."

But Snyder was gone, forever beyond the limits of mortal ministrations and sacraments. *How does Bill feel now,* I wondered? *Did his last, deep gaze into my eyes include understanding as well as goodbye?* Yes, Robert William Snyder was gone, but he was not forgotten. I did not forget him, nor, it seemed, did the surviving troopers of Charlie 1-5.

Gator revealed something of his esteem for Snyder about a month later. "Chaplain, I've quit smoking," he announced.

"Great, Gator," said I, "but why are you telling me? I never told you to quit smoking."

"No, Chaplain, but Bill Snyder told me to."

Later, a lieutenant asked me to help him deal with a moral problem and to straighten his life out in preparation for reunion with his dear wife. He, like Gator, credited Snyder's council and example for bringing him to see me. A private first class counseling a lieutenant. Now that's unusual.

I found a semblance of peace days later while I prepared to conduct a memorial service for Snyder and his fellow grunts. Bill Snyder had lived in accordance with God's will as he understood it, which truth I discovered in a spiritual, powerful, sure manner. Thus was I convinced that Bill Snyder had been chosen for higher purposes in God's plans, purposes in which he was already engaged, among the spirits of recently killed soldiers, American, Vietnamese, and many others, spirits with whom he held special standing. Snyder had served as a missionary in Canada for two years, then dutifully submitted himself for military service, which service he could have avoided simply by remaining in Canada to greet the hoards of draft dodgers who were flocking there.

Chapter Notes:

7 April 1966, 1435: "C Co is in contact with an unknown size force." 1450: "C Co engaged...trying to pull back." 1600: "C Co received 04 US KIA and 02 WIA...still in contact...received 05 60mm incoming rounds." 1637: "C Co is moving back to FOB about 200 meters to their west, enemy is following, still in contact." 1820: "C Co requests medevac at `11...completed at 1804 hrs...Contact was broken at 1720 hrs." KIAs: Hoover, Derda, Snyder and Allen. WIAs: Alfman -, Franklin-, Cole-, Heriot, McDonald, Castaneda-, Mahler, O'Neill and Wacker.

HQ, 1st Cav Div (AM) Journal, 1530 hrs: "At 1425H C/1-5 made contact w/est en plt... Contact broke 1444h. Neg. assess. Neg frly cas. 1500H. C Co began sweep of area...1800 hrs. Contact w/en was reestablished w/est 4 to 5 indiv. Rec SA & AW fire...4 to 5 rds 60mm mort...Res 4x US KIA, 2x US WIA. Contact continues." 1830 hrs, Item 46 [foxhole strength]: A Co., 2-65; B Co., 3-80; C Co., 2-62; D Co., 3-92; E Co., 2-39.

Chapter Eight

RENEW THE ATTACK!

In the wee hours of April 8, Captain Cain placed Charlie 1-5 on full alert, just in case the NVA tried to take advantage of our depleted stamina and resources. No attack came, though. What came instead was an order from battalion for Charlie 1-5 to renew the attack after dawn. We few who knew of the new orders waited in silence for the dawn and wondered what the new day held for us. We took some comfort from the promise that Air Force bombs would attempt to soften up the target prior to our assault.

Sergeant Clark came to me just after dawn. He looked very somber. "Chaplain, when I looked at my men this morning, some of them had no features where their faces should have been. It was like no soul existed behind each blank face." Clark interpreted the illusion, if illusion it was, as an omen that those particular soldiers would soon die.

I'd heard reports of this sort of "vision" during the World War s and Korea. Though I was inclined to not give much credence to Clark's premonitions, I remembered an Indian trooper, Prentice LeClair, who had come to me about premonitions of his own death just days before he died on 9 August 1967. Because of this and other experiences, I found myself unable to shrug off Clark's impressions as meaningless.

In fact, several of Clark's men would give their lives in days to come, but he wouldn't be around to confirm whether those who died were the same faceless ones in his "vision." Clark had about six hours to go in the field at the moment he shared his premonitions with me.

Combat doctrine, I was told on high authority, called for at least 500 meters distance between friendly troops and Air Force bombing targets. But we were only 200 meters from our objective. So to insure that the air strikes would be more effective than those on the previous day, Captain Cain gave our position as about 250 meters farther away to the west. Consequently, seven air strikes came in at half the "required" distance between friendly troops and the bombing target. I had thought that eight-inch shells at fifty meters were horrendous, but they paled in comparison to 500 pound and heavier bombs at 200 meters.

The circling Air Force forward air controller (FAC) warned us that the first bombing run was coming in. Casually we took cover in holes or behind trees just before the jet screamed across our front from the south, and almost instantly the jungle floor slammed like a sledge hammer into our chests or whatever body part we rested on. Concussion and the sound of the exploding bombs came so close together that I couldn't tell which arrived first. Waves of concussion swept over us with such power that even the largest trees seemed to lean away. The blasts were so loud that I doubted our tender eardrums could survive. Waves of shrapnel and debris flashed straight outward from the blasts, over and around us, sounding like thousands of giant, angry wasps. Secondary shrapnel and debris rained straight down from the sky moments after each concussion wave swept past us.

Faces paled in awe before the terribly destructive powers unleashed so near to us. Many eyes focused on Captain Cain, and behind those eyes lurked traces of hope and suspicion—hope that the terror of the bombs would spare us more intimate terror when we assaulted, suspicion that our leaders up above might kill us with the bombs in order to save us.

Spaced moments to minutes apart, six more air strikes followed, each just as impressive as the one before. *Surely any NVA left alive are too stunned to resist us.* Not so, as we soon discovered.

Following the concussion and initial sweep of shrapnel from one of the latter air strikes, Captain Cain dropped his helmet between his folded legs to relieve a terrible headache. He got them frequently, the result of an earlier wound, which I'll explain later. "Jim," I chided,

"You're setting a bad example for the troops, taking off your helmet at a time like this."

"Right," Cain said, with just the trace of a sheepish grin, as he replaced his helmet on his head. His hand was still on the brim of his helmet when a chunk of hot shrapnel fell from the sky and caved in his steel helmet a good half of an inch.

"Thanks, Claude," Jim said simply. Enough said.

We assaulted eastward right after the last air strike, moving steadily and unopposed for a hundred, which brought us to the north-south running ditch with the new NVA fighting positions that we had found the day before. After a brief pause at the ditch we moved forward with the men on-line across a thirty-meter front with Cain, the lieutenants and me about ten feet behind the line. Perhaps we were feeling more confident than was justified following the bombing.

Sure enough, the NVA opened fire across our front with AK-47's before we'd moved more than 50 feet. Three troopers fell wounded in as many seconds.

For the next hour we lay where we were and exchanged sporadic fire with the NVA—they seemed content to stay where they were too. Two more troopers were wounded during that hour. Finally on Cain's command, Haines called in ARA to attempt to end the stalemate. It was doubtful that ARA could make much difference, considering the fight still left in the NVA after those bomb strikes.

During the ARA attack, we were lying on our stomachs facing the enemy when shrapnel wounded the man to my left and a bullet laid open the left cheek—nose to ear—of the man to my immediate right. It took a very brave or an extremely foolhardy NVA soldier to rise up and fire so effectively with those ARA rockets raining down on him.

A trooper lying about ten feet to my left escaped bodily injury when a bullet cut a path in the ground beneath his prone body. The bullet, perhaps fired by the same NVA who hit the man on my right, drilled a cigarette case—top to bottom—in one of the trooper's upper blouse pockets and passed on without touching his flesh.

Charlie 1-5 moved forward again a little past noon and advanced unopposed for a hundred meters. We skirted the northern edge of the area where we had fought the day before, and stopped atop a steep bank that dropped to a debris-choked stream. Bombs and artillery had literally destroyed the jungle to the east of the streambed. A single dead NVA soldier lay in plain sight by the stream.

After a momentary pause the Second Platoon crossed the stream and reconnoitered among the fallen and twisted trees. When they drew no enemy reaction, Cain swung the line of troops south for a sweep through where we'd fought and been pinned down the day before. He halted the company in and around a small clearing east of and separated by a thin line of trees from the large clearing that had been on our right flank during the fighting the previous day.

Taking advantage of the stop, I sat down and leaned back against the termite hill that Cain had taken cover behind. For several minutes I stared, deep in thought and with churning emotions, at the spots where Snyder, Derda, Hoover and Allen had given their all. Suddenly, heavy small-arms fire shattered my contemplation, just as I was about to take pictures of the scene.

With all thoughts of a pictorial history temporarily forgotten, I rushed past the hole from which the NVA machine gun had given us so much grief the day before, turned south and dashed across a clearing to where a medic who was tending Sergeant Clark. The two were behind a large tree near the south edge of the small clearing and about ten feet from where Clark's men lay on their stomachs and poured automatic fire into the jungle to the south.

A moment before the shooting had begun, Sergeant Clark had raised up, much as he'd often done during the fighting the day before, to get his reluctant troopers moving to the south. Standing there and facing south, Clark looked over his right shoulder at his unmoving men, and with a follow-me-forward swing of his left arm he said, "Come on. If Gooks were out there, they would already have shot me." Bam! His arm signal was cut short by a shot from about twenty feet to his left front. Keeping his feet, Clark swung around, yelled to someone to take charge, then ran back and dropped behind the tree where I joined him and the medic.

An AK-47 round had torn through Clark's left wrist and buried itself and parts of his wristwatch in his left shoulder, which was bleeding profusely. Sergeant Clark was very calm.

The medic had a bandage on Clark's wrist when I reached them. A moment later sniper fire interrupted our joint efforts to tend to his shoulder. The single-fire rounds came from some trees about fifty feet to our left—from the east. The troops on the line couldn't help us; their hands were full. Across the clearing behind us were several troopers that didn't seem so occupied in the fight. I caught their attention, pointed eastward and yelled "Snipers in the trees!" They never reacted. So, assuming they could not understand me above the din of battle, I ran toward them with the intent of directing their fire against the snipers. What I did instead was draw the snipers' fire away from Clark and the medic. More than one sniper was shooting at us, no doubt about it.

I had covered about ten or fifteen feet when suddenly I realized that I was at the center of the focus of several snipers. In the same moment, I spotted an empty NVA fighting position off to my left front. I dived into the position with bullets cracking all about me. That's when I became aware of Clark's M-16 in my left hand. So I popped up just enough to blast away at where I thought the latest sniper fire was coming from. I didn't do the snipers any harm, though.

After the fight, several grunts expressed amazement that I wasn't hit. "Dozens of rounds followed you into the hole, Chaplain Newby, and they continued to pepper all around you until we finally realized where the shots were coming from and hosed down those trees," said a trooper to agreeing nods of his buddies. I'd been shooting in the wrong direction, betrayed by my ears, again.

After the men put a stop to the sniper fire, I helped the medic with Clark and the other wounded men until the company, down to 48 men as I recall, pulled back to the position we had occupied the night before. From there we evacuated the wounded.

In the quiet of the following night, I recommended to Captain Cain that Clark be put in for the Distinguished Service Cross, the second-highest award our nation gives for valor in combat. Cain declined to support my recommendation, so I recommended Clark, Snyder, Hoover and Derda for the Silver Star—Cain wrote up Allen—and later was assured the awards were approved, posthumously for all but Clark.

The NVA mortared us during the night, but the incoming ordnance made very little impression on my memory.

Probably, some will criticize me for taking up arms in three instances during the engagements of April 7 and 8, but I offer no apologies or excuses. What I did was done reflexively, for what seemed very appropriate causes under the accumulated heat of those particular battle conditions. It was, perhaps, another case of former infantry training and reflexes kicking in and overcoming chaplain education. The Geneva Conventions were definitely not on my mind.

It occurs to me that I've said almost nothing of my family since I began to describe the first month of this tour. Suffice it to say, I wrote almost every day, often in the dark out in the jungle. Helga and the children wrote, though incoming mail was as sporadic and unpredictable as incoming mortars.

Helga's letters came in bunches, with painful gaps in between. Still, they were filled with love and spiritual support, which is what counted. The mail also raised some concern about things on the home front. For one thing, Helga kept threatening to miscarry. I lived with the premonition, the certainty almost, that I would never see this baby alive in this world. Concerns for Helga and our children helped me to appreciate the cares and worries that so many troopers went through, and perhaps helped me to minister to them more effectively.

True to my call, though, I resisted the urge to quit and find a way to go home to Helga and the children. Actually, I'd never entertained the idea of going AWOL. Even as an enlisted man, I had always been paranoid about sometime being AWOL because of events beyond my control.

Chapter Notes:

8 April 1966, 1-5 Battalion Journal: 1113, "C Co is now receiving S/A fire from their front...one burst of AK-47 fire 15-20 meters away, from the southeast...01 US WIA."

1137: "C Co received another burst of automatic fire...believes fire is coming from a bunker instead of a tree. The bunker is center of mass of C Co line...will swing right and left and try to frag bunker."

1204: "C Co had made repeated attempts to maneuver on bunker, with negative results. there appears to be more than one individual firing...Enemy has two well-placed auto weapons and has been throwing chicom grenades."

1850: "C Co in contact today, had 05 US WIAs, 02 were wounded this morning, 03 were wounded this afternoon...medevac completed at 1825 hrs. C Co pulled back...tomorrow, C Co will sweep area. WIAs: Mario Trevino, Eddie Ellis, Raymond Clark, Richard Higgins, Donald Phillips and Douglas Barron.

April 1969 2-12 Operational Report: On 8 April contact was heavy. [In] A Co...claymore mine was detonated, causing 1 US/WIA... [later] point element engaged 2 NVA...found 2 additional claymores...minutes later ran into 5 individuals...while they were moving from LOG site, point element tripped a booby trapped claymore mine resulting in 1 US/KIA and 7 WIA. B Company made contact...resulting in 1 US/KIA, 8 WIA and 1 MIA. Next day B Company was in contact area and again received heavy fire, Results 10 US/WIA. On 11 April A Company made contact with enemy in bunker. Results, 5 US/KIA, 9 WIA and 1 NVA/KIA.

Chapter Nine

CIRCUIT RIDING

—Area Support—

On April 9, after conducting several small group worship services (small, to avoid bunching the troops) I returned to LZ Dolly. Over the next five days, I divided my time between efforts to get LDS troopers to a conference in Bien Hoa and quick visits to conduct worship services for companies in the field and on LZ Dolly and LZ Grant. Charlie 1-5 must have returned to LZ Dolly soon after I did, following the fighting on April 7 and 8, for there I conducted a memorial service for twelve troopers, including Allen, Derda, Hoover, and Snyder. Meanwhile, Bravo 2-12 still hadn't received its General Christian Easter Service.

Three days later, at 0820 hours, Alpha 2-12 moved by foot away from LZ Grant. An hour later they reported finding new graves and said the company was moving on. At 1150 hours, the RTO reported that the company was in a firefight and had sustained two wounded from small-arms fire. A few minutes later he radioed that the company was receiving heavy automatic fire and had one grunt dead and two more wounded. By 1301 hours, the American casualty count was two killed and four wounded. The company was still engaged in heavy fighting. Two hours later the count was three killed, nine wounded, and three missing in action. At 1710 hours, Lieutenant Colonel Boon reported from his command chopper that he had found two of the three MIAs.

While all this was happening to Alpha 2-12, I completed my first month in the field with Bravo 1-5 elsewhere in the jungle. Sometime that day I left the field for a religious retreat at Bien Hoa. I stopped on the way and picked up a contingent of 1st Cav troopers, including Sergeant Elvin Jackson and my nephew Earl Dyer. We flew to and from

Bien Hoa on an Air Force Caribou that I had laid on for the retreat. By invitation, I spoke during the retreat and turned one session into an informal memorial service for Bill Snyder and others.

Following the retreat, the Caribou dropped some of the troopers at Phuoc Vinh and dropped the remainder at Tay Ninh—we arrived there after dark. On the way from the airstrip to the 1-5 Cav rear area, Jackson and I stopped by to see Chaplain Black in his combination office and sleeping quarters.

When we walked in, Black tore into me angrily, without any courtesies or preliminaries. He was very put out that Bravo 2-12 was still waiting to receive a non-Catholic Easter service. "I didn't let your men go without an Easter mass, and Black Gold still hasn't had a service."

I explained about the heavy casualties and subsequent events in Alpha 1-5. Clearly from his religious perspective Black considered Easter services to have precedence over casualties. I didn't agree, but we parted on good terms and remained so for the duration.

The next day, April 13, I conducted several worship services for the 2-12 Cav at and around LZ Grant. One of the services was a belated "Easter Service" for Bravo 2-12, for which Chaplain Black thanked me profusely. "The men say you are just great, that you speak just like me," he said. This compliment I took as Black's peace offering.

Following the field services, I hitched flights to Ton San Nhut via LZ Dolly. Elder Ezra Taft Benson, former Secretary of Agriculture in President Eisenhower's cabinet and a very high ecclesiastical official in the LDS Church, was conducting the conference. The conference was more than half over when I landed at Ton San Nhut.

Out on the street, dozens of military vehicles ignored my outstretched thumb. Finally, I ran what seemed like a mile to get to the service, laden with full rucksack and field gear. Come to think of it, perhaps the traffic passed me by precisely because of my laden, scruffy, filthy, sweaty appearance. Fear of being mugged?

Elder Benson was delivering the concluding talk of the conference when I sneaked in and took a seat on the back pew. Among the things he spoke of were the importance and divine origin of the Constitution of the United States.

After the session, I held back from the crowd that gathered around Elder Benson because I knew that I smelled rather strong compared to everyone else. This self-awareness did not equate with any sense of being inferior or subordinate to the others, except Elder Benson. Like most of the front line troops that I served, I felt a bit superior to rear-area soldiers, because of my combat experiences and existence. I appreciated the sacrifices that many rear-area soldiers made, and understood how impossible our situation at the front would have been without their support, but it was hard to avoid this attitude.

Well, Elder Benson shook my hand in passing, but never commented on my aroma and appearance.

Between April 17 and 23, I concentrated on the companies of the 2-12 Cav, but not exclusively. My journal got behind, so consequently I must fill in the blanks with vividly remembered incidents, without positively linking them to dates in every case.

It was during this time with the 2-12 Cav that several well-remembered actions and events occurred. One involved a young lieutenant in command of a company, reinforcing the concept that preparation makes a difference. Another action exposed the hope- and promise-shattering vagaries of war. Yet another incident shattered any illusion that chaplains lead charmed lives.

About mid-April, I joined Alpha 2-12 for an afternoon and a night. The company was receiving supplies when I arrived. It had a temporary perimeter near the eastern end of an east-west running swath of open terrain. A recent B-52 bomb strike (Arclight) had recently created that swath in the jungle. The NVA demonstrated that they knew precisely where the company was by firing an occasional 60mm mortar at it. Fortunately for the grunts that were not dug in, the NVA mortar man was a poor shot.

The new company commander, a lieutenant about to be promoted to captain, appeared oblivious to the risks he was exposing his men to. He kept his company in the open for three hours following my arrival, to receive and break down supplies.

To make matters worse, this new commander—I believe he was John F. Kopacz, but can't confirm that—used up the last hour and a half of daylight to move his company toward the westward end of the bombed-out area. There he stopped the company for the night in plain sight of watching eyes around us in the jungle. While the perimeter was being laid out, I picked a spot near the center of mass and started digging a one-man foxhole. A few minutes later I gave myself a break and looked around. To my dismay I was the only one within my sight who was digging. Everyone else, it seemed, had things to do that they considered more important.

The troopers, following the lead of their commander, were wasting the remaining daylight on personal comforts, reading mail, erecting rain shelters and sorting out C-rations. Calling the CO aside, I offered some unsolicited advice. "Lieutenant, you are setting a bad example for the men." With that "tactful" opening, I told him why.

"You tend to your business and I'll tend to my company," he retorted as he turned and stomped away in a huff back to his CP group.

Shortly after dark, a subdued commander came to my foxhole, the only decent hole inside the perimeter. "I apologize for reacting the way I did, Chaplain. I'd appreciate it if you would explain what you meant," he said.

I gladly complied with his request, beginning with a critique of how the unit had stayed too long in the open while receiving supplies, and how he selected the FOB out in the open when he knew the NVA were watching. Then I pointed out how he and the troops had squandered the remaining daylight hours on creature comforts and then settled in for the night with poorly planned defenses and no overhead protection.

"Overhead cover isn't a big concern out here in the open tonight, but it is very important in the jungle and prevents mass casualties from mortar and rocket bursts in the trees," I explained.

The lieutenant acknowledged the wisdom of my observations and then impressed me by asking, "What do you recommend I do?"

"First, pray we are not hit tonight. Second, include in your re-supply list for tomorrow picks and shovels to distribute between the platoons, and several empty sandbags for each man in company. Third, starting tomorrow and from then on, put security before creature comforts," I advised.

"Why the picks and shovels? How do we use the sandbags?"

I explained how the 1-5 Cav and other 2-12 Cav companies developed a FOB. Perhaps the lieutenant said his prayers. We had a quiet night and Alpha 2-12 got itself out of the open first thing the next morning.

After we had moved a good ways into the jungle, we learned another 2-12 company was having a very loud morning following a quiet night. Boon radioed me to meet him at LZ Grant, and sent his C&C chopper to pluck me out of the field. While we waited for the chopper, the troopers blew down some trees to create a PZ. In the process, a trooper stuck his head up to watch the explosions. For his curiosity he caught a piece of shrapnel that might have cost him the sight in one eye. He left the field with me on Boon's C&C chopper.

Lieutenant Colonel Boon met me at his helipad, just outside the south side of the LZ Grant perimeter. Boon wanted me by his side when his dead troopers arrived. Soon a chopper came into sight from the southeast, made a 180-degree turn to the right and settled on the pad before us, facing east, with rotors turning. A detail of men ran forward and started unloading the chopper. A moment later, five poncho-wrapped bodies lay out on the ground in a neat row, their feet toward the chopper. At the last moment before taking off, the crew chief of the chopper tossed a wadded-up poncho out the door. The wadded poncho came open when it hit the ground. Its contents rolled out and came to rest at the feet of one of the troopers on the unloading detail. Dead eyes "stared" up at the trooper from the severed head lying at his feet—the eyes of one of his closest buddies. Understandably, the young man almost lost control of his emotions. And undoubtedly the memory is never far below the surface of his mind, assuming he survived Vietnam.

After we'd done what we could there on the helicopter pad, Boon had his chopper drop me off at the company of my born-again friend, where I got the rest of the story.

The night had been quiet, but for the usual defensive artillery fire. Next morning, the company broke camp and prepared to reconnoiter in-force to the west, in a column, with flanking security.

Unknown to my friend, the NVA had left him alone during the night in favor of a more elaborate plan, an ambush designed to catch the company outside the FOB between two forces of NVA. The captain said that his company might have been annihilated except for the nervous trigger finger of an NVA soldier in one of the NVA elements.

As the lead element of the company moved west, the remainder of the company gravitated toward the west side of the FOB. About half of the company was still inside the FOB when an NVA soldier opened fire on the point element, prematurely triggering an L-shaped ambush.

Simultaneously, the second NVA force attacked the company from the rear with heavy small-arms fire, hand grenades, and RPGs. This attack came from the foxholes on the east side of the FOB, holes the NVA had slipped into as the company abandoned them.

Thus, while the guys in the lead platoon fought off the ambush and dragged their dead and wounded away from the kill zone, the remainder of the company counterattacked to expel or destroy the NVA on the other side of the FOB. It was during this battle inside the perimeter than an enemy RPG decapitated the trooper.

The company commander was understandably dejected that his faith and prayers had not protected his men as he had promised them. Though I tried, there was little I could do to console him. I never saw him again after that visit to his company. A few days later at LZ Grant a hand grenade went off on a trooper's pistol belt or load bearing suspenders while my friend was checking some of his men in formation prior to them going out on ambush. He and several of his men fell, wounded severely.

Word came that my captain friend died of his wounds, but I can't confirm it. Boon insists only one of his company commanders was killed, in different circumstances than those described here. Another problem I have with this account is that, though I saw the bodies and got the story firsthand, I can find no official record of an engagement quite like the one described to me. The lack of records doesn't mean the fight didn't happen the way the captain said. I just wish I could verify the details.

It was mid-April and I was in a chopper at about 2000 feet elevation with a squad of infantry. We were southeast of LZ Grant headed toward LZ Dolly. Eight or nine infantrymen plus their chaplain with all their gear was more than a full load for a Huey helicopter. I sat crosslegged on the floor with my knees sticking out of the open left doorway directly behind the copilot's seat. While I was watching jungle and bomb craters sweep beneath us, the helicopter suddenly, without warning, banked sharply to the right and went into a steep dive. Only the quick reflexes of those sitting back from the doors kept others and me from being flung from the chopper to certain death. Our saviors had kept us in the chopper by grabbing our packs and suspenders.

At LZ Dolly the pilot apologized and explained. He'd been forced to perform the violent maneuvers because 37mm anti-aircraft guns had targeted us. The 37mm anti-aircraft gun, he explained, was aimed and fired electronically, during which process it emitted three electronic beeps. The first and second beeps occurred when the gun's targeting device gathered some aspects of the target's height, speed, and direction. The third and last beep signaled completion of the aiming process and firing of the gun.

"When we hear the distinctive signature beep of a 37 mike-mike, we react instantly and violently to thwart its electronic brain. We don't wait around to see if what we heard was the first or the second beep, for if we miss one and hear the third beep before we react, it is too late," the pilot explained.

Another night, Chaplain Black and I were both in the jungle with Charlie 1-5. The next day the company patrolled from the jungle eastward through the northern edge of the Michelin Rubber Plantation. Captain Cain was suffering one of his frequent and severe headaches. His eyes were glazed over and his demeanor and countenance broadcast a man on the verge of screaming. During a stop, Cain sent a squad along our back trail for rear security, then forgot to call it in before we moved on. The error was soon noted, and a platoon returned and brought in the lost squad.

Cain had been wounded twice before I joined the battalion. Once his RTO accidentally shot him with a .45 pistol; the round entered the lower abdomen and exited the hip. The other time, Cain took a piece of shrapnel in the face. The hot steel entered the side of his nose and lodged under the skin above the nape (back) of his neck. This injury accounted for his blinding, agonizing headaches.

After retrieving the lost squad, we moved farther east and into the edge of the jungle. There under the trees just outside the rubber plant, we established a FOB. As we dug in, I saw VC punji stakes for the first and only time in War Zone C—this was quite different from the highlands in 1966-67, when punji stakes had been a common threat.

Cain and I discussed the dilemma of headaches from the perspective of command and career. He very much wanted to finish his six months in command, but in light of his error earlier in the day, he worried that another mistake might get people killed. Still, he believed it could end his military career if he requested his own relief from a combat command. He believed his career concerns were justified because Peterson had reprimanded him for leaving his artillery FO in command when he was medevaced out from his company after being wounded.

The next day, with Cain's reluctant permission, I talked with Lieutenant Colonel Peterson about Cain's demonstrated courage, efforts, and performance, and the debilitating effects of his headaches. I recommended that Jim be reassigned short of the completion of six months in command for medical reasons. Cain was reassigned to the battalion staff ahead of schedule and replaced by Bill Kehoe, a newly promoted—or about to be promoted—captain in the TOC.

The division sustained a chaplain casualty about this time in April. Chaplains James Carter and Nicholas Waytowich, like Black and me, shared coverage of two battalions, but with a different modus operandi. Waytowich and Carter focused almost exclusively on providing worship services. Normally, the pair traveled together, hopping from company to company to provide concurrent or consecutive Catholic and Protestant services. Often they spent a night in one or the other's rear-area accommodations.

Waytowich and his assistant's sleeping quarters in Tay Ninh were in a rectangular room at the back, south end of a building. The middle and north end of the building served as a unit chapel. This was but one of several identical buildings aligned with military precision in rows running east to west near the north perimeter.

The sleeping area contained two cots, one on each end, with enough space between them for cots to be set to accommodate guests. Steel and sandbags enclosed the cots at the east and west ends of the room, leaving small openings for getting in and out of bed. During a visit with Waytowich and Carter, I concluded that I did not like the bunkered-in cots. But events were about to prove them quite effective and worthwhile.

Waytowich and his assistant went to bed one evening a few days after my visit, each in his own cocoon. Chaplain Carter bedded down in the guest cot. During the night their building took a direct hit. An NVA 122mm on a delayed fuse crashed through the roof and floor and exploded in the ground beneath Carter. The rocket's entrance or explosion took off both of Carter's legs at the hips. Waytowich and his assistant were shaken but unhurt. Carter lived and received a medical discharge.

Chapter Ten

MIND YOUR OWN BUSINESS

On Wednesday, April 23, I accompanied Delta 1-5 on an air assault into the western part of the 2-12 Cav AO. Delta Company was temporarily under the operational control (OPCON) of Lieutenant Colonel Boon and the 2-12 Cav. The next morning, following a hot and uneventful night, the company split into platoons. I went with First Lieutenant Larry Dee Brock's platoon. About midmorning, Brock received orders to find a PZ. We did so, and shortly were picked up and flown to the southwest, where we became OPCON to a mechanized company of either the 11th Armored Cavalry Regiment or the 25th Infantry Division.

When we arrived, the tankers were in the process of destroying a Sheridan tank, one the NVA had disabled with an RPG. The Sheridan had been declared unsalvageable under current combat conditions. The tankers finished stuffing the Sheridan with explosives. Then they (with Brock's Platoon atop tanks and APCs) moved off a kilometer to the northwest. From that distance, an M-60 tank fired a single HE (high explosive) shell at the disabled Sheridan, with very impressive results. The turret flew upward about one thousand meters, as I recall, and returned to the earth through a rising, mushroom-shaped cloud.

We spent the rest of the day riding atop tanks and APCs, with occasional stops. Snipers usually took advantage of these stops to take potshots us from distant tree lines. On the move, standing behind the turret of the lead tank with Brock and his RTO, we watched a long ugly gash being torn through the virgin jungle as small trees and forest giants yielded to the irresistible power of the M-60 tank. It seemed that nothing nature-made could resist "our" tank as it rumbled forward with its cannon pointed slightly off to the right or left. As I recall, the mechanized unit moved in two or three columns, each with an M-60 tank in the lead to cut its own swath through the jungle parallel to ours.

At one point a five-inch-diameter limb shook loose from a falling tree. It broke across my helmet, knocking me to my knees. Three factors combined to spare me injury: my helmet, a hard head, and the fact that the limb was rotten.

A little later, our column turned south along a swath in the jungle that had been made previously by these or other tanks. The going became much more difficult for both tanks and APCs because we were moving against the lay of the fallen trees, opposite from the direction they had been pushed down.

Lieutenant Brock of Oklahoma City, Oklahoma was sitting on a tanker's waterproof bag atop the right side of the turret as we rumbled over and through this mess. Suddenly, the forward movement of the tank drove the sharp end of a small, broken tree into the bag on which Brock sat. The scene was reminiscent of a medieval knight driving his jousting lance into an opponent's saddle. The bag catapulted into the air with Brock on it. Reflexively, I caught Brock as he flew over my head, and dropped him with a thump onto the tank. This rescue may or may not have kept Brock from being crushed beneath the treads of the second tank in the column, from breaking bones on fallen trees, or impaling body parts on broken limbs and splintered tree tops. Brock believed it did, and thanked me profusely. I felt great satisfaction that I was able to react quickly enough.

Well past twilight the tanks and APCs stopped for the night. I recalled anew one reason I hated working with tanks. Armor types had a habit of continuing until dark, stopping too late for accompanying infantry to dig in properly. Digging in was no big deal for the armored people. They had the equipment for the job.

To establish an impressive FOB, the mechanized folks simply used the tanks to knock down the local flora to clear both the areas inside of the perimeter and fields of fire. This done, they drew into a circle like a herd of musk-oxen, front armor and cannons outward, with the tanks interspersed among the APCs. As final preparation, the tank gunners loaded their cannons with flechette rounds and lowered them for direct fire. Defensive matters attended to, the tankers and APC crews attended to personal matters, preventive maintenance, and equipment repair routines, with very little concern for light and noise discipline. The tank and APC crews were content to spend the night inside their armor.

Cringing at all the noise, with images of NVA swarming toward them, the grunts dug in as best they could in the darkness or made do on the open ground. One thing experienced infantrymen weren't about to do in an attack on the perimeter was take cover beneath a tank or APC. Proximity to tracked combat vehicles greatly increased the odds of ending up crushed, punctured, or burned—tanks were like magnets to enemy rockets and they burned hot when their ammo load and fuel cooked off. We had a quiet night, fortunately.

The next day, April 24, Brock's platoon rejoined Delta 1-5. I remained on the chopper that picked us up and had it deliver me to Bravo 1-5, in the jungle northeast of LZ Dolly. Newly-promoted Captain King (an assigned alias) had recently taken command. All day, King's men kept turning up fresh sign that the NVA were active in the area, but the enemy themselves remained elusive.

King stopped his company at 1630 hours, in one of those rare areas of old-growth forest that reminded me more of hardwood forest back home than jungle in Vietnam. The trees were huge and the undergrowth was sparse, which meant good fields of fire for us but also an easy approach for any NVA who might want to attack us in the night.

A chopper resupplied us soon after we stopped for the night. My assistant and I, with no other pressing duties, commenced digging a foxhole. Something was bothering me as we dug. A quick glance around the perimeter during a rest from digging told me what it was. Every man in sight was busily sorting C-ration and care-package goodies, reading mail, or constructing a rain shelter. None was digging or filling sandbags. My first thought was that the forest-like surroundings had pacified the troops into a false sense of peace and security, but the real problem was something else. Captain King, having stretched a hammock between two trees, was testing it for comfort as he surveyed his new command—leading by example, deadly example.

I called King away from the CP and said, "You are setting a bad example for the troops, and it's going to get them hurt or killed."

"What do you mean?" he demanded testily.

"When the troops see you relaxing, they relax, assuming you know more about the situation than they do. When you spend the remaining daylight attending to creature comforts, the troops do too," I explained. King's facial muscles tensed up. He just stared at me silently. I added in essence, "By using a hammock out here you do more than set a back example. You also place yourself right in the line of grazing fire and in the most lethal path of shrapnel from bursting mortars."

"Mind your own business chaplain," King snapped, "and I'll take care of my command. Besides, when the mortars start popping I can be out of my hammock and into my foxhole as fast as anyone on the ground can."

So my assistant and I attended to "chaplain stuff," which stuff never pleased my assistant. "It doesn't seem necessary for us to be the only ones digging in," he opined. We dug, and only then did we set up a rain shelter.

Perhaps it wasn't so, but for the first and only time among a CP element in a combat unit, I felt unwelcome. I avoided the CP and spent the remaining daylight with grunts on the perimeter and talked with three visitors, actually four counting a beautiful German Shepherd scout dog. Division had attached a scout-dog team and a chemical specialist to the company for this operation. A civilian reporter had attached himself for his own reasons. The trooper from Division Chemical packed a fancy, non-regulation chrome-plated Army .45-caliber pistol in an army-issue leather holster.

The night was quiet. Sometime the next day I returned to LZ Dolly without another word exchanged between King and me—we'd never have another chance. I've often wished we had parted on cordial terms

On Friday, 25 April, Bravo 1-5 continued to follow fresh sign of enemy activity, right into a recently-vacated NVA bunker complex. None opposed their entry into the complex, so they commandeered it for a FOB. Perhaps King was pleased with all the overhead cover just waiting for new occupants. There would be very little digging of foxholes for a second night.

An embankment about two to three feet high meandered through the center of the complex from southeast to northwest. In its center the embankment turned sharply north and then swung westward, creating a crescent around a cluster of bunkers and a well. King chose these bunkers with their overhead cover for the CP element and visitors. Re-supplies arrived and were distributed. Among the re-supplies was a lot of CS gas. The trooper from Division Chemical used the gas to conta-minate the well and deprive the NVA of water. Some of the troopers on the perimeter had to dig fighting positions, while others like the CP pressed NVA positions into service for the night.

True to current leadership style, many of the troopers settled in casually. King again erected his hammock, this time between two trees. This arrangement put him about four feet from a bunker, on the oppo-site side from the entrance. The rest of the CP got comfortable among the cluster of bunkers about the well. The dog handler tied his German Shepherd on an unnecessarily short leash to a tree root that protruded from the bank, then settled down for the night.

The NVA mortared the FOB fourteen minutes past midnight on April 26. First came the frighteningly familiar *thump, thump, thump* of mortar rounds leaving tubes out in the nearby jungle. "Incoming!" yelled several troopers on the perimeter. Experienced grunts slipped under cover even as they snapped awake. Some of the less-experienced troopers frantically scurried about the middle of the perimeter in the darkness in search of the cover that they'd thought was well-fixed in their minds when the went to sleep.

No one knows how Captain King reacted. One of the first incom-ing 82mm mortar shells exploded beneath his hammock and decapi-tated him.

The dog handler and reporter made it to cover. The dog died at the end of its leash with its body stretching toward the entrance of the bunker where its handler had taken cover. The trooper from Division Chemical was killed. His .45 pistol was missing.

The ARVN scout/interpreter (not Sergeant Van Nie, I think) came close to dying when he jumped up instead of going for cover at the yells of "incoming!" He was understandably perturbed that no one had explained the meaning of the term to him.

On the south side of the perimeter, a mortar shell exploded on the overhead cover of a foxhole, wounding PFC William Brown and destroying an M-60 machine gun.

Back on LZ Dolly in the early morning light, Captain Jay Copley asked me to accompany him on the flight that would take him out to replace Captain King.

Copley had entered the Army from Kentucky in 1949 as a private. He went into combat as an infantryman on July 31, 1950 with the 5th Regimental Combat Team. He left Korea as a WIA in May 1951 and returned to combat in 1952. In May 1967 he joined the 1st Cavalry in Vietnam as the Sergeant Major of the 2-5 Cav operating out of LZ Uplift, just a few kilometers south of my unit on the Bong Son Plain. He received a battlefield commission with the rank of captain in February 1968 and moved across the LZ to take command of C Company, 1st Battalion, 50th Mechanized Infantry, 173rd Airborne Brigade. On May 1, 1968 he sustained gunshot wounds to the neck, right lung, and shoulder blade. After several months in military hospitals, Jay Copley arrived back in Vietnam just when Bravo 1-5 suddenly needed a commander.

Copley and I offloaded from the chopper in a small clearing. We moved quickly out of the way of a detail that waited to load poncho-wrapped bodies onto the chopper. Moments later a cursory look around the FOB told the story. King had ignored common-sense advice and gotten himself killed. By accepting NVA hospitality, he'd placed his command in a position with which the NVA were intimately familiar. They responded by lobbing in twenty 82mm mortars, almost without having to pause to adjust fire. Every shell exploded inside or on the perimeter.

One of Copley's first actions was to order a search for the late Division Chemical trooper's chrome-plated .45. It was found off in the bushes. Copley ordered that the pistol be sent to the rear and placed with the trooper's personal effects.

As soon as the casualties were evacuated, Copley had his men check the immediate area and then move out on a company-size recon toward the east. We continued to see lots of evidence that the NVA were very active in the area, but got through the day and following night without a fight.

Beginning at 0832 hours the next morning, choppers flew a series of round-robin sorties to concurrently move Bravo 1-5 to LZ Dolly and to combat assault Delta 1-5 from Dolly to a point a little east of where Bravo 1-5 was picked up. This rotation was timely, though it had been planned at least a day earlier. A week on and around LZ Dolly would allow Copley and his new command to get used to one another and get over some of the shocking events of the previous night.

I returned to Dolly with the first group to prepare for the worship service Copley wanted his men to have as soon as possible. With the change of command, I was again welcome in the Bravo 1-5 Command Group.

At 0856 hours I hopped off the chopper, ducked low beneath the whirling rotor blades and headed up a gentle grade toward the TOC and my bunker. Captain Patrick Greiner, Delta 1-5 Company Commander, and Lieutenant Larry Brock met me halfway up the hill. "Sir, Chaplain Newby saved my neck the other day on the tanks," Brock declared to Greiner, and described how I'd grabbed him in mid-air to keep him from falling off the tank.

Pat Greiner thanked me for keeping his lieutenant out of trouble and asked, "How about making the air assault with us this morning? We'd really appreciate it."

"I promised Bravo Company a service as soon as we're all on the LZ. I'll conduct the service and come back out," I promised. I headed for the TOC to get word out about the service. Pat and Larry Brock boarded a chopper with the first lift and went to war.

It was hard to put Greiner off, but the men of Bravo 1-5 desperately needed immediate spiritual support, interlaced with specific counsel about vigilance in the jungle.

Most of the Bravo 1-5 troopers attended the worship service as did Lieutenant Colonel Peterson and many others, sitting on the ground on a slope near the aid station and my bunker, facing south. The service was simple. My assistant passed out some laminated song sheets. We sang a song and I prayed, and was well into the sermon when a call from the TOC interrupted us.

"Sir, you'd better come quick. Delta is in deep sh—. Four friendly KIAs and lots of WIAs, still in contact," yelled a sergeant.

"Sorry, Chaplain," said Peterson as he took off for his TOC. For the remainder of the service, I gazed into the eyes of Bravo troopers that were filled with relief, remorse, regret, even guilt: relief because Delta 1-5 guys were in the fight and not themselves; regret, perhaps even guilt, because others were dying in their place.

The service over, I flew to Delta Company and helped load several dead and wounded men onto the chopper that delivered me there, including the body of Lieutenant Brock. Then I went looking for Captain Greiner and found him on the opposite side of a termite hill from where the ambush had occurred. He was wounded, but refused to be evacuated until his CP and Delta Company were reorganized. In Greiner's words, here is what happened:

"We were completing our week of base defense…when word came that Captain King had been killed…[in a] mortar attack….[He had been] sleeping in a hammock when the attack occurred.

"On the morning of 27 April, as we were preparing for a combat assault, Mateus -, one of my men, complained of trouble with his eye and asked if he could stay behind to get it treated. Reluctantly I turned him down, explaining that we were very shorthanded. As we lifted off from LZ Dolly, I continually rubbed the silver spoon I carried to eat my C-rations with—a kind of joke that had become my good luck charm. The combat assault was uneventful. The first element, which included my CP, landed without opposition or incident, even though we landed forward of the planned set-down point because of heavy smoke and dust that had been kicked up by a massive preparation fire from artillery and Blue Max ARA gunships.

"Once all the company was on the ground, we moved out to the east toward our objective, to check thick jungle, trails, and small streambeds for hiding places that could not be spotted from the air. Almost immediately, our lead element encountered bunkers. We stopped and formed a perimeter and sent out cloverleaf patrols. We weren't about to walk carelessly into something big.... At this point Sergeant James Meyer led his Third Platoon out, and just minutes later he radioed that they had come onto a t-intersection trail (a trail where another trail joins it) and running into heavy sign of recent activity—a 'Gook' latrine that had recently been used. We continue to check the area.

"A few moments later all hell broke loose—heavy fire and explosions accompanied by the dreadful realization that the majority of it was coming from the enemy.

"At first there was no response to our radioed request to 3-6 for a sitrep [situation report]. Then after what seemed like minutes but was probably about 30 seconds, the call came back. 'Six! Six! We are hit! We are hit! We are all down, need help!'"

"Translated, this meant thirteen wounded or dead grunts were pinned to the ground in the kill zone of an enemy ambush by a continuous heavy volume of enemy fire.

"I immediately ordered Lieutenant Brock and his Second Platoon and my CP forward, and directed the First Platoon to attack more or less straight ahead toward the enemy's left front. I intended that these two platoons would force the enemy back so they could recover the dead and wounded 3-6 troopers.

"As I was positioning my CP behind a termite hill, Brock's men moved on past and immediately began to lay down a heavy volume of fire on the enemy's right front. By this time many wounded and pinned-down members of 3-6 element were also returning fire.

"The enemy small-arms and B-40 rocket fire continued without letup, but now we were firing back with everything we had. And Lieutenant George T. Prosser, my artillery forward observer—call sign, Birth Control Four-Niner—was adjusting artillery and ARA fire. It looked like we were quickly getting the situation under control. But just as our artillery began firing for effect, a B-40 rocket landed in my CP. It detonated as best we could determine on the point of my rifle, which at the time I was holding lightly in my right hand as it lay beside me on the ground.

"The instant the round hit I saw a ball of fire by my right foot at the same time that I was thrown back. My first thought as I pulled myself up was that our own artillery—a short round—had hit us. 'No,' Prosser assured me. The rounds he called in had exploded on target a few seconds earlier.

"As I looked around I noted Brock's horribly-mangled body, but didn't recognize him. Among the wounded were all the radiomen in the CP, Brock's RTO; and Lieutenant Wendling and his RTO who were attached to us to field test some sort of secret coding device.

"My rifle peppered me when it exploded, but the wounds were minor, kind of like getting stuck a hundred times with a lead pencil.

"The next few minutes were a blur. But during those minutes we directed the troopers and they continued to lay down a strong base of fire, while we popped smoke and marked our position for Blue Max that continued to direct along with the artillery support. Soon, Prosse r had the gunships spray the trees around the contact area, which allowed us to break contact—total elapsed time was probably thirty minutes that seemed like hours.

"As we pulled back to the LZ that we'd assaulted into an hour or so before, I lugged one RTO's radio and Prosser another one. On the way we added a machine gun and other assorted gear that our dead and wounded had dropped. Back in the enemy bunkers, we huddled for protection as fighters swished overhead and each dropped their six 750-pound bombs on the contact area. Prosser directed those too. His coolness and professionalism under intense enemy fire saved a lot of lives that day.

"When the first Medevac arrived, I was both pleased and surprised to see Claude Newby walking my way. I always thought Newby was really a frustrated infantryman. He knew infantry tactics and was quick to provide his opinion when he thought it appropriate. I had no problem with this—I needed all the help I could get, both tactically and spiritually, and Claude gave good advice on both accounts.

"Among the wounded I saw Mateus lying on his back on top of a bunker. He was alive but had a sucking chest wound. 'How are you doing?' I asked him.

"'Well, my eye doesn't hurt anymore, Six.'

"As we completed the evacuation and regrouping, my XO Lieutenant Ash - arrived and took command."

Pat Greiner's account as given here agrees mostly with what he told me that day on the scene, except that I distinctly remember him updating me at the very spot where the B-40 rocket killed Brock and wounded Greiner. I recall concluding from the nature of Brock's wounds that the rocket hit him in the back from the rear even as he faced toward Greiner and the enemy out beyond the termite hill. I remember as Greiner described these events, I looked around for a likely place for the rocket to have come from. I concluded that it had to have come from high in the largest tree in the area, about twenty meters behind the mound. With that conclusion came the eerie feeling or impression that another B-40 rocket waited in the tube on an NVA soldier's shoulder, just waiting for him to get his fill of satisfaction from the results he'd already achieved before he let fly another blast of destruction. My impression was taken seriously. I'd finished relaying it when several grunts hosed the tree with M-16 and M-60 machine-gun bullets.

Lieutenant George T. Prosser, Greiner's FO, provides this graphic description of the engagement. "Chaplain Newby...I am sure Pat's account is accurate in every way, with the exception that in his modesty he does little justice to his own role. We all know the commander is vital....We expect him to be a major factor...[under] duress. I'm convinced we dodged a much worse outcome (I'm talking overrun) without the leadership we had to have and got from Captain Greiner. He very casually dismissed his own wounds. Let me tell you, he was a mess, [and] in pain. He did not have the use of his weapon or his hand....[For a time] the bad guys had fire superiority and it was possible Pat was going to have to fight with [one useless] hands.... While Greiner was shredded and bleeding, [and] covered with matter from Lieutenant Brock...we didn't know that the partial body in our CP was Lieutenant Brock....Captain responded like the seasoned veteran he was. How...he remained calm and capable of giving coherent directions is beyond me—if he had not, the results would have been appalling. [Nothing] can take away from...the amazing bravery of our troops in that war....That they displayed if they had direction. That's what got us through—Pat Greiner's cool direction under intense fire [despite his own] intense pain.

"First Lieutenant Brock died doing his job...an incredibly brave man. I remember in several conversations with Larry that he knew he would not survive the war. I don't know why he felt that way; he didn't resent it; he just knew it. How we wish he had been wrong!

"I remember the terrifying realization that the enemy was in the trees. [My] recon sergeant [Rodriguez] and an RTO [Francis, a Navajo] with me...[we] fell to the ground...with Rodriguez between Francis and me.... I first realized we had a tree problem [when] Rodriguez was shot, while Francis and I were spared. That is extremely bad news in triple-canopy jungle.... I have to give immense credit to the Blue MAX [gunships] for saving us from that most diabolical and dire situation.

"As a forward observer I recall many times when we had high explosives...explode in close proximity. Only once, that day, do I recall [that] air support [jets] so close that I tasted the cordite before I experienced the flash/bang/concussion. I don't know if that is even possible, but I know it happened—I can still taste it after thirty-one years.

"Finally, I remember the bodies lined up, covered with ponchos, awaiting removal after the wounded had been evacuated. Then, and how do you make sense of this, I remember it rained that night—a slow, drizzly, soaking, mournful rain; the first rain we had seen in months. The rainy season had begun."

In retrospect, someone on the NVA side that morning and the night before possessed excellent tactical skills and lots of combat savvy and insight. These traits he demonstrated by how he (one leader might have orchestrated both actions) anticipated Captain King's decisions the day before and Greiner's reactions this morning. The NVA ambush was superbly placed and executed. And it was eerie that the NVA leader had possessed enough insight to cover the likely place for our men to take cover.

Consequently the NVA ambush and subsequent attack killed five great soldiers, including Lieutenant Larry Brock, and wounded about thirty-three others and a civilian reporter. Except for a few blood trails and an occasional piece of NVA equipment, there was little evidence that the enemy had paid a price for their success. The Delta 1-5 First Sergeant would become a casualty of this action in a very unusual, unexpected way.

Meanwhile, Lieutenant Brock's death left me pondering, coming as it did within an hour of his heaping praise upon me for saving him from serious injuries, injuries that might have saved him from a violent death four days later. *Did I get Brock killed by rescuing him? Would things have turned out different had I accompanied Delta Company instead of delaying on LZ Dolly to provide a worship service for Bravo Company?*

Reason quickly dispelled these doubts, and unreasonable guilt yielded to spiritual solace and relief. Right there where Brock sacrificed his life, a powerful sense of peace and confirmation poured into me, bringing with it reassurance and insight. In an instant, I saw clearly that I'd done the best I could with Brock on the tank and later with him and Greiner on LZ Dolly, limited as I was by mortal foresight and reasoning powers. And I "knew" that my presence during the ambush and fight would have changed nothing, except perhaps for my family and me. I knew deep inside where it counts that I'd done right to keep Brock from being thrown from the tank, as he would have done for me, had our roles been reversed. No, my actions on Thursday did not make me responsible for what happened on Sunday. Ever since that moment there by the termite hill, I've been free of any conscious guilt for Lieutenant Brock's death—not grief, but guilt. Consequently, I've been better able to hear and counsel other long-suffering veterans during times of grief.

After a quiet night to lick their wounds, except for the frequent "swoosh" and "karrump" of friendly artillery, Delta 1-5 swept through the area where it had been ambushed the day before. Where giant trees and thick foliage stood twenty-four hours earlier, now stood splintered tree trunks, some with a few bare branches still attached and dangling. The ground was littered with fallen, mangled foliage.

In the midst of all this destruction and bad memories there appeared something quite beautiful and seemingly out of place. An amazingly colorful, crow-size tropical bird perched on the branch of a small, shattered tree. Apparently the bird was shell-shocked, for it did not react when a trooper took it in hand and checked it for injuries. It appeared to be unhurt. Those battle-hardened troopers evacuated the beautiful bird to LZ Dolly and made it Delta Company's mascot.

At LZ Dolly, Delta Company's first sergeant built the bird a cage in his bunker—he usually stayed on the LZ to coordinate and insure adequate support for Delta Company out in the field. I saw the bird in the cage a few days later. It appeared to have recovered from its ordeal in battle with Delta Company.

A few days or a week or so after that found me waiting in the early morning darkness on the "dust off" pad at the hospital in Cu Chi. I had come to visit some of my troopers and then spent most of the night trying to hitch a ride back to the 1st Cav AO.

About 0300 hours, a medic alerted me that a 1st Cav chopper was coming in with a fever-of- unknown-origin patient. The odds were small that the chopper was from my battalion AO, but I prepared to board it to get back to the Cav AO where I'd have a better chance of getting to one of my battalions.

The Medevac chopper landed and medics quickly offloaded the first sergeant of Delta 1-5. He was comatose—encephalitis, inflammation of the brain. The first sergeant was evacuated to the states, and word came back that he was a "vegetable" for life, however long that might be. The medics believed the First Sergeant caught the deadly disease from vermin living on the beautiful tropical bird that he'd made a home for in his bunker.

Chapter Notes:

26 April 1969, 1-5 Battalion Journal: 0020, "B Co received 20 rds of 82mm mortar in FOB, resulting in 02 US KIA and 02 WIA...evacuation of wounded will be at first light. Note: One of the KIAs was their C.O. B 16 has shrapnel wounds and is assuming command of company. Also B Co lost M-60 as a result of direct hit...Scout dog wounded, seriousness unknown at this time." KIAs: CAPTAIN [name withheld] and J. Balou [James D. Valov from "the Wall"] WIAs: 1LT James Joyner, Sp4's

Roger Mendell and David Boudeau; Pfc's William Brown and Irvin Barnett. Also WIA were S. Theil, Division Chemical and John Bordas, a civilian reporter.

0945: "Questions and answers between Bde S-3 and Div 6-B:

1. What time did unit move into RON position? A. 151600 April.
2. Distance to LOG pad? A. No Log pad, between 1720 and 1810, they took a kickout of 2 sorties, 100 meters away. Also had penetrator medevac at 1850 hrs.
3. Was unit dug in? A. The 2 KIAs were sleeping above ground-the rest were dug in with OHC [overhead cover].
4. Was FOB used previously? A. Negative.
5. Status of noise and light discipline? A. Status good-no unusual violations.
6. Readout: Area had been used by 1-3 individuals in last 2-3 weeks.

27 Apr 1969, 1-5 Cav Journal: At 1125 hours they [D Co] came into heavy contact...enemy probably in bunkers. The 36 element was in the lead and what they hit appears to have been an ambush. The 26 element moved forward quickly and also came under heavy fire...mostly B-40 rockets and small arms...B-40s causing the most casualties. Contact broke at 1158 hours...3 NVA killed by air strikes. 1300: "D Co became in contact with unk. number of NVA's while searching bunker complex. Contact began at 1137...stopped getting returned fire at 1150...friendly casualties, 21 WIAs and 4 KIAs. Delta 1-5 KIAs: 1LT Brock, Chambers [of Maysville, Oklahoma], [Pfc William W. Henderson [Lyndhurst, Virginia], Smith [Laconia, New Hampshire] and Bray [Paris, Texas) died later of wound. Delta 1-5 WIAs: Erford ; Crismore ; White, Rodriguez [of Fallon, NV], Davis, Erickson, Mougthty, Hunter, Meyers, Mateus, Gary-, Anthont, Ford-, Guss, Jardell, Actquilar, Gatto, Grandchamp, Sargent, Hughes, Karastory, Blehm, Bonimi, and Greiner (Company Commander). Other WIAs: Casey - and Wendling of HHC (medics) and Groves of B/1-77 (artillery FO); and Wigham for shell shock.

Left: PCC Earl Dyer and his uncle, the author. Dyer was on the receiving end of lots of enemy rockets and mortars at such places as Loch Ninh and Bu Dop. He operated refueling points at these and other locations in the 1st Cav AO. Refueling points and ammo dumps are lucrative targets on any battlefield. Phouc Vinh, March 1969

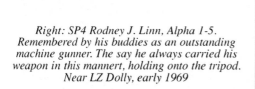

Right: SP4 Rodney J. Linn, Alpha 1-5. Remembered by his buddies as an outstanding machine gunner. The say he always carried his weapon in this mannert, holding onto the tripod. Near LZ Dolly, early 1969

A very relieved SP4"Terrence M. Brain shows off a bullet hole in his helmet. His only injuries: a bad headache and dizziness for several days. War Zone C near LZ Dolly, 1969

The author in front of the bunker that
served as his operational base on LZ Dolly,
Spring 1969

Below: Chaplain Newby (2nd from left),
LTC Booth (center), and Crew Chief
Erikson (far right), and others before
slick ship that was made available
to author each Sunday.
Phuoc Vinh, October, 1969.

It was by a crater in the bamboo like this one that the NVA caught Sergeant Elvin Jackson and his RTO in the open, stared straight at them, and turned and walked away without killing the two Americans. The grunt gives perspective and bears witness to the destructive power of a 500 pound bomb. Near LZ Dolly, Spring, 1969

A group of LDS soldiers pose beside the bunker shared by the author and battalion surgeon on LZ Dolly.
Sergeant Elvin Jackson (far left) Medic Bowen (5th from left), Chaplain Claude Newby (6th from left), PFC Ramone Banks (7th from left) and PFC Ted Pierce (8th from left).

The author pauses in the jungle while on patrol with one of his infantry companies.
War Zone C, 1969

Minutes before the NVA shot off a pointman's helmet as he passed the spot from which this picture was taken, moving right to left. In the background Captain Jay Copley's Bravo 1-5 troopers assault into the treeline from which the shots came.
War Zone C, north of LZ Dolly, May 15, 1969

Above: NVA and American APCs in background just took Delta 1-5 under friendly fire on the knoll. Chaplain (Captain) James Thompson, the author's replacement sits in the foreground. Nortwest of Loc Ninh near the Cambodian border, September 1969

*Above: Platoon Sergeant Elvin Jackson of Freemont, Utah following combat action with Alpha 1-5.
Near the Michelin Rubber Plantation, War Zone C, March 1969.*

Below: This Bravo 1-5 trooper smiles at the author in appreciation for the rucksacks that he is stacking on and about him to protect him from an airstrike.

The NVA soldier in the makeshift litter was wounded the previous midnight and left behind in a hammock with a Chieu hoi pass on his chest and his AK-47 by his side. Near LZ Dolly, June 1969

Below: These three Alpha 1-5 troopers are in the jungle a few days before Sergeant Tony Cruz, (center) died in the author's arms, of an enemy gunshot wound. Northwest of Quan Loi, September 1969.

Chapter Eleven

DOUBLE JEOPARDY

A season of less-intense combat settled over the 1-5 Cav AO for a few days. Consequently I focused a little more time and energy toward the 2-12 Cav AO, where more was happening. I ended my second month in the field—lifetimes compressed into sixty days.

On May 6, Alpha 2-12 was engaged in close, furious combat with a strong NVA force. American casualties mounted rapidly, and the Company Commander called in Medevac to extract the three most serious of its nine wounded infantrymen. The battle raged beneath triple-canopy jungle, so the most seriously wounded guys would have to be extracted by jungle penetrator—a buckle-in stretcher at the end of a cable.

Several minutes before 1700 hours, a Medevac chopper came to a hover above where the appropriate color of smoke trickled up through the trees. Over the next several minutes, the penetrator hoisted out two wounded grunts. Naturally, the NVA were busy too, trying to move into position to shoot down the chopper.

The third WIA had cleared the trees and was dangling below the hovering choppers when, at 1704 hours, the NVA opened fire. What happened next chilled the hearts of the troopers on the ground.

Concurrent with the NVA fire on the chopper, the troopers on the ground saw the chopper speed away, as their wounded buddy, wire litter and all, hurtled into the trees. "D— them...Gooks. They shot the cable in two!" a trooper shouted.

Later I learned different. And I kept what I learned to myself because I didn't want the grunts shooting down a Medevac chopper the next time they saw a casualty fall from the sky. By mid-1969, Medevac choppers were rigged with explosive charges so the penetrator cables could be *cut* in the event the chopper was about to crash onto a wounded patient or onto troopers on the ground.

Well, in this instance the chopper wasn't about to crash. Someone on board had apparently panicked and cut the cable at the first sound of AK-47 rounds cracking nearby. The wounded soldier fell into the trees and the Medevac chopper returned to Tay Ninh without any bullet holes in its skin. An hour and a half later, the grunts found their buddy in the wire litter, barely alive, hanging head-down from a tree. He may have survived.

On May 7, Platoon Sergeant Elvin Jackson and his men came upon a bomb crater in the jungle. The bomb that made the crater had also cleared the bamboo back about five feet from it. The platoon continued through the clearing one man at a time, skirting the edge of the crater on the left. Three squads had crossed safely when Jackson entered the clearing. As he started around the crater, three NVA soldiers appeared and knelt down in the edge of the bamboo just ahead of him and to his left. They were looking right toward him. "I quickly dropped into the crater and motioned for my RTO to get down too—he was following fairly closely to keep the radio handy to me," said Jackson.

Even in the crater, Jackson and the RTO remained clearly exposed to hostile view, and were certain they'd be cut down by bursts of AK-47 fire if they attempted to swing their weapons up. After a moment, the NVA turned around and disappeared back into the jungle. "It was as if blinders were placed on their eyes so that they could not see me, though I was in plain sight. It's hard to explain, but I believe God shielded me from the NVA, so they could not see me," Jackson said.

Jackson reported the incident to Captain Harrison, who asked, "Why didn't you open fire?" Despite Jackson's explanation that it would have been impossible to take out the NVA under the circumstances, and suicidal to try, Harrison said, "Sergeant Jackson, tonight I'm writing up charges against you for dereliction of duty." Harrison came down with malaria before the day was over. 1LT Phil Gioia took command of the company, and Jackson heard nothing more of the threatened charges.

The beginning of my third month in-country found me in Saigon. I had arrived there at 2200 hours on May 9 to attend a conference scheduled for May 11. I spent that night and May 10 with Major Rulon Paul Madsen, whom I first met in April 1967 at a conference in Japan. His billet in a hotel in the middle of Saigon was air conditioned and had hot and cold running water, maid service, and a hotel-style GI mess. I enjoyed a rare and long hot shower. The next morning a sedan, compliments of Madsen, delivered me to Ton San Nhut Air Base, where I spent the morning shopping for gifts for the family, a very neglected family the past two months.

At 1300 hours I attended an ecclesiastical leadership meeting. During the meeting Navy Captain Payne gave his farewell remarks—his tour in Vietnam was at an end—said, "Chaplain Newb y, you will never know what a wonderful effect you had on my family at the Mt. Fuji Conference in 1967. I will be ever grateful to you." A very kind tribute.

Paul Madsen inadvertently complicated my return to the 1st Cav AO by turning over to me an M-16 rifle, the old style with the open-pronged flash suppressor so handy for opening C-ration boxes. Madsen said he had no idea where the weapon belonged, and asked me to get it into the proper channels when I was finished with it. So, with an olive drab towel around my neck to hide my chaplain insignia, I hitched a ride to Bien Hoa with an Army chaplain and his assistant. My benefactor assumed I was an infantryman, an understandable and welcome mistake considering my grubby clothing and hidden insignia of branch and rank.

Early on May 12 the NVA simultaneously attacked the 1st Cav base camp at Phuoc Vinh and every battalion firebase in the AO except LZ

Dolly. I was asleep on the concrete floor of the Division Chaplain's office when the attack on Camp Gorvad (Phuoc Vinh) began. For the next hour I lay there and listened to the explosions of incoming rockets and the occasional rattle of shrapnel on the tin roof. From off in the distance came the sound of close combat, the unsynchronized fire of small arms, machine guns, and exploding hand grenades and claymore mines. An ineffectual ground attack was being beaten back at one point on the perimeter. Camp Gorvad was named in honor of LTC Peter Gorvad, the same who was killed back in March while I was still processing in to the division up at An Khe.

On the morning of May 15, following a quiet night on LZ Dolly, I entered the TOC for a sitrep. Based on skimpy intelligence reports, it looked like there would be no combat that day. Peterson was about to fly toward the area he thought any combat would be most likely. I boarded a slick ship (re-supply helicopter) and flew to Bravo 1-5, in the other direction. Bravo Company was on its third futile day of searching an area suspected to harbor a large cache of NVA supplies. Peterson would move the company unless it found something in the next few hours.

On the ground, the company commander and I decided to hold a worship service as soon as a squad-size patrol closed with the perimeter. After two or three nights in the same place, the FOB was taking on the appearance of a permanent camp, and the troopers appeared much too relaxed. In an instant, though, everyone was awake and looking sharp.

The returning patrol had just radioed in. "We're about two hundred meters to the west and coming in," when a burst of AK-47 fire added a stuttering exclamation point to the radio transmission.

The patrol leader, perhaps having lapsed into a false sense of security as the patrol neared the company, had led his patrol across an open field, the easiest, most direct route back to the FOB. The AK-47 opened up on the patrol even as the squad leader was delivering the radio message, just as the point man passed on the east side of a small clump of trees. The men hit the ground among the clump of trees and one shocked, happy squad leader gawked at his helmet. It had three bullet holes in it, but he was unhurt. A minute later, I arrived on the scene in company with the captain and reinforcements.

The captain sent two platoons, well dispersed in a wedge formation, across the clearing and into the jungle to the west of the clearing. We easily found where the NVA were hidden when one of them "couldn't" resist such an inviting target.

The platoon I was with scouted about fifty meters into the jungle and then turned right to skirt a small clearing, keeping it on our left. Chest-high grass rimmed the clearing, except for an eight-foot wide section that we had to cross. The NVA let a few troopers cross the gap in the grass unmolested, then fired short bursts at the rest of us as we dashed across the gap one by one. We all made it. Obviously this NVA was not the same soldier who'd hit the squad leader's helmet three times at ten times the range here.

We continued on along the north side of the clearing and soon discovered the outskirts of the NVA stronghold for which the company had been searching. Several times, we attempted to maneuver against the nearest NVA bunkers, but were driven back each time by Chicom grenades and bursts of AK-47 fire. The company commander ordered us back and called in artillery to pound the complex for the rest of the day. Meanwhile, Lieutenant Colonel Peterson flew over and radioed:

"Is One-Niner with you?"

"That's a 'rog'," the RTO replied.

"I knew it," answered Peterson.

Sometimes it seemed Peterson trusted my instincts more than he did Division Intelligence. Another time, following one of my rare orientations for replacements, Peterson said, "Chaplain Newby, having you is like having a second executive officer." I hadn't known he was listening in on the orientation.

In the morning on May 17, we swept back across the clearing and into the NVA bunker complex without meeting resistance at first. Apparently, the NVA had faded away during the night. Appearances were deceiving.

The CP of one of the platoons settled around and in a bunker while the platoons spread out and searched the area. Two troopers, for unexplained reasons, brought arm loads of B-40 rockets and Chicom grenades into the bunker where we waited in the cooler shade. I thought that was a good time to relate an incident that occurred two days earlier.

It happened on LZ Phyllis, south of the Fishhook and north of LZ Dolly nearer the Cambodian border. The NVA attacked LZ Phyllis viciously, then withdrew leaving lots of NVA bodies, rockets and shells scattered about. The next day a detail of troopers went about collecting the shells and rockets into a jeep-pulled trailer. Then for some reason the detail moved the vehicle and its deadly cargo inside the perimeter, where by accident or by NVA design the rockets and shells exploded. In an instant the lives of eight American infantrymen were snuffed out in a blinding flash of light and concussion. Ten other soldiers were wounded by the blast. A few days later I would visit abandoned LZ Phyllis and see the burned and demolished skeletons of the jeep and trailer that marked the exact spot where the eight troopers were blown away.

The platoon leader called a halt to the collection of enemy rockets. We got ourselves out of that bunker, just in case, and were putting some space between the bunker and us when B-40 rockets started exploding.

Apparently the grunts got too close to something the NVA wanted to keep hidden. So from a well-concealed position they fired three or four B-40 rockets, one after the other along the same trajectory. Each rocket penetrated farther through the foliage until the last one exploded in the midst of the Americans and wounded some of them, one badly. Other NVA opened up with automatic weapons in support of the B-40 grenadiers.

Under covering fire laid down by the rest of its platoon, the squad pulled back from the kill zone with their wounded. Quickly, we improvised a stretcher by chopping down and stripping two small trees and slipping them into a folded, snapped-together poncho. With me carrying the right rear corner of the stretcher, at the wounded man's right shoulder, we withdrew under fire to the edge of the jungle. Then, while 105mm and 155mm artillery rained down on the NVA positions, we moved across the open field, past where the patrol was fired on the day before, toward the company FOB. We were about halfway across the clearing when the trooper on the stretcher yelped in surprise and new pain. A large chunk of sizzling-hot shrapnel had hurled from the sky and buried itself in his right leg. Amazingly, he was the only trooper seriously wounded in the engagement— "twice" —first by the B-40 rocket, and then by friendly artillery at what was considered a fairly safe distance from the exploding shells. Little wonder the wounded trooper was anxious later, when we were ordered to get under ground for overhead protection because air strikes were coming in. He couldn't be placed in a foxhole because of his wounds. And I couldn't leave him like that.

Quickly, I stacked rucksacks all around and over the wounded trooper, leaving only his face partially exposed, then laid down beside him to wait out the air strikes. I have a picture of the trooper's grateful, smiling face, one someone snapped while I was barricading him. He survived the air strikes without sustaining any more wounds. The following sky troopers were wounded in that engagement (he was one of them): John Coates, Willie Chavez, Benny Wallace, Thompson, Gordon Holtrey, and Edward Schulnerrich.

Unknown to me, my old Delta 2-8 Cav became OPCON to the 2-12 Cav at 1840 on May 25. Soon after that, the *Angry Skipper* troopers were hit by fifteen B-40 rockets and perhaps some mortars. At 1930 hours, the point element walked into a claymore mine and sustained three killed and one wounded. Those killed were First Lieutenant John Preston Karr of Kenner, Louisiana; Corporal Richard Neal White of Golden Valley, New Mexico; and PFC Wayne Eric Garven of Mt. Vernon, Ohio.

Sergeant Stephen R. Atchley of Odon, Indiana, whose squad had the point for Delta 2-8 as it moved out that evening, tells what happened. "We left the firebase late in the evening of May 25, 1969. Choppers had dropped us off just as it was starting to get dark. We moved out with my squad on point. I was the squad leader of 2nd Squad [White Skull platoon].

"We soon came up on a bunker complex. It seemed to be empty [of NVA]. Captain Livingston, the CO, ordered us to keep moving, so we did and started finding stacks of mortars, grenades, and other ammunition, quite a bit of it.

"I thought we were getting into something bad, and reported what we were finding and my suspicions, and suggested that because it was getting dark we should pull back and set up, or set up where we were for the night. The CO said, 'No. We have to get to a certain place first.' He was green and had no idea what it was like to be on point, the time it takes to check things out, to cut a path...and then how all that becomes harder in the dark!"

Atchley continued. "We kept going and came upon a booby trap, a claymore mine—one of ours. We continued and soon came upon another booby trap and were trying to figure out what it was and how to get around it. All the time we were moving real slow, chopping through bamboo, and the CO kept calling to know what was taking so long, and pushing us to move on. SP4 Fred Metz butted in on the radio and started needling Lieutenant Karr by telling him it was the platoon leaders job to move up and see what was going on....Metz's squad leader shouldn't have let him touch the radio....Metz was too *gung ho*, most of the guys in White Skull thought. Karr trusted me to know what I was doing. I'd been there longer than he had.

"But anyway because of Metz's needling, Karr and Wayne came to the point...when they got up there to us there was a blinding flash and I felt great heat and pressure. Don't remember any sound. Don't know if it was another booby trap, a command-detonated mine, or what.

"I tried to get up immediately...couldn't hardly hear and was dazed. Wayne was on the radio to the CO. Kept repeating, 'The lieutenant's been hit! I think he's...I think he's....' Wayne just couldn't say that he thought Karr was dead—couldn't get it out. I'd crawled to Wayne when he passed out...had to use his radio because Dick's was destroyed. Called for a medic, then started trying to get the other guys posted around for security...it was kind of chaos.

"The medic arrived by the time I got the guys in position, but there was nothing he could do for John [Karr] or Dick [White] or Wayne [Garven]. He thought all three were dead, but...this young black kid noticed that Wayne was still trying to breathe [and] started giving him mouth to mouth....I took over and administered CPR...he [medic]...never checked Wayne out or anything, saying it was a lost cause. But I maintained a pulse for about twenty minutes.

"I had some metal in my leg, and my right knee was hurting badly....The next morning...I helped carry Dick, and returned us to the LZ where we stayed about three days."

Atchley was evacuated a few days later. A four-star general, perhaps Clayton Abrams, visited him in the Army Hospital at Tan San Nhut to pin a purple heart on him. "I asked him what Karr, Dick and Wayne were getting."

"Their families will get purple hearts."

"I told him [the general] to take my purple heart and 'stick it'."

"Son, you'll be sorry one of these days," said the general.

"I am sorry. I didn't get any of my medals. Nothing," said Atchley.

Chuck Hustedt, another participant in the Delta 2-8 action wrote, "Lieutenant Karr got a letter...his wife was pregnant. [Atchley was] hit by a B-40...command detonated. It appeared the Gook had suspended the B-40 above [Atchley]—there were wires hanging from the trees...looked like the wires suspended...the B-40 in the middle [over the path]."

Elsewhere, the last half of May was the quietest period of this tour to that point, but still plenty hot down at the grunt level. I was with Delta 1-5 one day during this "quiet" period when Alpha and Charlie 1-5 discovered a huge cache of food, weapons, and munitions. Delta Company was sent into the area to help them search the site. This was the sort of pre-positioned cache that the NVA needed for serious attacks on American or ARVN forces and population centers. Somewhat reluctantly, the NVA moved out of the cache site as we entered it. As I recall, Alpha 1-5 first discovered the cache and Charlie 1-5 approached later from a different direction to help search the area.

Terry Brain said, "Alpha Company entered a bunker complex that seemed to have been abandoned." Savaard and I jumped into a bunker to check it out and I heard a hollow sound when we landed. After jumping up and down to be sure, we alerted the CO. Then we pulled up a false floor and discovered a cache of weapons. About then, someone from another platoon called and reported that the men were finding all kinds of stuff."

A trooper in Charlie 1-5 fell dead to machine-gun fire as we entered the cache site a little later. About the same time, I came upon a fighting position that had been evacuated so hurriedly the ground still seemed to retain body warmth, and chicom grenades lay where they'd been abandoned by reluctant defenders of the cache.

A cache like this one drew generals and reporters like honey draws flies. Both types descended on the scene as soon as the area was pronounced secure. Those who came for pictures got them, and those who found the cache, the grunts, got to perform unaccustomed stevedore-like chores for the next couple of days, without benefit of heavy-lifting equipment. I'll not discuss the firefight Delta 1-5 got into—can't remember it.

Friday, May 30, nine Latter-day Saints, infantrymen and artillerymen and I, met on my side of a cramped bunker and shared the sacrament and our testimonies. We'd finished the Sacrament and begun sharing testimonies when a young Jewish officer, the medical platoon leader as I recall, stuck his head in the door. "Chaplain Newby ?" Upon realizing a service was in progress, he froze. I invited the lieutenant to finish his message. "I'll wait," he said. Instead of withdrawing to return later, he remained for thirty minutes, standing bent over, just inside the bunker doorway.

The service and testimonies completed, I thanked the lieutenant for waiting and asked what I could do for him, to which he responded, "Chaplain Newby that was the most meaningful religious service I ever saw."

I arrived on LZ Dolly one day about noon and while going from the chopper pad to the mess tent I passed two new troopers who were quietly praying over their food. Something was familiar about the way they did it.

The pair's blessing finished, I introduced myself and asked their names and from where they came. "I'm PFC Ramone Banks and this is PFC Theodore (Ted) Pierce [of Layton, Utah]," said the larger, fair-haired trooper.

So, in my usual style, my LDS affiliation hidden behind the anonymity of the universal Christian chaplain's insignia, I asked if the men were Mormons. They were, and they were replacements bound for Delta 1-5.

While I humped the jungles with Bravo 1-5 on 1 June, the men in Charlie 1-5 were following a strand of NVA communications wire. The NVA ambushed the point element and killed Sergeant Ray Edward Knoll of Michigan. The NVA, like any effective military force, were very protective of their communication assets.

The next day, June 2, Delta 1-5 engaged the enemy in the jungle not far from LZ Dolly and quickly sustained eighteen casualties—two KIAs and sixteen WIAs, including three medics. One of the medics died later. Private First Class Bowen - and I accompanied a chopper load of ammo out to Delta 1-5. Bowen -, who had recently arrived in-country, went to replace the three experienced medics.

The fighting was beginning to slack off when we reached the Delta 1-5. After helping offload the supplies from the chopper and with a cumbersome ammo box in hand, I slipped and slid off the muddy LZ, through the equally slippery and muddy jungle to the company CP. Later, after we settled down, I visited with Bowen - to help him adjust to being an instant replacement for three seasoned medics in a very violent environment.

Bowen - was concerned about his standing in the LDS church because he was also a conscientious objector. No problem, I assured him, for while the Church supported its members serving in the armed forces of their countries, it held very high the individual's agency and right to act in accordance with conscience. This counsel I had previously confirmed with the proper authorities.

Meanwhile, back on LZ Dolly, Platoon Sergeant Mario Grisanti waited at the helipad with some of his platoon for a chopper that was carrying someone who rated a welcoming committee. While they waited, one of his men, Arnold R. (Swamp Fox) Boggs casually drew his .45 pistol, pointed it at his own right leg just above the knee and fired. Grisanti said, "Swamp Fox had been growing increasingly agitated during the preceding days on LZ Dolly, getting more and more flaky. One day he started shooting hand illumination flares at the observation tower in the center of Dolly. I was having a real hard time keeping him out of trouble. Swamp Fox and his squad were at the LZ Dolly helipad to provide security for somebody important who was landing, when he calmly pulled out his .45 pistol and shot himself. I came running when I heard the shot and saw what had happened. After Boggs was taken care of, I dug the bullet out of the dirt. I've kept it for 30 years, hoping to run into Swamp Fox someday and return it to him."

Sergeant Grisanti was unusual in his own way in that he secretly humped a super-8 movie camera in his rucksack. With it he filmed quite a few of the things happening in and to Alpha Company. All this came as quite a surprise thirty years later to Phil Gioia and Steve Holtzman, who had been his CO and platoon leaders at the time.

Now back to Delta 1-5. The night of June 3 was quiet, surprisingly so, considering the NVA knew exactly where we were. Expecting an attack that never came, I stood two radio watches so the exhausted RTOs in the CP could rest, and to improve the likelihood the radio watch would be awake if someone yelled "incoming."

Early on June 4, we assaulted some NVA bunkers located less than thirty meters from the FOB. Here was where Delta 1-5 had fought a very costly battle the previous day. We took advantage of the NVA bunkers to call air strikes in closer than usual, almost as close as Captain Cain had called them the morning of 8 April.

The air strikes came in really close, and terror filled the eyes of the five or six troopers with whom I took cover in an NVA bunker, most of whom were new replacements. This seemed like an ideal time for an impromptu worship service. So with the eager consent of all present, we prayed and worshiped to a background of diving jets and exploding five hundred to one thousand-pound bombs. I like to believe a few violently trembling body limbs were calmed somewhat by the experience.

The enemy had pulled out, or they were killed during the air strikes. At least none made his presence felt as Delta 1-5 searched through the bunker complex and southward for the rest of the day.

The company dug in for the night about a klick from the site of the fight the day before. We held a worship service after everyone was dug in. Then at twilight I attached myself to the third platoon so Banks, Bowen -, Pierce and I could share the Sacrament, which we did beneath a poncho for privacy. Moments later the platoon, just sixteen strong, moved out about a hundred meters to set up an ambush at a point where a well-used path approached from the northwest, curved about 40 degrees and continued to the northeast toward the Saigon River. We met the trail at a point where the vegetation was relatively low and beaten down. A stretch of high grass and shrubs separated the path from a thirty-foot-wide, oval-shaped clearing on the south. Lines of shrubbery separated that clearing from similar clearings to the east and west. The near rim of a bomb crater came within a foot or two of the west side of the middle clearing. These details were just barely discernable in the thickening darkness.

The main body of the platoon set out claymore mines between the middle clearing and path, then settled down near the north edge of the clearing with about ten feet of higher grass and a fallen tree between them and the path. The main body included the lieutenant and five troopers, all of whom lay left of me with their faces toward the claymore mines and path beyond. The lieutenant had, I learned next morning, divided the remaining troopers between two five-man flank security positions, each near the path and about fifty feet to either side of us.

Not bothering to roll down my sleeves, I wrapped in my poncho liner and lay with my head toward the path, behind the trunk of the small, downed tree that lay parallel to the trail. The rain, which had begun at 2200 hours, stopped at midnight, which I confirmed by the luminous dial on my watch. I was feeling the usual appreciation for the poncho liner, which kept me quite warm though I was soaked. The stage was set for an up close and personal experience with the NVA.

Chapter Notes:

1 May 1969, 2-12 Battalion Operational Report/Lessons Learned (1 thru 30 April): Friendly Casualties: KIAs, 10; WIAs 54; non-hostile wounded, 7."

6 May 1969, 2-12 Battalion Journal: 1704, A/2-12; Medevac of 2 litter patients complete while third litter patient was being lifted out, bird took fire and patient was dropped...7 more [WIAs] to be taken out." 1825: "A/2-12; They found the missing man about 100m south from their location. He is line 2 [wounded]." 1925: "A/2-12 total of 13 line 2's [WIAs]; C/2-12 had 1 line 2, accident; D/2-12 had 5 line 2's and 2 heat casualties."

13 May 1969, Fm. Bde 3B, 2020 hrs: At LZ Phyllis, a great number of mortar rds and rockets were found around the LZ at the battle. These were policed up, placed in a trailer and brought into the LZ. One of the rounds went off somehow, exploding the pile of ammo and killing 9 while wounding 10 nearby. All...reminded of long-standing policy of blowing all but small arms ammo in the field ... preferably by EOD Team...ammo should not be gathered...nor should it be tampered with unnecessarily.

14 May 1969, 1-5 Battalion Journal, 1559 hrs: Fm B. Co: 26 ele...was engaged by 4-5 indiv fm tree line w/ak-47 ... Entire [company] moving to check out area...found small bunker complex...26 ele received AK-47 fire and 4-5 chicom grenades were thrown from a bunker 15 m to left of kitchen bunker.

15 May 1969, 1350, 1-5 Battalion Journal: Names of indiv...Rec #18 & 26: John Coates, Willie Chavez, Benny Wallace, Thompson, Gordon Holtrey and Edward Schulnerrich...treated at Dolly, Gordon Holtrey, Edward Schulnerrich. Four indiv wounded by shrapnel and remained in the field, 1Lt James Joyner, SSG Thomas, Newburn, Sp4 Jackie Burns and Pfc Aleya Hodroowich

25 May 1969, 2-12 Cav Journal, Item 92: Fm D/2-8, incoming...15 B-40 rockets (possibly a couple of mortars)...became opcon to 2-12 at 1840 hrs...at 1930 Hrs...point element walked into a claymore. Casualties 3 line 1 [KIA] and 1 line 2 [WIA].31 May 1969, Military Index: KIA Cpl. Landrus S. Taylor Jr. of Madison, Georgia].

1 June 1969, Military Index: KIA, Sergeant Ray Edward Knoll, Michigan.

2 June 1969, 1630, 1-5 Battalion Journal: "D Co 16 engaged 15-20 enemy in bunkers and trees...has 05 WIAs, still receiving sporadic fire." 1735: "D Co requests

medevac, blood, doctor and penetrator...Medevac 7 completed at 1719 hrs. Medevac 2 completed at 1731 hrs...02 KIAs were extracted on medevac bird. KIAs: Sp4's Duane Baumgardner [Cloverdale, California] and Jeffrey Geldin [Lindsey, Ohio] [both of whom are officially listed as having died on 2 Jun3 69]. Delta 1-5 WIAs: Whatley, Alicea, Booker, Smith, Spruill, Wright, Hansen, Overlee, Ashburn, and Hermandez ; 1SGT Prosser of B/1-77; and medics/ Pfc's Larsen, McFarland and Alonander [one of whom reportedly died of his wounds, but neither name is found on the Wall]. 1842 hours: Medevac requested at 1820...D Co contact today...GSW in leg. Also A Co. had 01 indiv shot himself in leg at LZ Dolly, D Co, Thoma[s?]; A Co, Boggs w/45 pistol.

4 June 1969, 1-5 Battalion Journal, 2310: "C&E 1-5, LZ Dolly, 2240H. Reports lightning struck several times in the perimeter, igniting several trip flares, fougasse, detonated several claymores...."

Chapter Twelve

DÉJÀ VU

It was June 4 and my watch read 0015 hours. I had just checked it and was about to turn over on the wet ground to relieve aching muscles. Suddenly, the RTO who was sitting radio watch next to me blasted off a full magazine from his M-16. He was shooting toward the rear.

"Gooks!" he shouted, and kept firing until his weapon clicked on empty. That's when he abandoned it and the radios and fled from sight around the rim of the bomb crater. Later we learned he'd run to the security element on the west flank, almost getting himself shot by friendly troops there in the process.

Simultaneously, the lieutenant and three troopers leaped over the small downed tree that lay crosswise between our position and the claymore mines we had set along the trail. The other trooper, Edward P. Woll, and I had the same idea—to stay put until we got a clearer idea of what was going on. Meanwhile, my left hand reflexively wrapped itself around the grips of a pistol.

There followed a moment of suspenseful silence, except the pounding of our own hearts. Then from the bushes near the bomb crater, we heard voices whispering in Vietnamese. A distinct, commanding voice said something. Another less-authoritative voice responded. One voice was obviously female. Into my mind flashed the image of a sergeant telling privates to do something dangerous and unpleasant, and of privates complaining about their orders.

Upon hearing alien voices so near, I retrieved four grenades that a trooper had laid out for the ambush, and passed them to Woll. Woll knew what to do. He lobbed the hand grenades into the row of bushes and beyond, in quick succession.

The grenades exploded about two seconds apart. A moment later, a shadowy figure moved from the bushes and dropped into the bomb crater. I could easily have dropped him, but I held my fire—the shadow might have been our RTO, and the muzzle flash from the pistol would have pinpointed my position. Besides, no one was threatening wounded troopers, so I felt constrained somewhat in my role as chaplain.

The moment passed and a shadowy head popped above the rim of the crater. A NCO-like voice barked something, probably a demand for us to identify ourselves as "friend" or perhaps to get us to fire at him and reveal our location.

Woll and I simultaneously took the NVA soldier's challenge as our cue to move, though no signal passed between us. Automatic fire tracked me as I leaped into the air and dove across the fallen tree into the midst of our comrades and the claymore mines. The burst probably would have caught me had I not twisted in the air to create a smaller target. Even so, the last AK-47 bullet cracked near enough to cause a stab of pain and momentary vacuum-like sensation in my left ear. As I landed in the grass, a Chicom grenade exploded within three to five feet of the spot Woll and I had just vacated.

There on the ground, striving to maintain perfect silence, with my wet body rapidly chilling in the absence of a body heat-retaining poncho liner, I mentally replayed what had happened. I concluded that the NVA unit had stumbled onto us as it came through the jungle to get on the trail. We had come close to being wasted because we had no rear security. This shortcoming surprised me, what with an OCS-trained platoon leader, new to combat though he was.

With six more hours of darkness to kill, I spent the first one carefully rolling down my sleeves for the meager warmth they offered, and for protection from the mosquitoes. The insect repellant was back in the clearing with the radios.

Meanwhile, the company commander was very concerned. He'd heard in quick succession an M-16 in panic mode, four American grenades, AK-47 fire, and a Chicom grenade. Then for six hours there was nothing. The RTOs had left their radios in the clearing and were understandably reluctant to return for them.

Later in the night, while Third Platoon lay silently at the ambush site, an NVA element hit the company perimeter on our side. This was probably the same unit that stumbled onto us, engaged in yet another unintended encounter with Delta 1-5.

Meanwhile, up on LZ Dolly Lieutenant Colonel Peterson probably wondered if he had lost an under- strength platoon. I doubt that the Delta 1-5 commander informed Peterson that he might have lost a chaplain.

Back on the ambush site, we lay quiet as death for six hours. At 0615 hours in the dawn's earliest light, the lieutenant stood up to see if he would draw fire. Instead of fire a mournful call of "chieu hoi" came from the jungle.

Carefully, we followed a trail of NVA packs and gear into the jungle, where we found a wounded NVA soldier in a hammock. His body was riddled with fresh shrapnel wounds. On the NVA's chest lay a Chieu Hoi pass—one of the open-arms certificates our psychological operations people spread around to entice the NVA and VC to come over to the South Vietnamese government side—and by his side an AK-47. America paid cash for surrendered weapons.

A few minutes later, I paced off twenty-three feet between where I had lain and the spot on the crater rim from which the NVA shot at Woll and me. This pacing I did while we waited back in the clearing for a chopper to evacuate the wounded enemy POW (later called EPW, for enemy prisoner of war). This experience was similar to the dream of death I had the night before I left home for this tour, except in real life the NVA missed me! We sustained no casualties during this engagement. Three months later, Woll would suffer a dreadful tragedy—the accidental killing of one of his buddies.

The chopper that came for the POW brought the new Second Brigade Chaplain, who stayed only long enough to pay his respects to the company commander. I accompanied the chaplain and POW to LZ Dolly, where lightning had struck the evening before with results similar to those during another strike when I was present.

LZ Dolly, in keeping with its defensive needs, was surrounded by a perimeter of bunkers, and with rolls and layers of concertina wire. These were supported by cleared fields of fire, trip flares, claymore mines, machine guns, CS gas grenades, and barrels of fougasse—a homemade napalm-like mixture of fuel and some thickening compound—set to be detonated on command by an explosive charge. The fougasse and other defenses frequently showed their value against attacking enemies. They were formidable weapons in the hands of determined troopers. Defensive plans included using these measures selectively, depending on the nature and ferocity of any given threat against the LZ. I doubt anyone ever envisioned the level of shock and noise should all these perimeter devices explode simultaneously.

The lightning strike that hit when I was present came about 1600 hours, a moment after Peterson passed my bunker headed toward the north. The lowering clouds threatened a monsoon downpour at any moment. I'd just greeted Peterson, stooped and gone inside and sat on the edge of my litter when a blinding flash illuminated the dank recesses of my bunker. Simultaneously, there came an earthshaking, ear-shattering blast from everywhere at once. A ripple of smaller explosions followed the big one.

Daisy cutter, I thought, one of those ten thousand-pound bombs the Air Force used to create instant landing zones in the jungle.

Outside, thick black horizon-blotting smoke billowed up all around the perimeter. A stroke of lightning had spontaneously ignited scores of claymore mines, drums of fougasse and most of the CS gas and flares on the perimeter. And nature continued to add its own voice to the tumult with each new bolt of lightning and simultaneous thunderclap; we were at ground zero.

Peterson hurried tearfully past me toward the TOC, his journey helped along from that point by the loan of my gas mask.

At 1033 hours on June 5, Alpha 1-5 engaged in a vicious, costly firefight that raged for more than an hour. The shooting began within a few minutes of my arrival on LZ Dolly with the *chieu hoi-* turned-POW.

Larry (Shorty) McVay described events leading up to the fight this way. "Just that morning I was moved over from Sergeant Jack Hatfield's Second Squad, Third Platoon to walk point for another squad." This would be his first time at point.

"We had been humping long enough that it was time to take a break, when I spotted the bunker complex. The complex had recently been destroyed by a B-52 strike. The NVA had moved right back in and built new bunkers and fighting positions under the brush and rubble caused by the bombing. They were waiting for us. I spotted something suspicious and reported it. Captain Phil Gioia called the company to a halt and sent out cloverleaf patrols. Sergeant Jack Hatfield of Ohio led his squad—my squad until a few hours earlier—into the bunker complex with Corporal David Mann of Iowa at the point. Mann moved forward as cautiously and carefully as he could, with Hatfield backing him up, but it was not enough. The NVA held their fire until Mann and Jack were well within the kill zone. The patrol hadn't been out but minutes when gunfire and explosions began."

McVay continued, "Jack and David were gut shot. David died instantly, cut in two by a 30-cal water-cooled machine gun. Jack died slower. The last thing he said in this life was, 'Mother,' and he closed his eyes.

"Benny Swan, a husky black man and Hatfield's assistant machine gunner, rushed forward.... The rest of the 2nd Platoon and a few men from other platoons rushed forward to support Hatfield's squad. Benny was like a man possessed—like John Wayne to me. Although being severely wounded, Benny poured accurate fire into the enemy positions and kept them at bay until our KIAs and WIAs were pulled back. There was much bravery that day. The KIAs could have easily been left behind but these brave young men fought until all their buddies were brought back."

Sergeants Elvin Jackson and Robert Fussell of South Carolina were among those heroes from other platoons that rushed forward into the jaws of death to help rescue the wounded and recover the dead. For their actions that day, Jackson received the Bronze Star for Valor and Fussell the Silver Star.

SP4 Tom Holcombe said, "He [Fussell] was next to me when the fight broke out with Jack Hatfield's squad on the fifth of June. He got up and took off to help, even though it was another platoon and they were handling the situation—he didn't have to go but he did. But that was Fuzz."

Only after Hatfield, Mann and all the wounded were recovered did Gioia pull away from the contact area so they could be medevaced and the area pounded by artillery and Cobra gunships, and napalmed by Air Force F-4s. Then about dark Gioia moved his company to another nearby site and set up a new FOB. He wisely avoided returning to the positions Alpha 1-5 had used the previous night.

"As I recall, the NVA mortared the position we had stayed in the night before," said McVay, and continued, "Claude, I remember it well. As corny as it may sound, I felt for years that I should have been on the patrol with my squad, from which I'd been gone only half a day. The fourth of June 1969 plays over and over in my mind while sleeping and awake. I've been treated for post-traumatic stress disease at the VA....I am doing okay now....I also accepted Jesus Christ as my Lord and Savior."

McVay's guilt is typical, unjustified, and definitely not corny. Though he never said it, added to his guilt feelings is the haunting fact that his alert led his squad buddies to enter the ambush without him and to the horrible deaths of Hatfield and Mann, close buddies; he'd joined the company about the same time as Mann.

Those who fell wounded during the attempt to recover Hatfield's and Mann's bodies included Platoon Sergeant Fussell (1st Platoon), William S. Haj, Swan s, Theil, John Stumpt, and Charles Spliker.

Fussell was awarded the Silver Star and went on to become a platoon sergeant before being severely wounded in the leg and medevaced to the states. Back home, following a long and painful convalescence and rehabilitation, he married and became the father of three sons. These days, he walks about performing his duties as the pastor of a

Friendship Baptist Church in North Carolina, aided in his efforts by a special built-up shoe.

The Army downgraded Sergeant Jackson's award to an Army Commendation Medal for Valor. He would become a platoon sergeant and be wounded, though not seriously enough to cut short his Vietnam tour.

Blissfully unaware of the action Alpha 1-5 was engaged in or of the casualties they sustained, I arrived at Ton San Nhut Air Base in Saigon about 1800 hours. A few minutes later, I dined with Paul Madsen.

After dinner I returned to Madsen's hotel room to write letters and prepare a monthly report. The next day was a rare goof-off one for me. The day after that, between 1300 and 1505 hours, I attended the ecclesiastical meeting that brought me to Saigon. By evening I was in Lai Khe in 1st Infantry Division (Big Red One) AO, and quite ill. On June 8, I went to the hospital in Cu Chi, where a doctor diagnosed strep throat. I visited twelve of my wounded troopers while I was there and spoke in an LDS service, with thirty-three members of the 25th Infantry Division (Tropical Lightning) in attendance.

Feeling ill wasn't unusual. The weekly big (as opposed to the daily little) malaria pills usually made me sick, which explains why I sometimes "forgot" to take them. Frequently I got fever blisters and sore throats, and numbness in my left big toe would continue to interfere with humping during most of this tour. And there were the rashes, constant sores and irritations to sensitive body areas in consequence of sleeping most nights in dirty clothes and going weeks, day and night, with my boots on. On the other hand, my metabolism worked well in combat. These were the only years since about age thirteen that I could eat without concern for weight gain. Still, I had it easy compared to the men in the companies. At least I could change clothes during stops at LZ Dolly.

On June 9 I returned to LZ Dolly, intent on joining Charlie 1-5. When that proved impossible, I flew on to Tay Ninh, and was there when my third month in the field ended. The beginning of my fourth month found me recuperating from strep throat to the tune of exploding rockets and mortar shells and the rattle of shrapnel against the roof and walls. I endured the rattling because I felt too ill to take cover in a bunker. While I slowed down to nurse my health, the action was hot for the 2-12 Cav the next day, June 10.

On June 10, Bravo 2-12 moved into a bunker complex and in exchange for one American life and seven wounded, captured a one rifle, ten bicycles, and other assorted items of NVA equipment. While that was going on, Alpha 2-12 made contact with a battalion-size force of NVA and sustained three killed and twenty-eight wounded. The Alpha Company troopers killed fifteen NVA that they could confirm. On June 11, another unit entered the area and found twelve more NVA bodies.

At 0545 on June 11, I snapped awake on LZ Dolly to the distant sound of mortar shells leaving tubes from too far away be ours. Several seconds later, the barrage rained down on LZ Dolly and wounded two troopers on the LZ. One had arrived in the battalion as a replacement the previous day and was slightly injured while he pulled perimeter guard. A senior NCO "jokingly" expressed envy of the trooper's "easy" Purple Heart on his record.

The enemy mortars, though they did little damage, validated my avowed belief that the NVA could precisely target LZ Dolly up there along the crest of the ridge.

Bravo 1-5 got through a mortar attack on its FOB on June 12, but wasn't so fortunate a day later while crossing a draw. One man was killed and another seriously wounded during the crossing. At 1300 hours on June 13, I joined Bravo 1-5 for a sweep along both banks above the draw. The NVA were gone or lying low.

From the draw, the Bravo 1-5 troopers pressed on and did a battle damage assessment on a bunker complex located just beyond the draw.

The BDA turned up scattered pieces of equipment, clothing, and bodies parts amid a wild tangle of downed trees, craters and angry red ants. None of the body parts was large enough to join together as a body, had the troopers been so inclined. It would have been hard to tell that the body parts were human but for the occasional pieces of clothing attached to them. An NVA helmet with a hole in it lay among ruins. I passed it on to Madsen to fulfill a promise I had made him.

That evening Bravo 1-5 dug in near the bunker complex, after which we held a worship service at twilight. Afterwards word came that Charlie 1-5 had sustained one dead and one wounded when two of its patrols bumped into one another.

With Charlie 1-5 the next day, June 14, I got the details of the fatal mishap the day before. The company had moved early into a night position and each platoon had sent out the usual cloverleaf patrols. Somehow in the featureless jungle, one of the patrols stopped in the path of another. Moments later, the point man heard the other patrol stealthily approaching his position. His patrol leader got on the radio and requested that all friendly troops freeze in place. The sounds of movement continued to draw nearer, even after confirmation was received that all friendlies were stopped.

Thus reassured, the point man on the patrol-in-waiting blasted away with his M-16 when the first shadowy figure broke through the underbrush. He killed instantly the point man on the other patrol and seriously wounded another man, who soon died of his wounds. Killed by friendly fire were PFC Theodore Heriot Jr. and SP4 James Burton. One of them had been a best friend with the shooter.

As best I could, I consoled the trooper who killed Heriot and Burton, but don't know whether I had much effect. "I didn't kill and wound my buddies. My leaders killed them by losing control and by assuring me no friendlies were moving in front of me," he said with calm and cold logic; he had a point.

About this time in June, I became upset because the CP group and some other elements of Alpha 2-12 bunched up badly in an open area. Later in the day, I got some negative feedback for raising my concern durin g a worship service. A trooper, and former LDS missionary to Hong Kong or Japan, said that some troopers in attendance griped that it wasn't my place to chasten them for bunching up.

My informant had his own sad story to tell. Back about February or early March, he'd been in night position beside a bomb crater. He and his buddies were licking their psychic wounds following a nasty fight. Out of the night he heard movement on the other side of the crater. His whispered challenge drew no response. He opened fire when a human shape rose up before him, silhouetted by the starlit sky. A fellow trooper fell dead, one that presumably had played dead since the earlier fighting and was making his way back to the company. Perhaps he'd been too shell-shocked to respond to his fellow trooper's whispered challenge.

While many accidents ended in tragedy, some had humorous properties, like what happened to a visiting chaplain. I ran into this chaplain on a firebase and commented on a large bandage across his nose: "What happened to your nose?"

"I was sleeping in the field and a grunt stepped on my nose and broke it. He was on the way to relieve himself," the chaplain explained.

Tactlessly, I said, "Man, you were lucky."

"What do you mean, lucky? Look at my face!"

"He could have stopped a step or two sooner."

Chapter Notes:

5 June 1969, 1-5 Battalion Journal: 1410, "A Co WIAs...Fussel US5394112, Haj US54835253, Swan s RA11870487, Theil l US51804226, Stumpt US51910289, and Spliker US56986800. Two KIAs: Hatfield US51838218 and Mann US56665583. 1411 hrs: A Co received AK-40 and MG fire at 1033 hrs from approx 10-12 indiv in bunkers...contact broken at 1144 hrs, most...resulting in 02 US KIA and 05 US WIA. Enemy losses, 05 NVA KIA.

13 June 1969, 1-5 Battalion Journal: 1124, "C Co made contact w/unk size enemy ele, friendly cas-1 line 1 & 1 line 2, contact broke at 1126 hrs."

1230: "C Co request medevac at 1135 for 1 ind...request doctor, Ind has wounds in the chest. Names, Pfc Theodore Heriot Jr. and Sp4 James Burton.

1253, Readout: "C Co, 36 element was...securing a trail...the 26 element was given the coordinated mission of swinging down the same trail... The 36 lead element setting in place, heard movement and opened up. CPT Cain is appointed as investigating officer."

Chapter Thirteen

FRAGGINGS

Though I saw more combat action with the companies of the 1-5 Cav than with the 2-12 Cav, I provided about the same number of worship services for each battalion. Early in June during a visit to Alpha 2-12, I learned of threats to frag a company commander. Several troopers confided to me that most of the men in the company believed Captain James Robert Daniel of Atlanta, Georgia, cared very little for what he put them through. "Plans are afoot to "frag" Captain Daniel next time the company's in a fight," I was told.

The phrase "fragging" came into use early in the war and described the rare practice of troops killing unpopular leaders, by tossing a hand grenade in their hooch or whatever. I knew personally of no fragging incidents during my first tour in Vietnam, but I heard of two or three alleged incidents—all involving rear-area personnel. The closest I came to a fragging, or anything like it, during my first tour was when troopers allegedly attempted to kill a fellow grunt for reporting an atrocity, the Mao incident.

But this was a different war in a different time, and we heard of fraggings almost weekly, some quite close. By 1969 fragging meant killing friendlies by any means, including shooting leaders and others in the back. This evolution of definition made sick sense considering the different conditions between the rear and the field.

In the rear, the grenade was often the weapon of choice because small arms were more carefully controlled than in the field. Usually, with patience, an unpopular individual could be found alone and blown away without anyone else being hurt. And hand grenades left no tell-tale fingerprints and rifling marks to lead the Criminal Investigation Detachment (CID) back to the guilty party(s).

In the field, on the other hand, small arms, which were in abundance, were weapons of choice for fragging. This made morbid sense. First, in the field it was difficult to isolate an individual from his RTO and others for a grenade attack. Second, it was extremely easy to shoot backward or sideways at the targeted individual during the heat of a firefight. Finally, even if a fragging were suspected, an adequate investigation under field conditions was very difficult, and successful prosecution was unlikely. Rifling marks on full-metal jacket M-16 bullets and markings on shell casings didn't carry the same evidential weight in the field as these would in rear areas.

Knowing all this, I alerted Captain Daniel and Lieutenant Colonel Boon about the fragging threats, and assured them the threats were serious, based on my confidence in my sources. Captain Daniel reacted with, "Chaplain, there is nothing I can do about that, and worrying won't change it. If the troops frag me, they frag me. I'm doing my job the best I can." Another tragedy intervened before we could find out how these fragging threats might have turned out.

On June 17, the Deputy Division Chaplain accused me of neglecting my battalion and troopers. This chaplain took almost every opportunity to show hostility toward me, whether for personal, professional or religious reasons, I knew not. But this accusation was too much.

The chaplains in the division had just completed a conference and I yet basked in good feelings over a moment of praise that the USARV Chaplain had just given me in the presence of the 1st Cav Chief of Staff. The compliment was for my work while at Fort Bragg. A few minutes later in the officer's mess, the Deputy Division Chaplain joined two other chaplains and me at our table. I hoped this chaplain, by joining us uninvited, meant to signal more openness and cordiality toward me. Not so, I soon discovered.

"Chaplain Frank, Chaplain Martin wants to send me an LDS chaplain assistant. Does Division have any problem with that? Do you?" I asked.

His response shocked me. "Chaplain Scott is considering moving you out of the division because you are neglecting your assigned battalion."

What? I couldn't believe what I was hearing. "Why?" I asked.

"Because three times in your weekly report, you showed more LDS services than Protestant ones," Frank said.

"Those instances don't mean I've neglected my battalion. To the contrary, they reflect the once-per-month occasions when another chaplain came into my battalion and provided communion services, while I went about the division AO conducting sacrament services for as many LDS troopers as I could reach."

This practice, I insisted, showed concern for the religious needs of my men, without bias. "Besides, I could legitimately have lumped LDS and general services together to impress you. Instead, I reported them separately to give you a clearer picture."

Chaplain Frank said he understood and accepted my explanation, then added, quite out of context, "Your being selected for promotion to major from the 5 percent zone means nothing. You don't fit here."

The next day I discussed my weekly reports and the threat of a transfer out of the 1st Cav with Chaplain Scott, the Division Chaplain. Chaplain Scott said he thought it unfair to isolate me in a battalion rather than assign me at a headquarters above division so I could minister to LDS personnel over wide areas.

We discussed this concept from my perspective. First, I reasoned that LDS members were well organized and empowered to care for one another. Second, in my present assignment I was chaplain to men of all faiths and those with no faith, which was what my church expected of me. Third, the chaplains would have a difficult time convincing my chain of command that I neglected the unit or could be better used elsewhere. Chaplain Scott promised to not try to move me from the division.

Thus, the matter was settled, at least on the surface. But the hurt simmered long. It tore at my heart to be accused of neglecting those whom I loved and tried so hard to serve. Considering the source of the accusation helped a little to ease the hurt. Chaplain Frank's irrational hostility toward me continued.

On June 18, while Chaplain Hugh Black went to the only 1-5 company that was receiving log (being resupplied), I conducted a memorial service for Bravo 1-5 on LZ Dolly— don't recall who the service was for. Next, I conducted three field services for companies in the 2-12 Cav, in their positions on the rocket belt (the area around a target from which rockets can effectively be fired) around Phuoc Vinh. In the evening I taught a lesson to some LDS troopers about the virtues of possessing a forgiving heart. My treatment at the hands of Chaplain Frank was on my mind.

The next day, June 19, a spur-of-the-moment decision saved my life. The fateful decision occurred at Phuoc Vinh. Boon's 2-12 Cav had moved from LZ Grant to assume palace guard around Camp Gorvad, the Division Base Camp. Battalions on palace guard kept one infantry company on the perimeter near the battalion headquarters and TOC, while three companies lived and patrolled beyond the perimeter to suppress rocket and mortar attacks and to deny the NVA opportunity to mass undetected for ground assaults. The line companies took turns spending a few days on the perimeter, where they enjoyed rare hot showers, three hot meals per day, cots, and other trimmings of rear-area life.

About 0900 hours, June 19, having conducted three field services, I flew back to the 2-12 and entered the 2-12 TOC to seek a ride to Captain Daniel's company. There I found Daniel and Major Robert William O'Keefe of Davis, California preparing to depart on Boon's Charlie-Charlie. I accepted a seat on the chopper, only to change my mind for some long-forgotten reason. The pilot of the Charlie-Charlie promised to return for me in a few minutes.

Ten minutes later, at 0940, Alpha 2-12 reported seeing a chopper explode in the air. Boon's Charlie-Charlie had collided with a 105mm artillery shell. Captain Daniel and Major O'Keefe were dead, along with the four-man crew of Boon's chopper. This I learned a few minutes later when I reentered the TOC.

So mangled were those bodies that had been blown out of the aircraft that we could not tell by sight to which body some parts belonged. The bodies of those who rode the chopper into the ground were mangled and severely burned, skulls exploded from the heat.

Understandably Boon and many of his staff were deeply distraught. After ministering to Boon as best I could, I went seeking solace of my own, solace which wasn't easy to find. One might expect my heart to be filled with gratitude for having been spared. Instead, my heart, mind and senses reeled, my emotions all mixed up, and terrible smells lingered inside and outside of me. I was in no mood for what happened twenty minutes later at LZ Dolly.

At Dolly, I stepped into the medical aid station for a cold soda. The only other person there, a medic and sergeant, reacted badly when I took a soda from the blood box. "Chaplain, no disrespect, sir, but you're just a big, — —," he said.

All my pent-up emotions burst inside of me. Instantly, I wanted to demolish that sergeant, who at the moment epitomized every rear-area snob I'd ever met. Just barely, I suppressed these destructive impulses and said: "Sergeant, you are taking advantage of me. I want very much to stomp a mud hole in you, but I can't do so because I'm your chaplain."

"I'll gladly ignore your rank and position if you will," the sergeant snapped back.

His offer was sorely tempting, but of course we had no barn or other private place to go behind. Anyhow, while considering the sergeant's invitation, I collected myself. *How did I offend him so,* I wondered? So I asked him.

"You come in here like you own the place and help yourself to other people's sodas," he said.

"You don't understand. I contribute to the soda fund so I can have an occasional cold drink when I come in from the field," I explained.

The sergeant's apology didn't help much. I had arrived at LZ Dolly with my feelings and reflexes on supercharge because of my near miss and what had happened to those on Boon's chopper. These factors combined with the confrontation with the sergeant and a lack of mail from home— it had been days since I got a letter—affected my mood for the worse. So I joined Alpha 1-5 in the field for a day and two nights of humping, during which time I managed to get my feelings into a precarious balance.

Sometime in May or early June there occurred an incident that lives vividly in my memory, but for which I can not find records that the final outcome is as I remember it.

Three troopers in one of my eight line companies refused to go on an ambush. Their company had remained for a second night in a FOB near where one of its ambushes had been very successful the previous night, having killed several NVA without taking any casualties.

The ambush had been set up along a well-concealed trail about fifty meters from the FOB. As part of its preparations, the ambush team aimed a 90mm recoilless rifle straight down the trail, chambered a flechette round, and waited.

About midnight the point element of an NVA unit came along the trail. The troopers fired the recoilless rifle. At first light they found several dead NVA on the trail. One was literally pinned to a tree by flechette darts. The surviving members of the NVA unit had retreated leaving their dead behind. An NVA unit, probably the same one, dogged the company the next day. I joined the company as it was digging in for the night.

The company commander directed one of the platoons to put an ambush on the trail, the same as the night before. The platoon leader designated a squad for the ambush, and three squad members refused to go out. "It's stupid to put an ambush in the same place as last night. We'll be killed if we go," a spokesman for the three had insisted.

The company commander said, in essence, "I hate it, Chaplain, but I've no choice. If they don't go on ambush, I must bring charges against them. Would you talk to them?"

I found the three sullen men in a small, clear spot beneath the bamboo. "Don't try to change our minds, Chaplain. We'll be killed if we go out tonight," one of the three said.

"I don't intend to change your minds. All I intend to do is help you consider the alternatives and consequences. Yes, you might be killed if you go out tonight. It's very possible. On the other hand, if you don't go on ambush tonight, you *will* go to LBJ [Long Binh Jail] tomorrow and you *will* face a general court martial. That is a certainty. You three are the only ones left with any choice. You can go out or stay. The Company Commander has no choice. He can't back down, no matter how much he understands and sympathizes with you. You made sure of that when you openly refused his orders."

In conclusion, I asked the three troopers how they'd deal with it if others died in their stead, and added, "I wish I could promise you'll be okay out there tonight, but I can't. But if you decide to go on ambush, I'll go with you."

The three troopers looked back and forth at one another in silence for a minute or so. Some signal must have passed between them, undetected by me, for their spokesman said, "We'll go out on ambush Chaplain Newby, but you can't come. No use you being killed too."

The three troopers went on ambush with their squad. During the night the NVA attacked viciously, its assault focused directly on the ambush site, which led me to suspect this was the same NVA unit our ambush had hurt the previous night. The three troopers were killed.

Without self-recrimination, I grieved hard for the men who died acting on my counsel. I sorrowed long for them, wishing there had been another way.

On June 22, Alpha 1-5 moved through the jungle to a clearing. We were to be picked up by choppers to relieve Bravo 1-5 on LZ Dolly. While most jungle is indistinguishable from other jungle, this was different. I sensed I'd been here before as we neared a clearing that was designated for our pickup zone.

A powerful sense of awe came over me as we entered the PZ. Looking to the north side of the clearing, I suddenly knew why. Here, Snyder, Derda, Hoover and Allen gave their lives; here I came mighty close to dying. That day after Easter, two and a half months before, seemed to be in the far distant past.

Reverently, I walked twenty feet into the jungle and stood in contemplation and prayer at the spot where those great men gave their all. No longer did the events seem ancient. Memories and sensations flooded through me as if the experiences of that day had happened the day before, though much had changed and so many troopers had died and been wounded since then.

Even this sacred spot was rapidly changing, being reclaimed by the jungle. The termite mounds, trail and the caved-in NVA machine-gun position were still there. Otherwise, there was little evidence of the terrors shared and blood spilled on that frightful day.

On a whim, I looked at the scene from the NVA machine-gun position. The line of fire was perfect. The machine gunner couldn't have missed me. *Impossible.* He'd had a clear shot with nothing to deflect his fire, but he had missed me! Snyder, Derda, Hoover and Allen hadn't had a chance, either. *Why did the NVA machine gunner miss me and not the others?*

This would have been a good time to experience survivor's guilt, a malady so common to survivors of traumatic incidents. But instead I was having an indescribable, deeply spiritual experience. I understood, like Moses on Mount Sinai, that I stood on hallowed ground. I intend to return to Vietnam someday as a reverent pilgrim.

As I paused there and turned inward, deep into my soul, I appreciated more deeply than ever how unfathomable are the vagaries of war, and how the soldier can't always be responsible for them.

Sometime after the middle of June, I tallied the friendly KIAs and WIAs in the 1-5 and 2-12 Cav battalions, beginning with when I arrived in the unit and going through about the middle of June 1969, or three and a half months. One hundred and twenty-eight troopers had died and eight hundred had been wounded—though I can no longer find all their names in the records. Amazed at the number of casualties, almost all of them infantry and medics, I checked morning reports for foxhole strength to compare casualty numbers with the number of fighting men and medics actually in the field. The results were sobering.

Between March 11 and mid-June 1969, the combined strengths in my ten infantry companies hovered just below eight hundred, far below what the strength should have been. The flow of replacements couldn't keep up with the casualty rates. Thus, 800 wounded and 128 killed represented a casualty rate of more than 100 percent, albeit a skewed casualty rate because some soldiers were wounded, treated and returned to duty only to be wounded again or die. This brings me to one other major difference between 1967 and 1969.

In 1966-67 a wounded trooper could usually expect to be in a chopper en route to expert medical care in sixteen minutes, on average. In 1969 in War Zone C, the wounded waited as much as ten hours for evacuation by a Medevac chopper or slick ship. This change I attributed to the loss of so many great Medevac crews; exhaustion of the ones remaining; the difference between fighting VC and NVA regulars; and the affect of war protests on everyone, especially on the pilots, who generally were better educated than infantrymen.

At 0800 hours, June 22, I conducted a memorial service for Alpha 1-5, followed by a worship service. Though I was with the company when these troopers died, I can't remember the details of how the deaths occurred. Perhaps my emotions and mind had all the horrors they could deal with at the time. Still, I feel disloyalty to the dead whose names I can't remember.

Following the services, I flew to Tay Ninh and almost got hit by one of three 122mm rockets—it exploded next to the latrine while I was inside "reading." Next day I was back in the jungle with Second

Platoon, Bravo 1-5, searching the banks of the Saigon River on foot and via Army boats. Choppers had lifted boats in. This was one of the worst nights ever for mosquitoes. Those NVA mosquitoes along the Saigon River appeared to relish insect repellent; they came out in the daylight, too.

On June 24, a Delta 1-5 patrol discovered NVA "commo" wire within six hundred meters of LZ Dolly. We followed the wire and were pleasantly surprised that none of us got shot in the process. This time, the NVA had moved on, leaving the strung wire behind.

Delta 1-5 stopped for the night about halfway up the south slope, in the northernmost saddle of the razorback ridge, between LZ Dolly to the north and Dau Tieng to the south. In the afternoon I held a service for the company followed by a sacrament service with Banks, Bowen, - and Pierce. Later we entertained ourselves creating pizza from C-ration items. The night sky was brilliant, unusual for the rainy season.

All seemed so peaceful. I really needed this moment to contemplate situations here and at home. I was growing more and more concerned about Helga and the baby; her letters described increasing threats of a miscarriage.

Chapter Notes:

16 June 1969, 1-5 Battalion Journal: "0920, A Co had two claymores blown at it...2 WIAs, Sp4s Ronald Anderson and Thomas Spratt."

1400 "A Co, while checking bag of rice, booby trap went off...1 WIA, Gerald Peihl, eye.

18 June 1969, 1-5 Battalion Journal: B Co, Nickolas Rutvicror [?], appendicitis

19 June 1969, 0940; 2-12 Battalion Journal: "A Co 16 reports seeing a bird go down...probably the CC. Also probably hit by friendly arty.:

1035: "Medevac 6 extracted 1 line 1 and part of another body." KIAs: Major Robert O'Keefe [of Davis, CA]; Captain James R. Daniel, Warrant Officers Ralph Clime and Jerrold Pearlstein, and Sp4's Raymond Voss and Henry Matthews."

1300, D Co Heatstroke, Pfc Barry Overlee.

30 June 1969, 1-5 Battalion Journal: "1650, A Co WIA, Pfc James Beroney, frag leg.

Chapter Fourteen

GRIEF ON THE HOME FRONT

Delta 1-5 moved out early on June 26, and by 0930 hours we'd moved west through the saddle in the razorback, crawled through bamboo thickets contaminated with persistent CS gas, and were in position to assault a recently-discovered NVA bunker complex. The complex was near the base of the razorback ridge and almost within spitting distance of the southwest perimeter of LZ Dolly. Battalion thought we'd need more ammunition and medical supplies, so we delayed the assault to await re-supply.

Battalion Operations called about 1000 hours. "Is One-Niner at your location?"

"That's a rog (roger)."

"Instruct him to report to Phuoc Vinh ASAP. Emergency message from home."

A slick ship landed half an hour later. While his men offloaded ammunition boxes, the company commander, with the radio handset still to his ear, relayed a message from Battalion. "Get on the chopper, Claude. Battalion is delaying the assault to fly you to Tay Ninh, where you are to prepare for travel to CONUS [Continental United States]." Under the circumstances, I appreciated this gesture.

A few minutes and kilometers later at about two thousand feet in the air, the crew chief suddenly hustled out of his rigging and started erecting a jump seat; I was sitting on the floor, as usual. The seat ready, the crew chief hollered in my ear, "Buckle up, Chaplain! We're having transmission trouble and might crash." This was very bad timing. Helga needed me too much for me to crash now. We made it to Tay Ninh, "coming in on a wing (rotors in this case) and a prayer." On several prayers, no doubt.

At Brigade Headquarters the Red Cross director handed me two messages. The first message said a daughter was born and not expected to live. The second message said she had died. Somehow, I knew as I read the messages that our baby's name should be Suzanne Marie and that Helga would agree. Helga, on her own, had the same impression. We had never before discussed this name.

Many hours later I landed at Travis Air Force Base, California on the same day and close to the same hour that I'd received the first emergency message in the field, in consequence of crossing the international time zone in the middle of the Pacific Ocean. It took almost as long to go the 850 miles from Travis AFB to Utah, via San Francisco, as from Vietnam to California.

Bishop David Taylor met me at the airport and took me straight to Helga's bedside in the old Dee-McKay- Hospital in Ogden. Helga and I clung to each other for several minutes. It was a bittersweet moment. We were so glad to be together, even under the circumstances.

With her faith, Helga was handling Suzanne Marie's death very well, and so was I. We knew, nothing doubting, that our baby was beyond such conditions as I'd left in Vietnam and she was ours eternally, provided we lived for the blessing.

The children appeared to be doing very well too. They were accepting what was and what could be, or so it seemed. But James was hiding his true feelings, which I'd learn more than a year later in Germany. Meanwhile, the children had grown during my almost four-month absence.

Helga, the children and I had three days together before Suzanne's funeral, time to comfort one another and become reacquainted.

On the day of the funeral, I saw Suzanne Marie's remains in her casket. Her infant face is burned indelibly in my memory.

At 10:00 a.m., June 30, 1969, we held a grave-side funeral and buried Suzanne Marie in the All-To-Rest Memorial Park Cemetery in Ogden, Utah, a temporary grave because we intended to move her someday to wherever we settled after the retirement. Dallas Murdoch opened the service with prayer. Bishop Taylor gave an obituary and Lynn and Sharon Cruiser sang "I Stand All Amazed." Like angels they sang. Elder Marion D. Hanks spoke about faith, hope and God's love.

Suzanne Marie's funeral marked the completion of four months on my second tour in Vietnam.

Following the funeral, Helga and I spent a few days trying to help each other regain our physical and emotional strength. I had come home with the fabled "thousand-meter stare" common to soldiers too long in combat. Later I wondered how this leave with Helga and the children contributed to my being able to complete this tour, painful though the occasion was. We had several impromptu family home evenings, times to talk and share and watch and play, and to reinforce the truths of Christ's redeeming love. We visited Joan and Dallas Murdoch and played and fished and water-skied and worshiped. Helga and I clung to each other, spirit and soul, trying to give and receive enough strength and memories to carry us through yet another parting.

Elder Marion D. and Maxine Hanks, sensing our emotional needs, invited us for an afternoon in the Hanks' co-op swimming pool, followed by dinner at their home. The children loved the pool and the new Ping-Pong table discovered on our hosts' back porch. The Hanks showered us with hospitable kindness and showed sincere interest in Helga, the children, and my experiences in Vietnam. About 10 p.m., as we prepared to leave, Elder Hanks folded the new Ping-Pong table and tied it atop our car.

We think the *Hanks' Table,* which is how we thought of it, followed us four times across the Atlantic Ocean and at least as many times across the American continent. Finally in 1981 we donated its shaky remains to a poor, struggling seminary teacher in Orem, Utah.

The parents of one of my troopers called the day before I left to return to Vietnam. He had written home about my leave. It meant so much, I knew, to the parents to talk to someone who had recently "touched" their son, to receive reassurance firsthand that his assignment was as "easy and safe" as he claimed it was.

Fortunately, before I had to answer their inquiry about the dangers, the mother diverted me with a more delicate question.

"Sonny [assigned alias] said his company just got in a lot of —s. Embarrassed, I got around the question with some vague comment and a promise to *visit* Sonny the moment I returned to Vietnam. Her question gave me an idea for a sermon for all the troops, about avoiding the use of certain acronyms and phrases, especially in letters home.

As I recall, Bill Snyder's brother visited us during my short leave, seeking a personal account of how Bill served and died. Sergeant Elvin Jackson's brother also visited.

Sometime during the emergency leave a reporter from the Deseret News, a Salt Lake City afternoon paper, interviewed Helga and me in our home. *Almost a Legend in His Own Time* was the heading for the somewhat accurate article that resulted from the interview. I about had to get a new helmet.

My mind refuses to release the details of our final parting on July 15, except the pain. Though I had to go and was being pulled back to Vietnam, leaving was so hard. It was probably harder for Helga than for me, weakened as she was by giving birth and losing her precious daughter.

I departed Travis Air Force Base, California at 2300 hours, July 15, and was back with my unit at 1600 hours on July 17. During the return flight I decided I would take a rest and relaxation (R&R) with Helga in Hawaii at the first opportunity, to take her away from the pressures of home and help her through her grief.

At 1600 hours on July 17, I arrived back in-country. The 1-5 Cav had replaced the 2-12 Cav on Palace Guard. LTC Ronald R. Rasmussen had replaced Lieutenant Colonel Peterson as Battalion Commander. It was almost too good to believe that the 1-5 and 2-12 Cav battalions had sustained just one KIA while I was gone! Very sad for the fallen trooper's buddies and family, but what a relief that there had not been more.

Chaplain Hugh Black had been sent to Korea and replaced in the 2-12 Cav with a non- Catholic, which ended our reciprocal support arrangement. As the leaders said that chaplain support had been inadequate in my absence, I felt especially grateful for unusually low casualty rates during this time. The new commander, LTC Ronald R. Rasmussen, and other leaders welcomed me back with enthusiasm and surprise. I wasn't due to return for another two weeks, but Helga and I both knew we couldn't leave the unit without its chaplain for so long.

Private First Class Robert F. Bacon of Alpha 1-5, from Phillipsburg, New Jersey, was killed by a sniper's bullet within minutes of my return to the battalion. Two men were wounded with him. We almost made a combat assault my first evening back, in response to Bacon's shooting, but it was called off after we were aboard the choppers.

When I met Lieutenant Colonel Rasmussen, he said he'd heard only nice reports about me. He asked me to go over a sympathy letter he'd just roughed out to Bacon's wife or parents, and to rewrite it if necessary. I recommended he change the word *lost* to *gave* in the phrase, "your husband lost his life while..." to better express the sacrifice every trooper stands ready to give when he answers the call of his country. This characterization fits Bacon, who according to other sources was a schoolteacher and thus could have been exempted from the draft. Rasmussen liked the change, and we became instant close friends who shared comparable ideas about and respect for the troopers we led and served.

Casualties remained low and the action light for the 1-5 and 2-12 Cav battalions between July 18 and August 12, thanks at least partly to palace guard duties and rain hard enough to discourage even the NVA. I took advantage of this to increase the number of worship services for small units, to counsel soldiers, send sage counsel to my children, tighten up denominational leadership, get troopers to a conference, and arrange R&R in Hawaii. I recall but one personal close call during these days, when a sergeant almost shot me in the back.

On my first full day back from leave, July 18, I conducted two pla-toon-size worship services in the field. Over the next two days I visited the new 2-12 Cav Fire Support Base (FSB) O'Keefe. About this time, a high-ranking general ordered that henceforth battalion-size firebases would be called fire support bases and the designation Landing Zone (LZ) would be applied only to temporary landing sites out in the field. Unofficially, we continued to designate places like Dolly and O'Keefe as LZs.

LZ O'Keefe was named in honor of Major O'Keefe, the same who was killed when artillery blew Lieutenant Colonel Boon's chopper out of the sky back in June. Colonel Barker (from Fort Bragg) arrived at LZ O'Keefe as I was tromping about through mud and heavy rain. We met, and he seemed pleased to see me. He said he would get me as his brigade chaplain, provided he could arrange a transfer. Though it would probably have been a great career move, I hoped he would not succeed. I didn't know it then, but position would count for more than combat experience in the future peacetime Army. Even had I known this, I think I still would have wished to be left with my battalions, which wish I confided to Chaplain Scott.

On July 21, a shot-up helicopter limped in for an emergency land-ing at LZ Ike while I was stranded there. At the control was the same pilot who had interrupted my Easter service by crashing into a nearby bomb crater. We were pleased to see each other alive.

Eventually I got off Ike, only to be stranded again on LZ Dolly, where Delta 1-5 was engaged in the destruction of what remained of the firebase. The work of demolition stopped while we held a memor-ial service for Bacon, followed by a worship service, and then a sacra-ment service with four in attendance.

Later in the day, stranded again by weather, I spent the night at Lai Khe. That evening on Chaplain Allen's television we saw Neal Armstrong make footprints on the moon, a "giant step for mankind...the greatest event in the history of mankind since the creation," exaggerated President Richard M. Nixon. I made a mental note to remind the troopers who created the moon and placed it there.

On July 24, frustrated in my efforts to reach a 2-12 Cav company (none were receiving log), I gave up trying and tackled an administrative backlog. After writing several official letters and counseling several troopers, I went to Saigon to celebrate Pioneer Day.

At Ton San Nhut Air Base, I attended meetings with Colonel McPhie and USAF Chaplain Robert Christiansen. Afterward, the three of us celebrated the day over steak and a special cake at the officer's club, quite a different celebration from the one near An Khe in 1967.

A counseling moment of note occurred on July 25. It involved a young officer who sought spiritual counsel because he, a married man and a Christian, had gone with a prostitute at the coaxing of another officer. This reminded me of the destructive, wasteful nature of short rounds—artillery, mortars and bombs that land off-target and harm friendly troops and non-combatants. Short rounds would be my sermon topic the next day.

On July 26 I made a rare trip via jeep, to visit a 1-5 Cav unit which was protecting a major bridge on the Song Be River. The unit was down in the dumps because the muddy, swollen river had swallowed up a rucksack-laden grunt, never to be seen again, as I recall. I say "as I recall" because though I've been unable to find any record of a trooper being drowned at that time, I find records of troopers drowned a month earlier, and suspect a trick of memory here. We held another memorial service in the driving rain for Bacon and (presumably for) the drowned trooper. The service I'd held several days earlier had been with a smaller element of the company. A worship service followed the memorial service.

Elsewhere in the rocket belt, the Third Platoon of Bravo 1-5 combat assaulted into a hot LZ. Another platoon was boarding choppers to reinforce it when I arrived. Captain Copley asked me to go along. We loaded into Chinooks in terrible flying weather.

A Chaplain Allen and I had an interesting conversation at Lai Khe the evening of July 27. The exchange began with his challenge of my operational methods. He insisted that staying in the field and accompanying units on combat operations had negligible benefit to the troops, though it earns lots of points with commanders. Allen offered two arguments to back up his premise. First, it is too hard on unit morale and effectiveness to have the chaplain become a casualty. Second, he argued, the chaplain is too valuable an asset to risk losing in close combat.

My response was that the chaplain, in order to influence the soldier and unit, must accompany the soldier wherever duty takes him, as far as that is possible. He must share the soldier's experiences and fears. "Only in this way can the chaplain's influence remain with the soldier when he is not there, as a constant reminder of higher values and hopes," I insisted.

I countered the arguments about effect on morale and effectiveness and the chaplain's value as an asset. First, the chaplain is negligent who waits for the soldier to come to him in the rear, for the field soldier seldom has the opportunity to do so. Second, the soldier heeds the sermon he sees, and what he sees influences what he hears. Third, the chaplain's voluntary presence with the soldier during hardship and danger preaches a mighty sermon about the soldier's worth and lends credence to what the chaplain says and stands for. Finally, those things the chaplain represents are reinforced for the soldier during times of terror.

In conclusion, I insisted the chaplain is a valuable asset precisely because, and only if, he accompanies the soldier wherever the soldier is sent. Thus, the chaplain's life is worth risking for the sake of the soldiers' souls and well-being.

"Besides," I added somewhere in the conversation, "I know the safest place for me to be is where I should be, for then if I die, I live in the Lord."

We cordially discussed these topics without either of us noticeably changing his opinion or without Allen attempting to change my modus operandi by force of his position. This exchange gave *me* more clarity and helped me focus myself in ways that prepared me for future duties as a combat developer (yes, chaplains do combat developments too).

Chapter Notes:

17 July 1969, 1-5 Battalion Journal: A Co KIA, Pfc James Bacon, sniper; WIAs, Robert Davidson and Occheuzzie US273367132. Sgt. Timothy Dagin was evacuated from the field with FUO.

27 July 1969, 1-5 Battalion Journal: 1013 D Co, head, Gerald Lawton.

Chapter Fifteen

BEGINNING OF THE END

President Richard M. Nixon visited Vietnam and got a sanitized tour. USARV pulled 1st Infantry Division company onto a firebase and issued each man a new, clean uniform and jungle boots—even new helmet camouflage covers, free of short-timer calendars, salutations, crosses, peace symbols and the like.

Meanwhile, other companies were shifted around in-country so the president could visit the squeaky-clean companies on secure firebases. I spent the day with a 1-5 Cav company patrolling out beyond a firebase near Bien Hoa to suppress enemy activity during Nixon's visit.

Having moved by Chinooks to an area south of Bien Hoa, we transferred to liftships and combat assaulted into a swampy area interspersed with clumps of jungle. Our mission was to suppress any rocket and mortar attacks that might threaten the president.

This was a bad day, not because of enemy action, but because the troopers behaved as if the enemy were all elsewhere. Perhaps the guys acted this way because we were south of Bien Hoa Air Base and a great distance from War Zone C.

Never had I seen such slothfulness among 1st Cav troopers. Troopers talked loudly, laughing and joking as we patrolled the area. Some even hung items on their packs to rattle and clang about. Under these conditions I had another close call with death by non-hostile means.

We'd been patrolling to the south but a few minutes, and had just entered a patch of jungle, when a shot rang out almost in my ears. Ignoring the principle of dispersion, plenty of space between soldiers on patrol, the platoon sergeant had closed within a yard of me and accidentally fired his M-16. Fortunately for his conscience and my health, the bullet passed harmlessly over my head or shoulder. The accidental shot was the only one we heard all day, except for artillery and ARA.

The whole Nixon visit agitated me, all the scrubbing and polishing to create a false image for him. It would be much better, I thought, for him and all the visiting commanders and politicians, to see conditions as they really were.

But as matters turned out, I deduced what the President saw was irrelevant, for he came not to see but to tell. His visit provided a dramatic backdrop for announcing the beginning of the American withdrawal from Vietnam and "peace with honor."

Thus, I considered President Nixon's 1969 visit as the official beginning of the end. I would soon conclude that his visit marked the beginning of a rapid decline in unit cohesion, combat discipline, dedication, aggressiveness, and general racial blindness among the front line troops. These negative changes, marked by a rapid increase in disciplinary problems, reflected a loss of *sense of mission* by the Army, concurrent with a growing, collective unwillingness to waste life in a lost cause. But the war still continued hot and furious for my units and men.

Back at Phuoc Vinh that evening, after a day of patrolling to support the President's visit, my nephew Earl Dyer met with two troopers who also served as LDS missionaries. Earl returned to his unit with lots of new questions spinning in his head.

Now, I always exercised extreme care to avoid the very appearance of unethically misusing my position and influence to convert soldiers of other faiths, as all chaplains were supposed to do. Earl is close blood kin, so I made an exception when he asked me specific religious questions.

Combat was light August 2-5, and so were casualties in my two battalions. Private First Class Johnson became my chaplain assistant in

July, and promptly announced that he wanted to accompany me to the field and "see what it is like." He soon got his wish, a combat assault with Bravo 1-5.

Unchallenged, we made the assault and jumped off into waist-deep water, in a spooky area of dead trees—victims of agent orange spraying. Johnson and I linked with Second Platoon and moved out to the east on a company-size search for an NVA bunker and village complex that was supposed to be in the area. We waded in the chest-deep water for several hundred meters to reach wet ground, there being no dry ground nearby.

We continued eastward the next day, until late in the afternoon, when the point man began reporting signs of NVA—tracks, fighting positions, finally bunkers. As we moved among the fighting positions, I, in a whisper, pointed out and explained tell-tale signs of the enemy's presence to Johnson. Johnson appeared increasingly uncomfortable the deeper we moved into the NVA complex. Finally, Johnson crept to me, holding his stomach. "Chaplain Newby, I don't feel well. My stomach really hurts."

"Know what you've got?" I asked.

"No. What?"

"A severe case of fear," I diagnosed.

"Really? That's what fear feels like?" Johnson seemed relieved and satisfied, even pleased to know how it felt to be afraid.

Well, his fears were for nothing. The NVA chose not to fight. While the grunts pushed on to the east side of the NVA complex, where the flooded area began anew, the CP set up for the night among the bunkers. They soon wished they hadn't. The complex swarmed with little red leeches; they rose from the ground wherever one looked.

We'd been in the complex an hour or so when from the east side of the perimeter came the dreaded cry, "Medic! Medic!"

The company medic and I rushed toward the sound of the alarm, wondering what could be the matter. We'd heard neither shooting nor explosions. Just beyond the complex and undergrowth, knee-deep in water, stood a very upset trooper.

A leech had crawled inside him. The unwelcome guest was discovered when a buddy asked the trooper why his trouser-front was covered with blood. The leech had sucked blood until it burst and kept right on dining.

We could do nothing for the poor trooper. A lighted cigarette to the head of the leech was out of the question, as was a squirt of insect spray and other tried and proven methods of making a leech turn loose.

The trooper's medical evacuation, which began when he climbed into a chopper hovering over the flood waters, ended at Walter Reed Army Medical Center, in Washington, D.C. There, surgeons removed the unwelcome guest from the trooper's anatomy. What a way to get out of Vietnam early.

Meanwhile, back among the leeches, none envied the trooper his unusual method of escape.

After the medevac was completed, Johnson and I made a rain shelter and settled in to wait for the dawn, which I thought would never come. All night long, I imagined leeches crawling on and into my body, especially into the more sensitive parts. Vainly I tried to sleep while limiting contact between my body and the ground. Great was my relief next morning after Johnson and I checked each other and found we were free of leeches, except in the mind.

Sergeant Elvin Jackson came in from the field the evening of August 7. He showered and donned dry underclothing for the first time in 57 days. The next day he and I hitched a ride to Bien Hoa on an *Air America* (Central Intelligence Agency "Airline") fixed-wing aircraft. At Bien Hoa we treated ourselves to some commercial food and a movie and then visited until midnight. This day, August 8, held special religious significance for Helga and me. I began and ended that day reflecting on our blessings, and feeling especially close to her despite the distance between us.

As the concluding speaker at an LDS conference, I paid tribute by name to Sergeant Jackson and many others the next day. My remarks led many rear-area people to a clearer understanding of the nature of the war and to a greater appreciation for the sufferings and sacrifices of the faceless men they supported. At least that is what several of them told me afterwards.

Following the conference, I placed a call to Helga via the MARS system, and waited until 0300 hours the next morning for it to go through. The call went something like this: "I love you. Over...."

Six hours after the call I was in the field conducting worship services for the platoons of Delta 1-5, followed by two more general worship services for other units and two LDS services, all at different sites.

The pace of war increased the night of August 12. NVA forces attacked American firebases throughout the 1st Cav AO. In response to the attacks, the 1-5 Cav was pulled off palace guard and air assaulted into the jungles northwest of Quan Loi, near Cambodia. I moved forward with Alpha 1-5 to LZ Shirley at An Loc h. There we offloaded from Chinooks and stood by on the airstrip to await the Huey choppers that would carry us on the air assault.

The terrain was fairly clear for about 2000 meters west of the north-south running airstrip, which airstrip was just inside the firebase perimeter. The Alpha Companies of the 1-5 and 2-5 Cav battalions were spread out along a descending embankment on the west side the airstrip. Lieutenant Colonel Rasmussen, the Sergeant Major, the operations officer and their RTOs huddled in a sandbagged gun pit several meters east of the runway.

Without warning a 90mm recoilless shell exploded about eight feet behind the huddled CP group, followed by the sound of a round being fired from the west. More shells followed. I became edgy because the two companies of infantrymen were bunched up and very exposed. So I dashed across the runway, followed by two companies of infantrymen, who knew a good example when they saw one. Of course, we were bunched up again, but not as exposed.

The incoming shells exploded among positions fifty feet behind us at the rate of two per minute. We counted our blessings; the NVA weren't targeting the unprotected infantry along the airstrip. Then to the north I saw something that would surely bring the shells nearer.

A C-130 cargo plane, laden with infantry I later learned, was on final approach. It would stop beside us. Those around me did not appear interested in the approaching plane, nor in the likelihood that its arrival would draw enemy shells onto the infantry.

Hoping I knew what I was doing, I ran onto the runway and, with incoming recoilless shells whizzing overhead, I waved the cargo plane off. Apparently, upon seeing me, the pilot refused to land until the enemy fire ceased. Soon friendly artillery rained onto the area to the west and the 90mm shelling ceased. Captain Gioia's memory of this morning differs from mine in two ways. First, he is certain that Rasmussen and his CP did not arrive at An Loc while we were there. Second, he recalls personally waving off some choppers because of incoming 90 recoilless fire. He doesn't recall the C-130 being waved off, and I don't recall the choppers being waved off.

Soon after that the choppers arrived, and I accompanied Alpha 1-5 on a combat assault into heavy jungle within four kilometers of Cambodia. Though the jungle we moved through was somehow different, eerier than any other jungle I'd seen in Vietnam, we made no contact with the enemy as we humped the rest of the day, dug in for the night, humped another day and dug in again. We saw little sign of enemy forces in the area or of recent American ground troops having been in the area.

Termites attacked during the second night and ate holes in some heavy rubber air mattresses. While the termites feasted, NVA mortars rained destruction on the 1-5 Cav's LZ Eagle One, which had opened on 12 August. The bombardment of LZ Eagle I began a few minutes past midnight and continued for an hour. The enemy tubes fired from about five hundred meters east of our position, almost on-line between the firebase and us.

Repeatedly, we called in coordinates and requested counter-fire on the enemy mortars, but never got it. Meanwhile, I quit counting the mortar shells at one hundred. On the firebase, the battalion sustained several casualties, mainly because of unfinished defenses on the new LZ.

The next day, August 14, I conducted worship services for Alpha 1-5 and shared the sacrament with Elvin Jackson before returning at noon to Phuoc Vinh to prepare for R&R.

I spent August 15-17 at Bien Hoa and getting to Ton San Nhut for my R&R flight, which flight got off to a bad start on August 18.

We boarded an air-conditioned commercial airplane about mid-afternoon, eagerly anticipating a quick takeoff and smooth flight to Honolulu and into the arms of loved ones. I sat next to a window on the left several rows forward of the rear door of the aircraft. The engines, and with them the air conditioning, stopped several long minutes later: "Sorry gentlemen, but we have a little light here that we shouldn't have. We'll take off after it is checked out. Meanwhile, Customs says everyone must stay on board. Relax, gentlemen. The smoking light is on," said the pilot in his best *don't worry, everything's all right* voice.

Once the air conditioning was turned off, the passenger compartment quickly became a torture chamber in the intense heat and humidity. It was no place for a nonsmoker to be trapped in starched khakis. I spent the next one hundred and eighty minutes sweltering with my head beneath a wool Blanket, as I tried to filter the effects and disgusting stench of tobacco. I dreaded the assault this stench would have on Helga when we next embraced at the Honolulu airport.

Many hours later in Hawaii, the torture chamber forgotten, I passed through customs and hurried into Helga's waiting embrace. She seemed hardly to notice my smoke-cured aroma. In my journal I described the moment: *18 Aug 1969...Hawaii...To see Helga was joy beyond description...very romantic, lovely, and memorable...only regret...temple is closed.*

On this R&R, like the one in 1967, we spent a wonderful, romantic, memorable six days and five nights. Helga grew stronger physically and emotionally day by day. Alas, all too soon the adventure was over and the sorrow of parting was upon us. But we appreciated what we had between us and knew it was worth the pain of another parting.

Helga recuperating on R&R in Hawaii with her husband.
August 1969

On August 25 I returned to the 1-5 Cav. The fighting was similar but less frequent and intense than it had been in the Spring and early summer, but morale and esprit de corps, spirit of the unit, were falling at an almost discernable rate. Racial tensions were mounting even in the foxholes, though nothing like they were doing in the rear areas. Back there blacks and whites glared at one another with hate-filled eyes. White troops averted their eyes as black *brothers* exchanged the closed-fist black-power salute, or "dapped" one another with their imaginative handshakes. Things were changing for the worst, the first signs, I think, of the impact of President Nixon's announced American withdrawal from Vietnam.

An attack on Quan Loi two days before I returned from R&R inflicted casualties in every unit in the 1-5 Cav, except Echo Company.

My first night back from R&R I spent under the stars at LZ Eagle 1. My assistant hadn't constructed a shelter or cover for us in my absence. The LZ enjoyed a quiet, wet night, nothing like what was in store for it the next night, when I would be in the jungle with Delta 1-5.

The NVA launched a heavy mortar and rocket attack on LZ Eagle 1, beginning at 0030 hours, August 27. Two troopers died and several others were wounded. I monitored the standoff attack by PRC-25, from out in the jungle.

Phil Gioia described the attack: "Terry Brain (my paceman, also known as Biggy) and I were sitting on the sandbag ring around an 8-inch howitzer on LZ Eagle 1; Foggy Day [Alpha 1-5] had that afternoon been airlifted into the LZ. The very first round of an incoming sheaf of mortars or rockets hit right inside that gun pit, killed several members of the gun crew, flipped the gun on its side, and blew Terry, myself and a couple of other people into the side of a bunker. Dazed, shaken and temporarily deafened, we quickly scrambled to cover in one of those hasty-bunkers that consisted of a half-culvert laid on the ground and covered with sandbags.

"Terry, I believe, lost a kidney (or so we heard later), and was sent back to Ft Lewis, WA, where he sorted mail until the Army let him out. I wasn't scratched, but to this day I have serious hearing loss in my left ear, which was toward that 120mm mortar or 122mm rocket. We were so close to the explosion that I didn't hear a thing when it went off…just remember a blue flicker, like when you switch on a fluorescent light tube. Couldn't hear anything out of that ear for days afterwards. Still have a constant ringing in it."

Said SSG Elvin Jackson : "I was in a bunker with another soldier when a mortar round hit outside of it. RTO Carl Bahnlein was in a bunker some 20 to 30 feet from ours. Shrapnel hit me in the shoulder and arm when I ran from my bunker to check on my men. That's when I found Bahnlein lying half outside and half in his bunker. He was seriously wounded in the chest, the result of shrapnel. A trooper, the company mail clerk, who had been stranded on Eagle 1 for the night, responded to my repeated calls for assistance, and he and I carried Bahnlein to the medics under a continuing barrage of heavy mortars or rockets."

After we left the medics, the mail clerk began crying. "I've lost my weapon! I can't find it," he told Jackson.

"I gave him my weapon, and told him to watch the perimeter. He stayed on watch there behind the sandbags all night, and was still guarding the perimeter when I checked on him at dawn. In the daylight, we found his weapon and he returned to his job in the rear. I was very impressed with his courage and willingness to help me under those dangerous conditions. I hope he got a medal," said Jackson.

Three troopers were with Bahnlein in the bunker just before he was hit, Platoon Sergeant Mario Gristani, Larry Smith, and a blond medic. "Bahnlein had just come back to the field after recuperating from previous injuries, and had just started humping an M-79 that he was dying to shoot. We were having movement around LZ Eagle, and he kept pestering me to let him shoot it, but I said no. Then when the NVA started mortaring us, I said 'Go ahead. Knock yourself out.'

"Bahnlein was just running out of the bunker when a mortar round landed right in the doorway and blew him right back into the bunker. Smitty looked down at him and said, 'Oh my God! A sucking chest wound!' and I thought Bahnlein would go into shock."

Jackson received word the next day that Bahnlein had made it out of the unit alive, but he didn't know how long he lived. "It wasn't until 1999 that he and I made contact again. He is alive and well, but badly scarred, and living in near Washington, DC," Jackson said.

Bahnlein told Jackson that, "Working in a VA hospital, I know that I had but minutes to live with the kind of wound I had, and I would have died if you had waited until the mortar barrage stopped before you came out to help me."

This is how Terrance Brain (pace man) remembers that morning. "As we came into the LZ earlier, the NVA kept popping up, shooting a few rounds at us and disappearing. That night I was sitting between two of those bunkers made out of half-culvert corrugated steel—first time I saw bunkers made that way— and reading my mail in between mortar and rocket attacks. When the barrage started, I headed for a bunker, then turned aside to grab a radio that was separated from the CP— Captain Gioia needed two radios, one to communicate with the perimeter and one to coordinate fire support.

"I grabbed the radio and headed at a crouching run for the bunker about 12 feet away. There was a big explosion and something slammed into my back just as I reached the entrance, threw me right on top of Captain Gioia. He and the medic, a large black man and really nice guy, kept telling me to quit putting my hand in my wound...they had to turn me around inside the long narrow culvert/bunker so they could get my head up...burned and pained awfully. The blast didn't just ruin my kidney. It completely destroyed, disintegrated it—nothing left.

"Because one of the troops was too badly wounded to wait, a Medevac chopper crew braved rockets, mortars, and small-arms fire to come in and hover while the worst wounded were loaded. I also got aboard, wrapped in a blanket and sitting upright.

"A few minutes later at one of those blow-up medical places, probably the 2nd Surg, I sat next to a wall and observed the medics chasing around and trying to find a really seriously wounded guy. No luck. A doctor said, 'He's got to be here. He was on that chopper. Start checking the medic tags.'

"Soon, a medic reached inside my Blanket and pulled out my tag. 'Here he is!' he shouted. That's when I knew I was in trouble...Later, at a hospital in Saigon, a doctor told me I was going home. 'No,' I said, 'I'm going back to my unit.'

"'You're badly wounded, son, and you are going home.' I came home."

Between August 27 and 29, the battalion sustained at least seven more KIAs, including three more on LZ Eagle 1 and one at Quan Loi. At Quan Loi a 107mm rocket burst in the battalion rear area. The field trains had recently moved there from Tay Ninh. Also, on the night of August 27 the NVA viciously attacked Bravo 1-5 in its FOB. I can't recall the outcome.

On August 30, I left Delta 1-5 and headed for Quan Loi via LZ Eagle 1. My objective was to visit the troopers of Bravo 1-5, who had come in to "enjoy" a 48-hour stand-down in the Division "VIP" Center there. The VIP Center was nothing more than a place to provide the grunts, a company at a time, two days and a night away from the constant patrols, ambushes, bunker building, and firefights, where they could get a real shower, eat a little better and drink if they wanted to. I came to the VIP Center to provide the men a rare opportunity to worship as a company and to help restore their spiritual strength and stamina.

One look at the VIP Center and I wished these men were somewhere else. Sure, they had showers and cots, but very inadequate overhead cover. *They will have little rest and recuperation here*, I thought, correctly as the next hour proved.

I'd barely left the VIP Center to visit Chaplain Lamar Hunt at his nearby hooch when several mortar rounds and rockets came in. I hurried back to the VIP center, but a 107-mm rocket beat me there by mere seconds and exploded in the branches of a tree. Hot shrapnel and debris wounded three troopers. This "break" from the field was the first for Bravo 1-5 since late in April.

The next night was another bad one for Delta 1-5. The company had stopped early, dug in well, built overhead cover and set out plenty of claymore mines, trip flares, LPs and ambushes. None of these things kept a very capable NVA unit from sneaking right up to the FOB without being detected until an NVA point man finally tripped a flare. The instant the flare popped, the NVA point element opened fire, killing a trooper as he scrambled for his foxhole. Reacting almost as quickly, the men in Delta 1-5 killed several NVA soldiers, including the point man, who fell between two perimeter foxholes.

On September 1, I passed the halfway mark on this tour, grateful to have escaped the threat of being reassigned to a rear area unit, as was customarily the fate of captains and above. The troopers in Alpha 1-5 marked the new month in a much more dramatic way.

Captain Gioia grew tired after waiting several hours on LZ Eagle 1 for choppers to arrive to carry Alpha 1-5 back into the field. "We are infantry. We will walk," Gioia said, according to Larry McVay.

Tom Holcombe said, "We simply walked off Eagle 1 in the usual two-column company formation with my squad about in the middle of the left column. Around midday we came upon a field that was too large to go around. We were about halfway across the field when one of the men farther back in my squad passed up word that he'd spotted NVA out to our left front. I got on the horn and reported this to Six [Gioia], who stopped the company and sent a large patrol ahead to check the sighting out. The patrol moved forward in two columns, with half of my squad at the head of each, and me in second position on the left."

Holcombe continued, "We took off at a fast walk trying to overtake the enemy and had gone about 400 meters when Ed Atkinson, point man for the right column, spotted something and signaled the patrol to stop by raising his hand, palm forward. Ed signaled Bob Ahern to come forward with his M-79. Meanwhile, Lt. Williams moved everyone on-line and I positioned my men to provide fire support for Ed and Bob. 'Open fire at the first shot from either side,' I whispered. Then I stayed kneeling on one knee in the waist-high grass so I could watch Ed and Bob. After a moment, Bob Ahern saw the NVA Ed was pointing at and fired. Instantly, both sides opened up, and the B-40 and small-arms fire seemed to last forever."

McVay added, "As Ahern's squad leader in the First Squad of the Second Platoon, I was standing right beside Ahern when he fired the first round, and Holcombe was to my left. Despite the intense small arms and rocket fire we were taking, we swept forward. During the charge Lt. Williams, our platoon leader, fell seriously wounded...I was hit too; however, I didn't realize I was hit until it was all over."

"My squad's M-60 machine gunner and point man and Lieutenant Williams were among those evacuated. McClelland went home. The point man eventually returned to the squad. Several others were wounded, including some who rushed forward from other elements in the company to reinforce us," said Holcombe.

"I believe we killed a couple more with small arms before the NVA made a hasty exit," McVay said.

It is amazing that Americans did not die in this action. Things were definitely in the enemy's favor. They were in hiding and the Americans were moving toward them in the open, which gave the NVA the element of surprise and a better fix on the Americans. That Atkinson saw the enemy soldier lying in the elephant grass at all is extraordinary. That Ahern got off the first shot, and by so doing thwarted the ambush and wrought the most damage in the fight is almost beyond comprehension, given the other factors. "The enemy had fared much worse before they pulled back from the ambush they had attempted to draw us into. Bob Ahern's first M-79 grenade hit one of the ambushers right in the face, killing him and the poor soul next to him," said Holcombe.

According to Shorty McVay, "Lt. Williams...was wounded and returned to the states...I received shrapnel from a B-40 rocket...stayed in the field. Also wounded were Robert Braud...remained in the field...[and] Charles Robbins. May have been others. Some of the A1-5 troopers dubbed this action the 'Ahern Ambush'."

On September 3, in the field with Alpha 1-5, everyone dug in with zeal, spurred on by fresh NVA sign and the occasional clank of metal-on-metal in the nearby jungle, that distinct, nerve-stressing clank of a gun barrel against mortar tube or base plate. Obviously the NVA knew our location, and lately they'd shown little reluctance to engage us up close.

Shortly after full darkness, Sergeant Tony Cruz of Phoenix, Arizona took his squad and set an ambush about 100 meters north of the FOB. We settled in, fully expecting to be mortared, and perhaps hit by a ground attack. I dozed off once sometime after midnight, only to be snapped full awake by the clank of metal against metal out in the jungle. The clanking came from the east of our perimeter, and close.

Captain Gioia put us on 100 percent alert at 0355 hours in response to a whispered radio message from Sergeant Cruz. "Gooks all around us! Heavy movement and Gook voices!"

Gioia considered ordering Cruz to withdraw his men into the FOB, but rejected the idea when Cruz reported hearing Vietnamese voices between his position and ours.

At first light, according to the plan, Cruz and his men would blow their claymore mines, which they'd rearranged facing in all directions. Then simultaneously, each squad member would throw two hand grenades and fire off a magazine in every direction except toward the FOB, then the squad would dash for the FOB along a narrow, specified lane between heavy covering fire by Second Platoon. "The tension in the minutes before I withdrew the OP/LP was so thick you could cut it with a knife…there was a big unit out there, moving across our front, and Tony and his people heard them very clearly. We shot artillery to cover their withdrawal into the main body of the company," said Gioia.

Preparations for the withdrawal went according to plan. Cruz and his men threw the grenades and each blasted off a magazine. But Cruz was hit in the back almost as soon as he and his men jumped up and began their dash for the perimeter. A green tracer round (red, according to an entry in the Battalion Journal) entered his lower back and traveled upward slightly to leave a fist-size exit wound in his chest, just right of center.

Seconds later Tom Holcombe swept forward with the rest of his squad in response to a radioed plea for a medic, and reached the ambush site in a few seconds—Holcombe had been Cruz's squad leader until Cruz got his own squad just before this action. "When I got there, one of the guys from the ambush was with him [Cruz] calling for a medic. He left and I stayed with Tony and tried to calm him. When I saw the wound, I knew he wasn't going to make it. All I could do was tell him help was on the way. I'm sure Tony knew he was going to die," said Holcombe.

The NVA withdrew without putting up a fight, for reasons known only to them.

The company medic and I reached Cruz within a minute, followed shortly by the company commander and first sergeant. For the next fifteen minutes, while some troopers provided security and others cleared an LZ for Medevac, I held Cruz's head and upper torso in my arms and literally watched his heart beat through the hole in his chest.

During those minutes, while I comforted Cruz and the medic attended him, his buddies pleaded for him to hang on. "You've got it made, Tony! On the way home, man." Standing by helplessly, the first sergeant vented his frustrations on Medevac for taking so long to reach us, which frustrations he expressed with obscenities sprinkled with a divine title.

"I don't want to die," Cruz gasped, as he looked into my eyes and grasped my right hand with his right hand. His grip became vise-like, superhuman as his life ebbed away. "I feel my life slipping away," he whispered.

Then turning his eyes on his men, he spoke a few words in Spanish, and died. "So long. I'll see you guys later," he said, according to a member of his squad. "Sal later translated to us that Cruz said 'see you in heaven,'" said Holcombe. "He must have died shortly after that while you were holding him, Claude. I remember that I was low on ammo that day and wound up taking Tony's...had to...wipe the blood off of each magazine."

McVay said of this incident: "Your [my] account of the day and night of Sept. 3, 1969 is just the way I remember it. I had Second Squad and Tony had the First Squad in the Second Platoon....I remember tying claymores up in trees...we were expecting to get hit...I also recall Sergeant Cruz calling in Arty most of the night. His Arty missions are most probably what kept the enemy off the FOB that night. Anyway, that's how I felt at the time and still feel today."

Contrary to the battalion journal entries about this incident, Tony Cruz was killed by a green tracer round and not by a fragment from friendly artillery that he himself had directed, nor from a grenade that he or his men threw. And he died on the scene, not on the way to Quan Loi. I know an exit wound made by a high-powered weapon when I see one.

Captain Gioia wrote, "I've always been convinced that Tony Cruz was killed by small arms... [I] shot artillery to cover their withdrawal into the main body of the company, and the staff types later inferred that he'd been hit by secondary frag (as though seasoned field soldiers didn't have the sense to stay down). But as you say—and I remember quite clearly—the other people in his group reported incoming green tracers as well."

About September 5, following a night on ambush with Echo 1-5, I held a worship service on LZ Eagle One. At the meeting were the Commander and the Command Sergeant Major of the 11th Armored Cavalry Regiment. The NVA shot down the Commander's C&C helicopter thirty minutes later, and the sergeant major was wounded.

Later that day I provided worship services for Alpha 1-5, then joined Delta 1-5 for two nights, during which time we conducted a memorial service, followed by some worship services. That evening Banks, Bowen -, Pierce and I shared the Sacrament. It was the last time with all of us present.

It was during this visit with Delta 1-5 that Lieutenant Colonel Rasmussen performed an act of leadership worthy of special mention because it contrasted so much with some other leader's examples. The Battalion Command Sergeant Major said that back in July and early August when the 1-5 Cav was on palace guard, the engineers demanded tribute of the infantry in exchange for water for the grunts' showers. He said that each afternoon the engineers expected a case of beer in exchange for a daily delivery of water to the battalion area on the perimeter. If the engineers found no case of beer waiting for them, the infantrymen received no water for showers the next day.

My upset over this system of tribute affected my reaction to what was happening on LZ Eagle One early in September— people were eating lots of ice cream, but ice cream was not getting to the field. An S-4 officer justified this. "We can't get ice cream to the field before it melts."

So I took my observations to Rasmussen and on September 6 he personally radioed Delta 1-5. SP4 Ted Pierce took the following message and relayed it to Captain Nishioka : "If you can find an LZ within the next thirty minutes, ice cream is on the way!"

We immediately stopped in place, set up a perimeter, and while patrols cloverleafed the area, other troopers went to work. Well within thirty minutes, an oval-shaped patch of sky appeared where triple-canopy jungle had reigned. Those highly motivated grunts created that hole by blowing down trees with plastique explosives. Compound-4 (C-4) was in abundance because most troopers, and I, carried a pound or two in our packs for "emergencies" like this and for heating C-rations, though using C-4 to heat C-rations was forbidden because C-4 fumes were—according to medical sources— hazardous to one's health.

Exactly thirty minutes after we received Rasmussen's ice cream message, a chopper settled carefully down through the hole we'd provided and kicked off a half gallon of ice cream for every man who wanted it, including me, very little of which was wasted. Ron Rasmussen made lots of troopers happy with this gesture.

Two NVA stumbled onto an Alpha 1-5 observation post early the next evening. One NVA fell with wounds to the body and the other one fled to the north. Moments later I passed the fallen NVA soldier, by which time he was quite dead from a shot to the head. A few minutes later back in the FOB, someone snapped a picture of me with two troopers, one of whom, I was told in privileged communication, had delivered the *coup de grâce* to the NVA soldier.

Chapter Notes:

18 August 1969, 1-5 Battalion Journal: Attack on LZ Eagle 1. [no names].

19 August 1969, 1-5 Battalion Journal, 1322: "C Co at 1145, w/2 WIA by friendly claymore, Schinowski, hand and Kellerhaus.

24 August 1969, 1-5 Battalion Journal: Casualties from Attack on Quan Loi, WIAs, "HHC, Pfc's Cook-, Rook and Hernandez ; A Co. L. F. [SSG Larry C.] Fields and (check with clerk for name; B Co, Hafley or Haeley, M. M. Morris, S. K. Kreiger, Trainer ; C Co, Phillips (Donald?); D Co, Wenick."

27 August 1969, 1-5 Battalion Journal; 0030: "Fr GM 1/8: Reports Eagle 1 was mortared w/unk no. of 120- mm mortars…Pfc Gardner Brown [Union, ME], Sgt. Guy Inkle [Beecher Falls, VT], both B 1-77 were working their 105mm howitzer when 01 120mm mortar impacted within the pit, killing both ind. instantly. WIA: Pfc Martin Butler, B1-77 ; Sp4 Joseph A. Gatto, D 1-5; Sp4 Carl Bahnlien, A 1-5; Sp4 Jesus

Jimenez, A 1-5; Sp4 Terrance Brain, A 1-5." Attachment to Journal: B Co. WIAs [lists thirteen by initials and nature of wounds, only].

29 August 1969, 1st Air Cavalry Division General Order 10571, Purple Hearts for Wounds received: 24 Aug. Sp4 Ronald C. Biaisdell ; 25 Aug, D 1-5 Sgts John P. Roland and Tyson W. Caitano, Sp4s Jerry E. Wilson, Edward F. Reddek Jr. and William D. Gahacyn, Pfc's James R. Neely and Benito L. Alba Jr.; 26 Aug. Sgts Henry W. Dickinson, Elvin C. Jackson and Jack D. Morrison, Sp4s William C. Scott, Carl B. Bahnlein II, Joseph A. Gatto, Jeses R. Jiminez and Terrence M. Brain, and Pfc Michael S. Asbury ; 27 Aug 1LT Dale D. Koonce, Sgt David T. Widey [sp] and Pfc Paul R. Wagers.

31 August 1969, 1-5 Battalion Journal: "...0410, D Co...several trip flares set off by small arms fire and B-40 rocket...enemy evaded N. E. some 600 meters, again engaged by 1-6 element w/claymore and smf. One friendly KIA, Pfc John A. Polefka, WIAs, Stroh, McCoy and Adams -. Five NVA KIA and 1 NVA WIA."

1 September 1969, 1-5 Battalion Journal: A Co, 4 WIA, no names; 5 NVA KIA.

3 September 1969, 1-5 Battalion Journal; 0355: "A Co 21 ele reports having movement. 0720: "A Co: A medevac was requested at 0645 hrs for 01 litter case. Individual was injured when A Co sprung an ambush...in response to heavy movement; a doctor and blood requested. the ind has fragmentation wounds. Medevac completed at 0710 hrs. 0800: "A Co 6 readout on 21 element. 21 ele blew their TT and received return fire. The 21 leader was hit in back by a red tracer and came out the front. A Co 6 thought the size of the enemy was about 30-40 ind." 0830: "65 Relay: Ind who was wounded in action in A Co became a line 1 [died]. Name; Cruz, Tony, E-5. It is not available as to what ind was wounded by, an autopsy will have to...determine cause of death...Ind died enroute [not so]." 1230: "GM6 : Readout on A Co contact...At 0706 medevac 14 picked up ind at 0710 was taken to Quan Loi...Dr pronounced DOA. The type of wound was frag wound to chest. Do not know if friendly or hostile."

4 September 1969, 1-5 Battalion Journal: 2201, C Co, 2 WIA, while on bunker guard, mortar short round, last of fifteen rounds fell short, WIA Millard Layne and Mason Sims."

5 September 1969, 1-5 Battalion Journal: "0305, LZ Eagle 1 taking incoming...8 to 10 mortar and 1 120 rocket, 4 WIA, Stanford and Eigel-, all frag wounds."

7 September 1969, Battalion Journal; 1932: "D Co reports one indiv wounded at 1825 hrs in stomach due to an accidental discharge of an old 45 pistol found in the rubble...man who found the weapon was trying to unjam it when it accidentally went off...Casualty: John L. Erford [Toledo, Ohio]...man who shot [him], Edward P. Woll.

Chapter Sixteen

YOUR NUMBERS ARE UP

On September 9 at Phuoc Vinh, Chaplain Scott announced he was transferring me from the infantry before "you are killed. You've used up all your 'numbers'."

"But, sir," I reasoned, pleaded, "I'm just at the point where my reflexes and skills improve my chances of survival."

Chaplain Scott, after putting up with my begging for a few minutes, promised to reconsider the transfer. But alas, during an afternoon meeting the same day, my finely honed survival reflexes betrayed me and brought Scott's reconsideration to a screeching halt. I sat in a circle in company with a dozen or so other chaplains. We were toward the front in the Division Chapel, between the altar rail and the pews. Each pew had hinged kneelers, rails used by Catholics and some other high-church denominations, which usually were turned up when not in use.

I came late to the meeting and reluctantly took the only chair available, which left me with my back to the pews and front door. Doors to my back tense me up.

During the meeting, a kneeler fell to the concrete floor with a bang. Most of the chaplains present seemed not even to notice the sharp crack. But as I left my chair, spinning toward the "threat," I noted a couple of them glanced over their shoulder in mild surprise, not at the noise, but at my reaction. "It's just a kneeler, Claude," laughed one of the chaplains.

"That's it, Claude. You are moving. Pick any available assignment, so long as it isn't infantry," said Chaplain Scott. My fine reasoning and heartfelt pleas fell on deaf ears from that moment on.

The non-infantry positions open or opening included the 8th Engineers, an aviation battalion and the 1-9 Cavalry Squadron. Without hesitation, I chose the 1-9 Cav because it was a combat unit, perhaps the most famous battalion-size unit in Vietnam, even though it operated out of forward-rear area base camps. Most importantly, from my perspective each of the three 1-9 Cav air-cavalry troops—same as companies in infantry battalions—had a platoon of infantry.

Chaplain Scott introduced me to my replacement, Chaplain (Captain) James Thompson, and allowed me a few days to introduce him and say goodbye to the 1-5 Cav. I felt very anxious. Thompson was quiet and nice enough, but I sized him up with the critical subjectivity of a father appraising a suitor to his favorite daughter's hand, not very generously. *Will Thompson feel about my men as I do?* Still, I yielded to the inevitable and took him under my wing, intent on taking at least a week to introduce him around the battalion. Rasmussen tried to block the transfer. His efforts were futile, as I expected they would be.

On September 10, I took Chaplain Thompson to LZ Eagle One and introduced him to Lieutenant Colonel Rasmussen and the TOC personnel. Ten minutes later, we attended a change-of- command ceremony and congratulated Captain Paul H. Reese upon his assumption of command of Echo 1-5, call sign Big Sioux Six.

About thirty minutes later, at 1240 hours, several explosions on the north perimeter interrupted visiting between Chaplain Thompson, the senior medical NCO, the battalion surgeon and me. The medic-sergeant and I dashed to the scene of the explosions.

Smoke billowed from a berm-protected pit as we broke from between the bunkers near the north perimeter, where enemy munitions had been collected and stowed following a recent attack on the firebase. Two bloody, mud-covered men were writhing in pain. They lay where the blast had thrown them, some 20 to 30 feet from the smoldering pit.

Fearful that the whole pit would explode, others were fleeing or backtracking quickly away from the pit and from the two men lying in the road, even as we came on the scene.

Splitting apart without conscious coordination, the medic and I each ran to one of the wounded troopers. As I hit the ground by the farthest soldier, I saw over my left shoulder that the medic was shielding Captain Reese with his own body. Quickly then, with the help of several men who had turned back when the medic and I arrived, we placed Sergeant Perra of Charlie 1-5 and Captain Reese on litters and hustled them away from the still-smoldering pit. I vaguely recall that the medic and I each carried a folded litter during our dash to the scene.

Paul Reese was wounded a half an hour into his new command. Sergeant Perra, whose company had base security, had been escorting Captain Reese on his first inspection of perimeter security. The two were apparently investigating a trace of smoke coming from the munitions pit when some of the dud shells or rockets exploded.

We hustled Reese and Perra onto Rasmussen's C&C chopper and the medic and I accompanied them to the 15th Medical Clearing Station at Quan Loi. Captain Reese was obviously the more seriously wounded, with a leg blown off and one eye gone. Perra had multiple shrapnel, debris and blast wounds, and internal chest injuries.

The 1-5 Cav's medical NCO and I helped the doctors and medics at the clearing station until Reese and Perra were stabilized. Reese had quickly lost consciousness, but Perra stayed awake and alert through all sorts of painful lifesaving procedures—slashed arms to expose veins for IV's, a hole in the right side to admit a large drainage tube, and so forth.

I'd often seen the tube-in-the-side procedure, but never when it took all the strength of two doctors to push the tube between the ribs, while four men pushed from the other side to keep Perra on the operating table. Perra endured this without benefit of anesthesia. I've no idea what Chaplain Thompson did during this emergency or what he thought about it. He never said.

The next day, September 11, I began Chaplain Thompson' introduction and my good-byes in earnest. We began with visits to the 93rd and 24th Evacuation Hospitals, where we checked on Reese and Perra.

Reese was conscious, barely. Perra was wide-awake and overjoyed see-ing us. "I owe my life to Chaplain Newby. He threw himself between me and the ammo pile and got me out alive," Perra said to a doctor standing nearby. Captain Reese died soon after this visit.

Next, we flew to LZ Kelly at Loch Ninh, where we landed on its PSP (perforated steel plating) covered airstrip at about 1600 hours. From Kelly we flew northwest to a field location where Delta 1-5 was co-located and operating with a mechanized company—APC-mounted infantry. The companies were set up in the southeast corner of a large clearing, between sections of old rubber trees, and very close to the massive NVA sanctuaries in Cambodia.

A cold, steady rain had been falling all day, and the red clay had been churned into a morass by the metal treads of the APCs. Chaplain Thompson was miserable from the start, but became downright dis-couraged when, following introductions to the company commander, we started digging our foxhole. Chaplain Thompson hadn't had time to acclimatize. Soaked and mud-covered as we were, he was in for a very miserable and chilling night.

The next morning, the infantry and mechanized companies split up. The APCs moved off to the east and Captain Nishioka's Delta 1-5 moved to a rubber tree-covered knoll just south of the position where we had spent the night. We intended to stop on the knoll just long enough to conduct a worship service under the cover of the rubber trees, at Nishioka's request.

The company stopped about 200 feet into the trees and established a temporary perimeter. Cloverleaf patrols went out to check the area on the east, south and west sides of the knoll. We'd been there only a few minutes when I got a strong impression that we were being watched. To Captain Nishioka, I said, "I recommend we not bunch up here for a service because the NVA are close and they have us in their sights."

Nishioka agreed and told his RTO to have the platoon leaders recall their patrols and get ready to move out. Thus, I maintained my perfect record of never having a worship service interrupted by an enemy attack. We also avoided taking heavy casualties among troopers gathered to worship.

Moments after Nishioka recalled the patrols, one of them made contact with an NVA unit. The patrol had come in behind the NVA unit as it was moving in to attack us on the knoll. The resulting firefight prompted us to dive for cover in very old weed-and spider-choked trenches that ran among the rubber trees—just in time, too.

We'd barely gotten in the trenches when other NVA elements swept the knoll with a heavy volume of 30-caliber machine gun and AK-47 fire. Moments later, we cringed at the sound of mortar shells leaving NVA tubes about 500 meters to our southwest—the trenches would provide us no protection from mortars burst above us in the rubber trees. Unexplainably, the mortar shells exploded harmlessly among the buttoned-down APCs that by then had reversed course in response to the heavy gunfire and were rushing to our aid.

The mechanized company took but moments getting back to the clearing we had all just left, where the APCs got on-line and charged toward our position on the knoll, with jumpy trigger fingers at the ready.

Again, the drainage trenches were our salvation, because another spattering of small-arms fire drove us back under cover. At that moment, a trooper waved at the approaching APC's crews to mark our perimeter. A 50-caliber machine gun on the nearest APC responded to the wave with a burst of fire. Sixteen M-60 and seven more 50-caliber machine gunners joined in immediately, and for a moment that seemed much longer, the slower chump, chump, chump of eight 50-caliber machine guns and the faster tat-tat-tat of sixteen M-60s resounded over us as thousands of hot bullets swept our knoll. None was hurt by the NVA and friendly fire that swept our position, thanks to those trenches and the sniper fire that drove us into them!

After the commanders got the friendly fire stopped—which didn't take long—the Mech Company Commander opted to stick around and cover us while we withdrew into jungle across and east of the clearing, rather than pursue the NVA.

We dug in among the trees at the edge of the same clearing we'd tried to sleep in the previous night. Chaplain Thompson and I conducted small-group, small-target, worship services and visited troopers for the rest of the day, to the accompaniment of frequent sniper bullets cracking and the pop of an enemy mortar shell fired from behind the knoll we'd just vacated. For some reason, the NVA shells fell on a Vietnamese Popular Force (PF) unit that was two klicks from us, though we offered a more lucrative target.

"Is it always like this?" Chaplain Thompson asked.

"No, not always. Sometimes it is rough," I answered truthfully, rubbing it in a bit. I wanted Chaplain Thompson ready to care for "my" grunts.

Delta 1-5 linked up with the mechanized company again the next morning, September 13, and we rode atop APCs back to the airstrip at Loch Ninh. Chaplain Thompson left me there and returned to LZ Eagle One. But before he departed, I arranged with him for me to return to the battalion for a day or two each month "to give you a break from the stresses," *and give me an excuse to return to my battalion.* According to LTC Ronald Rasmussen and several troopers,

Meanwhile, I joined Bravo 1-5, which was about to leave Loch Ninh, for one final mission with the battalion, as I supposed. We left Loch Ninh atop the same APCs I arrived on. The NVA mortared us half an hour later as we rode north-northwest toward Cambodia. Fortunately the mortar shells fell too short to force us into the APCs. We stayed atop the armored personnel carriers (tracks), suspecting the NVA were trying to drive us inside before they opened fire with rocket-propelled grenades. No experienced foot soldier wanted to be caught inside a thin-skinned APC should an RPG hit it.

After a few kilometers riding atop the tracks, we dismounted and the mechanized company departed. Bravo 1-5 patrolled to the west, with air scouts from the 1-9 Cav screening ahead of us in the face of sporadic 51-caliber anti-aircraft fire.

That afternoon we spotted NVA pacing us from the front. They were still there when we stopped and dug in for the night. While some of us dug, others kept watch on several NVA soldiers as they worked through the rubber trees row-by-row to within about 150 meters of our perimeter. The troopers fired at the NVA several times, but the NVA simply stepped behind trees or pulled back when the grunts pushed toward them, only to move closer when we returned to our perimeter. Apparently, these NVA soldiers were intent on staying close to us, correctly assuming they'd be safer from our artillery and gunships. Not once did these NVA return fire or snipe at us. They just stayed close and watched in silence, like they were taunting us to draw us out beyond our rapidly developing night defensive perimeter.

All night we waited for the attack we were sure would come. However, the closest thing to an attack was NVA mortars being fired from about 500 meters to the east, along our back trail. Those rounds, however, exploded farther away, perhaps on the mechanized company that was still out there somewhere.

Captain Copley's company broke camp at dawn and patrolled to the west until the afternoon. They stopped after we crossed a narrow, chest-deep, north-to-south running stream. Beyond the stream, we passed through a thin line of trees and thick underbrush into a wedge-shaped stretch of rubber trees. The rubber trees were bordered by jungle on three sides and very near to Cambodia. The clearing was about a 35 meters wide on the north end spread to about 400 meters wide on the south, and was about one kilometer long, with a slight rise in elevation to the southwest.

This afternoon was like the previous one in that the NVA crept close as we dug in near the narrow end of the patch of rubber trees. They came out of the jungle to the west. While out alone chopping logs for overhead cover, I spotted an NVA soldier about 30 or 40 feet away. Unbelievably, he just stood there next to a tree and watched me work. Not having many options, I kept a wary eye on him and continued chopping.

The LPs went out at twilight and we settled down for another night of waiting to be attacked. Some of the CP members settled down to rest and sleep without any apparent regard for where they laid down in relation to their foxholes. I suggested to them, "Always lie with your head oriented toward your foxhole. Then when incoming jars you awake, you'll automatically scoot into it without losing precious seconds getting oriented."

"I'm always oriented. I'll beat you into the hole when the shooting starts tonight," said one of the CP members, with a chuckle.

Some members of the CP group rearranged their sleeping positions as I advised. Attack was certain tonight, this near Cambodia, with our exact location known to the NVA.

At 2130 hours, dozens of mortar rounds began thumping from tubes in the jungle about 200 meters to our west. Instantly, I was in our hole, where the medic and an RTO had arrived even sooner. Moments later, my focus on a trembling trooper beneath me was broken by the noise of someone scurrying about in the darkness, bouncing off rubber trees and cursing, "where in h— is the d— foxhole?"

That individual, who shall remain anonymous, finally made it into a foxhole. He would have been too late had not the shells burst on a different unit farther away. All was quiet after that until just before dawn.

In the predawn gray on September 14, a whispered message came over the radio from troopers on the south side of the perimeter. "Beau coup gooks coming at us through the rubber!"

"It's too dark to see movement. You're seeing shadows, not gooks," someone responded.

The troopers on the line knew better. A trooper opened fire with his M-14 rifle and the attack was on.

Through the mist and dawn's early light charged about 100 NVA soldiers. Courageously, foolishly, the NVA charged across hundreds of yards of almost open ground beneath the rubber trees. From the south they came. Most were firing AK-47s from the hip without pausing, while others paused only long enough to aim and fire B-40 rockets from the shoulder. The ground inside our perimeter shook and trembled with the explosions of incoming rockets.

From well-placed and protected foxholes, the grunts met and repelled the attack with withering defensive fires laid down by small arms, M-60 machine guns and recoilless rifles. Accurate enemy mortars entered the fight too late for NVA purposes. Their shells began exploding in our midst about the time the attack began to falter. The mortars were no more effective against us than the ground assault had been, though shrapnel wounded three troopers on LP duty who had no overhead cover.

"Medic!" cried one of the wounded troopers, loudly enough to be heard over the din and tumult of exploding mortars and rockets.

Captain Copley and I quickly reached the wounded troopers amid bursting mortar shells. Fortunately, the barrage was tapering off. Upon finding that the troopers were only slightly wounded, we waved the medic back and withdrew with the wounded to our foxholes. That's when the second wave of the NVA attack came.

The second wave displayed much less enthusiasm and lots more respect for us. The charge fizzled out well short of where the first attack had stopped.

ARA choppers arrived and pounded the NVA mercilessly as they withdrew from the second attack. Our M-60 machine guns added to the retreating NVA soldiers' woes with devastating, tracer-marked grazing fire.

One by one, the troopers stopped shooting. We watched silently as NVA soldiers carried their dead and wounded across our front into the jungle, like ducks in a shooting gallery. It seemed that these young Americans empathized with their enemy for just a moment. These NVA impressed me for their courage, but not for good sense. *Surely, despite all their courage, they are not of the caliber of fighters we've faced the past days and months. Perhaps they just arrived from the north and have unseasoned leaders.* These were certainly some of the most brazen, unpredictable and seemingly uncoordinated NVA I'd ever seen.

It was suggested that these NVA mistook us for a Vietnamese PF or ARVN unit, a fatal miscalculation, if true. It was hard to imagine them attacking us the way they had, otherwise.

Even considering all this, I couldn't understand why the NVA attacked across a kilometer of relatively open terrain when the jungle offered concealment to within thirty meters of the west and east sides of our perimeter. Why did their supporting mortars delay until it was too late to influence the outcome of the attack? Often I'd seen the NVA act very courageously, but never this foolishly.

Though we confirmed only six enemy dead, sometime called "step-ons," NVA losses were heavy and would have been worse, had the troopers not withheld their fire while the NVA carried away at least as many casualties as they left behind.

It was a credit to Copley's integrity that he didn't pad the after-action report with *probable* enemy casualties. One could call our light casualties miraculous—only the three on an LP—especially considering that a foxhole took a direct hit by a rocket, and the rubber trees inside our perimeter bled white on all sides from hundreds of shrapnel cuts.

After beating off the NVA attacks, we linked up with an ARVN unit that had come to reinforce us. Next, we moved eastward, back across the stream. Then, circling to the right, we crossed back over the stream and searched the area from which the NVA had attacked us, then dug in for the night in an overgrown, probably long-forgotten, cemetery. Most likely, we would have moved the FOB, had we arrived while there was enough daylight to make out where we were.

It was a very miserable night for everyone, especially me, for I had given my air mattress and poncho to a trooper who lost his during the dawn attacks. Like everyone else, I was soaked to the skin and covered head to foot with red clay and mud. No pretty sight, we.

Late the next afternoon I conducted a worship service for Bravo 1-5 and delivered my farewell address. Most of the company attended, as we were well concealed.

Heavy sadness descended over me when it came time to go. The sadness was heavier than what I felt when I left the 2-8 Cav troopers back September 1967. This was so partly because, I believe, I no longer had any hope that our sacrifices would make a difference in the future of Vietnam or that our service and the faithful sacrifices would be appreciated by the nation which had sent us here.

I arrived on LZ Ann during a driving, frigid rain. LZ Ann was a secondary 1-5 Cav firebase opened that day to bring artillery nearer where the companies were operating.

Chapter Notes:

10 September 1969, 1-5 Battalion Journal; 1240: "B Co: 36 reports an explosion in the ammo dump near them (B Co rear)...some individuals were wounded."
    1325: "Fm GM 6 : "An explosion occurred at 1240 hrs at Eagle I in an area used to secure unserviceable ammunition prior to its being destroyed. The exact cause...unknown. Big Sioux 6 and leader of Fence Post 46 were both

injured and evacuated to Q. L.", WIA, Captain Paul Reese, E Co and Sgt. Perra, C Co 4-6.

14 September 1969, 1-5 Battalion Journal: "1800, B Co at 0700, 3 WIAs, Pfc's Stephen Taylor, Darrell G. Harley and Guillemet or Bellimet."

0845, B Co was in contact with approximately 100 NVA.

Chapter Seventeen

THE "REAL" CAVALRY

I left LZ Ann after spending only a few hours there and reached Phuoc Vinh by late afternoon or early evening, where I dined in the Division Officers Mess in company with the chaplain I was replacing in the 1-9 Cav. My unkempt, mud-covered presence drew stares and frowns from many patrons, perhaps because I left red smears on everything I touched.

Following dinner, my predecessor showed me where to bunk, shower and so forth. A few minutes later, my wristwatch disappeared while I was showering with real, steady, hot water. That watch had served me well in the field.

Well, wristwatch or no, I'd entered a different war and joined a unique unit, the First Squadron, Ninth Cavalry Regiment or "First of the Ninth" (1-9 Cav), also known in an esprit sort of way by its members as the *Real Cav*. I'd joined a unit that didn't quite fulfill Chaplain Scott's intentions of removing me from the field and away from combat situations.

Between 17 and 19 September, I turned gear in to the 1-5 Cav, drew gear from the 1-9 Cav, and settled into a four-man room in the 1-9 Cav headquarters area. A major had commandeered my predecessor's private room and a bunkered-in cot. I never objected, though I could have because as a chaplain I required private accommodations for counseling. But after all those months in the open, I didn't relish sleeping in a crypt-like, sandbagged bunk.

For sleeping, writing letters, and so forth, I had an area about seven by ten feet, just inside the front door against the east wall of a north-facing building. From my bed, a real cot, I looked out on a small quadrangle and beyond to the revetments which protected the Cobras, LOH, and Huey choppers of Headquarters and Charlie Troops, 1-9 Cav. The pilot on the other side of the door from me had a battery-powered Sony television set. An officers club, the unit's very own, was around the west end of the building. Yes, I'd definitely entered a different war.

Regular infantrymen and enemy alike recognized and respected the 1-9 Cav. One day in the fall of 1969 a pink team was flying in the vicinity of abandoned LZ Becky when the LOH crew spotted something that had not been there the day before. The NVA had pinned a sign to a tree. It read, "Welcome, Scouts, to battle."

On my third day with the 1-9 Cav, September 20, I conducted my first official duty, a memorial service for an infantryman—a Blue Platoon member—who had been killed by friendly fire. Afterward, the troop commander said this was the best memorial service he'd ever attended.

LTC James W. (Pete) Booth commanded the 1-9 Cav. Company-type units were called troops. The squadron consisted of a headquarters troop, three air cavalry troops, and one motorized troop. Additional assets included the divisional long-range patrol (LRRP) or H Company, 75th Rangers, and the 62nd Infantry Platoon (Combat Trackers [tracker-dog teams]). And the 98th, 151st, and 545th Transportation Detachments—helicopter mechanics—were each attached to one of the air cavalry troops to keep the birds in the air. During my time with the 1-9 Cav, its Headquarters Troop, Charlie Troop and Delta Troop were co-located at Phuoc Vinh, as was the H Company, 75th Ranger Company. The 62nd Infantry Platoon (combat trackers and their dogs) were at Tay Ninh with Apache Troop, and Bravo Troop was at Quan Loi.

Each of the identically organized and equipped air Cav troops had a complement of scout crews, cobra crews, and a platoon of infantry. The infantry platoons were known throughout the Division and Vietnam as the "Blues."

Delta Troop usually patrolled roads around the base camp, set ambushes, and provided ground security to motorized convoys.

The Blues were true infantrymen. They regularly carried out very dangerous missions for which they were often inadequately armed. But unlike typical infantrymen, Blues spent most of their nights in camp sleeping on cots, taking warm showers, taking in movies, partying in clubs, or whatever they wished. The Blues were generally credited with the second-highest number of enemy killed of any units in the war, second only to the 1-9 Cav aero-cav teams.

Before the introduction of the Cobra into the unit, machine gunners on Huey gunships were credited with being the most lethal American weapon in the war. The crew chiefs on the LOH quickly took over that distinction. On the LOH the crew chief, also known as the "torque," served as both crew chief and door gunner. Without question, the LOH crews' life expectancy was shortest of any in the division, except for infantry point men and perhaps grunts who happened to be following NVA commo wires.

In my time with the 1-9 Cav, the primary aerial scouting and fighting element of each troop was the pink team. A pink team consisted of a LOH and a Cobra Gunships. Fighting platoons were designated by color in Troops A, B, and C: infantry was Blue Platoon, scouts were White Platoon, and guns were Red Platoon. Red (guns) and white (scouts) equal pink. Thus, a team made up of at least one each gunships and scout bird was designated as a Pink Team.

During pink-team missions, the LOH flew near the earth to seek out the enemy and draw fire while the Cobra followed at a higher altitude. Sometimes, to cover distance or to arrive on top of the enemy before he could react, a pink-team LOH skimmed the trees at breathtaking speed. More often the LOH maintained an almost leisurely pace, the better to spot enemy sign and draw fire.

On-station over an objective or an area from which they received fire, the scout choppers moved slowly back and forth, sometimes hovering and even flying backward or sideways to blow foliage off trails so they could look for tracks. They even flew beneath the long branches of trees for the same reason. Often, from the ground with the 1-5 or 2-12 Cav, I'd been impressed as these little choppers buzzed about, dashing forward, backward and sideways like oversized bumblebees.

Normally a pilot or crew chief stayed with a pink team for six months, unless they volunteered to stay longer. Their chances during the six months were by my estimation about one in four of being killed, two in four of going home seriously wounded, and only one in four of going home whole or only slightly wounded. Those scout crewmembers that survived for six months tended to seek other duties for the second half of their tours. Because of the high mortality rate, I would conduct memorial services almost weekly in each of the Air Cav troops.

Notwithstanding the high casualty rates and almost daily contact with the enemy, the aircrews were distinctly different from typical infantry. I credit this difference in large part to the types of personalities drawn to flying and to their almost nightly return to the comforts of base camp life. Religious attitudes were distinctly low-key in the 1-9 Cav, compared to regular infantry. In the field, troopers flocked to worship services at almost every opportunity. In the 1-9 Cav, troopers practically shunned worship services, at least until they got to know me. Well, I knew how to become acquainted with my new troops— share their life and go with them on missions, except LRRP and tracker -dog missions, of course.

Early during my new assignment I watched would-be rangers, all volunteers, running around the airstrip at Phouc Vinh in the intense afternoon heat; they were each laden with a rock-filled rucksack and other equipment. Those young men would soon be going out on very dangerous and difficult long-range patrol missions, provided they survived two weeks of training. Two of those rangers that I visited may have been Kregg P. J. Jorgenson of Seattle and Jerry Clayton. of Downey, California. Both men had arrived in country in September— Jorgenson on the same day that I signed into the 1-9 Cav, September 17. Our paths would cross again.

Church attendees or not, the 1-9 Cav certainly supported my efforts. Each Sunday I had a helicopter and crew dedicated for religious support operations. With those assets I routinely conducted Sunday services across the 1st Cav AO, from Phuoc Vinh (Headquarters, Charlie and Delta Troops) to Quan Loi (Bravo Troop) and Tay Ninh (Apache Troop).

Between and after services at these key bases, I flew wherever else I needed to in the line of duty, which included ecclesiastical meetings and hospital visits in Long Binh and Saigon. SP4 Harold Lewis came with the assignment. He was LDS and a draftee from the Denver, Colorado Police Department. Lewis usually accompanied me on these Sunday rounds. Overall in this new assignment I think I had more freedom to move according to my own priorities than any officer in Vietnam, in part because Lieutenant Colonel Booth trusted me to do my job as best I could.

The basic pattern of the demands of duty became evident during my first week in the 1-9 Cav. As mentioned earlier, I began my new duties on September 20 with a memorial service for a soldier that was accidentally killed by a ranger. The next day, following my first Sunday services for headquarters, my departure from Phuoc Vinh was delayed because the chopper assigned to me was shot down. Eventually, in another chopper, I visited Tay Ninh and Dau Tieng, visited wounded Blues of Bravo Troop at Quan Loi, canceled worship services twice because the troops were in contact, and attended an LDS service and spent the night at Quan Loi.

On September 22, I traveled around the division AO making acquaintances with 1-9 Cav officers, noncommissioned officers, and troops. Over the next few days I flew to Tay Ninh and Quan Loi for worship services. Services were canceled at both locations because the troops were unexpectedly inserted into the jungle. One platoon went in to secure a downed aircraft and the other to rescue a team of LRRPs that was fighting off the NVA. At Tay Ninh that day, an Air Force FAC pilot invited me to accompany him on a mission and watch him orchestrate close air support (Air Force support) of infantry and bombings of enemy targets; he was shot down and killed before I could accept the invitation.

On September 24, I awoke on someone else's cot at Tay Ninh. At 1000 hours I conducted a worship service with twelve men in attendance. After the service I played chess with a pilot, then flew to Phuoc Vinh and attended evening meetings. I became frustrated because I couldn't get a flight to the hospital to visit the crew of a Bravo Troop scout LOH that had been shot down to the east of Quan Loi. The LOH had crashed into the bamboo, promptly broken off all four main rotor blades, which kept the destruction down, and come to rest on its nose, tilted over so that the rear end of the skids pointed upward and angled forward. A nearby LRRP team hurried to the crash site and found the pilot, WO Russel, with both legs broken and his knees being pushed into the ground by the weight of the chopper and crew. Four rangers simply lifted the chopper up while the fifth one pulled Russel out of the wreck.

At 0745 hours, September 25, I visited wounded troopers at Bien Hoa. Later at Lai Khe I was able to visit Warrant Officer Russel and Sergeant Fasthorse -. SP4 Early, the most seriously wounded crewmember of the LOH, had been evacuated to Saigon.

Back at Phuoc Vinh, I petitioned Booth to fly me to Saigon. We arrived there too late again to see Early. He - was already on a Medevac flight to the states. Late at night we returned to Phuoc Vinh where I fell asleep on my own cot.

The next day, September 26, I deployed with the Charlie Troop Blues to LZ Buttons where we remained on standby the whole day. I used the time to conduct services, and to visit and counsel with the Blues. Seldom did they have uninterrupted days like this one. At Phuoc Vinh for the evening, I attended a scripture study class.

On September 27 I accompanied the Bravo Troop Blues on an insertion to recover key components from Russel, Fasthorst, and Early's LOH. We followed preparatory artillery and ARA fire into a small LZ, then made our way through giant bamboo for two hundred meters to where we found the chopper. Anyone flying directly overhead would have seen the skids and underbelly of the aircraft.

That evening I attended an obligatory *hail and farewell*, where Booth jokingly introduced me as one whose sanity might be in question because I willingly accompanied the Blues into the field. Booth would make up for the less-serious part of the introduction in August 1995 by introducing me a former "real Cav" man, "the bravest man I know"—quite a compliment, coming from a former combat commander of the famous 1-9 Cav. Thus ended what was probably the quietest, least eventful week during my time with the 1-9 Cav, a week of unusually low American casualties.

At 0800 hours, September 28, I conducted a worship service for Headquarters, 1-9 Cav. Booth missed the service because of operational demands, a rare omission for him. Later at Quan Loi I conducted another service for three men, Harold Lewis, the Bravo Troop executive officer, and me. Having reached Tay Ninh, via II Corps and Phuoc Vinh, I reorganized the LDS group and offered an evening service for Apache Troop, to which no one came, due to poor communications and a last-minute mission, I supposed.

A couple of times during the first half of this tour, I had tried to visit my old unit, the 2-8 Cav, which at the time operated out of LZs Caroline and Becky in a nasty area north-northeast of Tay Ninh, between the Black Virgin Mountain and Cambodia. I visited LZ Caroline once shortly after its perimeter had been overrun by the NVA, but found no familiar faces. With the 1-9 Cav, I often flew over LZ Becky, which was abandoned and flooded by monsoon rains. On 29 September, upon learning the 2-8 Cav was pulling palace guard, I volunteered to augment its religious support during the palace guard stint.

It was during this period, I believe, that I visited Sergeant Major Wiley L. Watson, formerly First Sergeant of Alpha 2-8 Cav. Watson and I talked of acquaintances in common, rehashed shared experiences from 1967, and reported on what we'd each been doing since. Watson, I realized, felt out of place operating at battalion level, which I understood.

I spent the night of September 29 with Bravo Troop at Quan Loi, where I slept in the TOC. Next morning I held a worship service that was attended by twenty-three Blues, almost the whole platoon. The increased attendance suggested that the men of the 1-9 Cav were beginning to accept me. On Sunday, October 19, I conducted four services around the 1-9 Cav AO, with between eighteen and thirty-seven present in each service.

Other indicators of acceptance included invitations to go along on operations and to learn to fly. Frequently I got to handle the controls of a LOH from the left copilot or observer seat. I became adequate at flying straight and making gradual turns and changes in altitude, but never advanced to landings, which skill the pilots liked observers to have. Just in case.

In the 1-5 Cav, I'd counted off months beginning with March 11, the day I joined the unit. Now, in the 1-9 Cav, I counted off months from March 1, the day I left the states to begin this tour. Though I never counted the days, I was conscious of them, especially with the drawdown of American troops, which President Nixon had begun. Consequently I was ripe for rumors like most everyone else.

Word had spread throughout South Vietnam that each soldier's tour would be reduced so many days for each month he completed in-country. According to the formula described, I might be home by late January 1970. The "word" was everywhere, even in semi-official unit newspapers, until the bubble burst.

A reporter, according to the *Stars and Stripes*, asked a senior official at MACV or USARV to confirm significant tour curtailment based on months served. He quoted the official in essence as saying, "I'm sure the curtailment is official, though I haven't seen the order. I'll get back to you." Well, no such orders existed, the embarrassed official discovered. So applying his snooping skills, the journalist tracked the "word" to its source.

In northern South Vietnam, in or near Danang, two rear-echelon types, while seated on commodes, discussed the traditional source of Army rumors—the latrine. The discussion led to a plot to start a rumor and see how far it went. While their success surpassed their wildest expectations, it worked extreme cruelty on thousands, especially those lonely grunts in the field. As the rumor spread throughout Vietnam, it raised and then dashed the hopes of thousands of lonely soldiers, marines, sailors and airmen, and their loved ones. It also messed up wedding and planned conception dates and such. This was a true "latrine rumor" in every way, as such were known in less delicate terms.

Though I've intertwined discussion of family affairs with this combat tour much less than I did for 1966-67, Helga and the children always supported me, inspired me, pulled at me, and occasionally worried me. Often, I considered what price each family member would pay for my long absences during critical years in the children's development. Would these absences during James' and Jeannie's early teen years deprive them of an essential role model and maybe stunt their development—social, emotional and spiritual? *If I survive only to see my children become casualties of this war, is the price too high?*

To perhaps limit the damages and help the older children progress, I frequently sent each of them their own personal letters and reel-to-reel tapes, crammed full of love, encouragement, and counsel. Jeannie yet has some of the tapes I sent her, she says. Helga gathered the family around to listen to the first tape that I sent them. This was five-year-old Brenda Lynette's first experience with reel-to-reel tapes. So, recognizing my voice, she stared closely at the machine and demanded, "Come out of there, Daddy!"

On October 3, I operated with the Charlie Troop Blues, which gave me a good opportunity to compare a Blue platoon to regular infantry. I found among the Blues a sincere respect for the regular infantrymen, tempered with pride in being Blues and a hint of gratitude that they were Blues, rather than regular grunts. The Blues, though, didn't really appreciate and understand the lot of regular troopers, though they came closer than most to doing so. But no one can appreciate the life of a regular grunt unless he has been in the field continuously for days and months on end. Regular grunts and company leaders generally respected the 1-9 Cav, though many in the field never knew the Blues existed.

Operationally, the Blues were well-disciplined in the jungle, all the time, I hoped. Man for man, a Blues platoon member carried much more weaponry and ammunition than a regular infantryman. Blue troopers could afford to do so because they seldom carried rations and survival gear to last them several days, as it was rare for them to stay overnight in the jungle or to hump farther than a kilometer during an operation. In addition to their personal and team weaponry the Blues usually had very good air support of both the logistical and firepower sort, dedicated and on-station.

Blues lived on the edge of the war with frequent dashes into the middle of it. Regular infantrymen lived in the middle of the war with all the perils, stresses, and strains that went with it. However, they usually experienced less-frequent periods of actual fighting. The Blues usually knew where they were going and had some idea what awaited them there—downed aircraft, hot LZ, and such. Regular grunts seldom knew what was ahead and the fighting, when it came, was usually unexpected and a total shock to their souls.

The regular infantryman's combat tour was a year—if he made it all the way—of near-total misery. He was always wet and muddy or hot and soaked with sweat, engulfed in the stench of unwashed clothing and bodies. Often he drank water that was "fortified" with dead polliwogs and leeches; and he was accustomed to finding leeches in unpleasant places on his person.

Several factors rendered the regular field troopers' existence incomparable to that of anyone else. These factors included carrying everything they needed on their backs; constant vigilance around the clock; unending danger; spirit-draining, backbreaking, and exhausting labor; and an existence almost devoid of such creature comforts as frequent baths, clean clothes, beds, and uninterrupted nights. They humped and dug every day. They pulled perimeter guard, OP duty, or ambush every night, no matter what else occurred. All this was all interspersed with intentional dashes into combat and those totally unexpected times of terror during firefights and ambushes by the enemy. And with all this, the regular infantrymen got few breaks even during occasional stints providing firebase security or palace guard. Exhaustion and sleepiness were the grunts' constant companions.

The infantryman came to the war alone, committed to a one-year tour. If he survived the first battle, he was accepted as a veteran. He lived in unrelenting stress, and endured unimaginable horrors. Often he would carry the bodies of killed or terribly wounded buddies, sometimes for hours until they could be flown from the field; there was no escape from close companionship with death and maiming. Nothing compares to the regular infantryman's existence in combat, not in the Army and not in life.

A *Stars and Stripes* article unintentionally helps explain the disparity between all other troops and regular infantry. The article, in praise of the support provided to American forces, bragged that 93 percent of all meals served to US forces in Vietnam were hot. The piece failed to mention that this statistic applied mostly to troops located well behind the infantry line companies or that C-rations constituted at least two-thirds of the meals eaten by the grunt. It didn't mention that "hots" served to men in the field frequently consisted of the likes of cold or lukewarm, often watery potatoes and stringy beef served from olive-drab, oval mermite (thermos) cans.

Though I have no statistics on awards, I expect a disparity because the regular grunt's valorous actions were seldom witnessed by anyone but his buddies, buddies just as exhausted as he, and as unlikely to find a moment's peace to write up recommendations for awards. His actions, even when noted and written up, frequently became lost between pen and the awards board, or were depreciated by those who suffered from poor memory or who had never known the infantryman's existence.

All too often in the regular infantry, witnesses to a trooper's valor carried that knowledge to an early grave or to a distant hospital where names, faces, and deeds of valor took second place to personal pains and medical concerns. Just as often, acts of heroism, which in other environs merited recommendation for a Silver Star or higher award, passed with little notice.

Another factor working against the interests of regular infantrymen was that recommendations had to pass through several layers of command for final approval, and paperwork could get lost at every step. In the 1-9 Cav, on the other hand, only the troop and squadron commanders stood between the trooper and General Casey, who had approving authority for most impact awards. Even here things sometimes went awry. Once Booth contacted a master sergeant in Awards and Decoration to ask why no awards had come down for about a month. The master sergeant explained that a storm had blown a large stack of recommendations out into a muddy field and he'd had no way to identify which ones were lost or to reconstruct them. There is no way to tell how many well-deserved awards got lost in situations like this—a lot of them for certain.

Other factors influencing the awards system included proximity to the *flagpole,* uninterrupted esprit between members of unique units like the 1-9 Cav, and operational relationships. For example, the Apache Troop Blues worked closely day after day with the same Apache Troop pink teams and liftships, especially the LOH crews. Almost daily the Blues and aviators got one another out of trouble. And each evening, with few exceptions, both Blues and aviators returned to base camp, where deeds of valor could be written up without the distractions of ambush duty, radio watch, and enemy probes against defensive positions just meters away. Also, the exploits of Blues and aviators were more likely to be observed by officers from higher echelons that knew who they were by name, even reputation.

The well-deserved reputation of the 1-9 Cav had a distinct effect on the number of individual awards recommended and approved. The 1-9 Cav was there at the beginning of almost every major battle and most minor skirmishes that the division got into. The troopers and aviators of the 1-9 Cav earned their reputation the hard way. They accounted for highest number of enemy killed and consistently sustained the most casualties of any American unit in the war.

Having said all this, I intend to take nothing away from the Blues, LRRPs, aircrews, and leaders of the 1st Squadron, 9th Cavalry. I salute them for - their outstanding and effective exploits. I salute the regular ground troopers in recognition of their mostly unsung valor and for all they endured, routinely, "above and beyond."

On October 3, upon returning from the insertion with the Charlie Troop Blues, I traveled to Saigon with Captain John Thomas Kalunki, where we visited USAF Chaplain (Captain) Robert Christiansen. Tom Kalunki and I had a private showing of "2001: A Space Odyssey," courtesy of Kalunki's contacts with the media. He was Assistant Information Officer for the 1st Cav. For dinner we dined on steak in company with Colonel McPhie (Air Force) and Paul Madsen. Afterward, Tom and I visited until 0140 hours. My path would cross Kalunki's often in years to come. For example, I piggybacked my 1981 master's thesis on one Kalunki did in the 1970s.

In 1994, emotional exhaustion and a vague sense of depression would weigh down on me when I transcribed my war journals and memories into the computer. Later, these same sensations arose as I attempted to turn my journals into an autobiographical account of the war years. These sensations and emotions were replays of those I endured, especially in the last half of my second tour, as it became obvious America was throwing away our sacrifices in Vietnam in exchange for President Nixon's promised *peace with honor.*

From this point on, I will touch on the highlights of those last months in Vietnam. By doing otherwise, I would be repeating much that Kregg Jorgenson, Matthew Brennan, and others have already chronicled.

On October 7, I rode for the first time in the *middle* seat on Lieutenant Colonel Booth's gunships. As I mentioned before, the Charlie-model Huey Gunships bristled with rockets, a mini-gun, a grenade launcher, and M-60 machine guns, and was more potent and versatile than the newer Cobra gunships which replaced most of them, in the view of many aviators.

The Charlie-model gunships were crewed by four men, a pilot, copilot, crew chief in the left door, and door gunner in the right door; the chief and door gunner each manned an M-60 machine gun. Behind the pilots, against the back of the passenger/cargo section, a jump seat reached from door to door. I sat in the middle of this seat during flights on the Charlie-Charlie, so I could see ahead between the pilots' heads with a clear view out the open left and right doors. Of course, in the 1-9 Cav I had my own aviator helmet and nomax (fire resistant) flight suit. I used the helmet so I could listen in on and take part in onboard communications, but never wore the nomax suits because I preferred jungle fatigues. I appreciated these rides because it was cool at higher altitudes, no matter how hot the weather, and in the Charlie-Charlie chopper I knew what was happening to the Blues and flight crews. As an added bonus, Pete Booth and his successor LTC Clark Burnett were good company, as were their crews.

On October 9, I flew with Booth and his crew, which consisted of Warrant Officer Danner - in the left copilot seat, door-gunner Godfrey, and Svafen, the crew chief. We intended to visit Tay Ninh. We were barely underway when we diverted to the scene of a downed scout LOH. Tay Ninh would have to wait.

October 10 began like a replay of the previous day. After spending the morning on administrative details, I took off with Booth to visit crewmembers that had been wounded the day before. On the way, we stopped briefly at Quan Loi and LZ Buttons, and again, the NVA interrupted our plans.

"We received a report that a slick ship with about eight men from Charlie 2-5 had been shot down and was burning in a small clearing north of LZ Buttons near the Song Be River on the south side. The call came just after we lifted off from LZ Buttons in my Charlie-Charlie, a C-model Huey Gunships. One of Major George O'Grady's Saber pink teams (Bravo Troop) was en route to provide danger-close support," said Booth.

In the situation that was developing, Booth would show his savvy and skill as a commander. It is as natural as breathing for a commander to try to get near the action so he can know what is happening and ensure that adequate support is provided to subordinate commanders and leaders. Consequently during the Vietnam War C&C helicopters tended to stack up in the air over extended engagements. In a matter of minutes, the battalion or squadron C&C would arrive and start circling the battle at, say, two thousand feet altitude. The brigade C&C would follow shortly to circle a thousand feet higher. Then the commanding general or one of his assistant commanding generals would circle higher still. Unfortunately some commanders got in the way instead of helping.

We arrived over the downed choppers just behind the pink team, and Booth immediately began showing that he could support the commander nearer to the ground without usurping his authority and responsibility. The men down there belonged to Major George O'Grady (Saber Six) and it was his AO. As the situation developed, Booth ordered in Charlie (Cavalier) assets and turned them over to O'Grady.

Then he moved Alpha (Apache) Troop assets into the area to stand by prepared to become OPCON to O'Grady, if needed.

Below us a mangled chopper burned in a small clearing. Several apparently dead bodies lay on the south side of the downed chopper, opposite from where rockets from the pink team Cobra were already exploding and where a continual stream of tracer rounds from the LOH was impacting. As we watched, the LOH took hits and crashed near the burning Huey. Three crewmembers quickly scrambled out of it and joined the surviving 2-5 Cav grunts and Huey crewmembers who were hugging the ground among their own dead.

A second Saber pink team arrived on-station and added the firepower of another LOH and Cobra to the support of the troopers on the ground. As I recall, Booth's Charlie-Charlie also contributed firepower at this time. However, he doesn't remember firing rockets then or later. Captain Lou Niles, then Platoon Leader of the Bravo Troop (Saber White) aero-scouts insists that Booth held off on firing his rockets until a later, critical point when no other gunships were on- station.

Booth continued: "The Saber Blues, led by Lieutenant Maurice (Mike) Murphy (call-sign Saber Blue) of Peach Tree City, Georgia were just seconds out, en route to attempt to secure the crash site and rescue the survivors. With two choppers down in the small clearing, the Blues would have to rappel in because there wasn't room for the Hueys carrying them to land. Hovering over or near the clearing so the Blues could rappel in was out of the question due to intense enemy small-arms, rocket and machine-gun fire from very close range. To make matters worse, the nearest clearing that might serve as an acceptable LZ was at least fifteen klicks away. Fortunately a very small clearing with two overlapping bomb craters in it was about one and a half klicks from the clearing that the Huey and LOH had gone down in. Unfortunately, though, the potential LZ was barely large enough for a Huey to land. Limbless trees stood like telephone poles around the craters. The Blues would have to rappel in and then tear their way through trackless jungle to reach the downed infantrymen and chopper crews.

"Saber pilot Kenneth Caudill of Oklahoma hovered his chopper just high enough above the clearing to ensure that the rotor blades

LTC James P. (Pete) Booth (pilot-3rd from left), Svafen (crew chief-front left), and others pose before his Charlie Model Huey gunship.
Phuoc Vinh, Fall, 1969

cleared the surrounding jungle. The chopper crew lowered four ropes, two from each side, and the first four Blues rappelled to the ground.

"The second set of four Blues, one being Lieutenant Murphy, was standing in the doors and hooking up to go down the ropes when the NVA opened fire. Suddenly the Huey tipped sharply to the left and crashed straight down into the

This Bravo 1-9 liftship in the clearing came under fire as Kenneth Caudill hovered it above the clearing. It crashed, pinning a Blue trooper beneath it and almost throwing Lieutenant Mike Murphy into the rotor blades. Near Song Be River, October 10, 1969

This Bravo 1-9 liftship in the clearing came under fire as Kenneth Caudill hovered it above the clearing. It crashed, pinning a Blue trooper beneath it and almost throwing Lieutenant Mike Murphy into the rotor blades. Near Song Be River, October 10, 1969

clearing. The momentum of the dip and crash almost threw Lieutenant Murphy up into the main rotor blade. In 1998 Murphy told me [Booth], 'It threw me up almost into the rotor. Still attached by the rope, I landed on my back across the hot transmission and engine. It was *hot!*'

"Hot was nothing compared to what happened to one of the two Blues dangling from the left door of the crashing chopper. The chopper landed on top of him and pinned him against the side of a crater or depression, promptly covering him with a growing pool of inflammable JP-4 aviation fuel.

"Quickly scrambling off the hot engine, Murphy took stock of the situation and scurried into a crater both for cover from heavy enemy small-arms fire and to communicate with his troop commander, Major George O'Grady, who was nearby in the air. Murphy knew the trooper pinned beneath the chopper had to be gotten out very quickly. He knew it wasn't possible to lift the ship off the man with the manpower available on the ground and that the volume of incoming enemy fire would render that impossible, even if they could. Rescue efforts were further complicated, he realized, because the downed chopper took up most of the tree-studded clearing.

"The two remaining Saber liftships returned to Quan Loi to pick up more Blues. Coming in at Quan Loi, one of the pilots flared his ships too steeply and drove the tail rotor into the ground. George O'Grady now had one liftship left.

"About that time, while circling the contact areas," Booth continued, "I made a wide left turn and saw the big red ball of the sun just touching the horizon to the west and starting to sink. Thinking that *this is going to be a very long night*, I ordered Major Treadway to send me every available ship and also his Cavalier © Troop) Blues. I also ordered Apache troop to deploy from Tay Ninh to Quan Loi and stand by on five-minute alert. Next, I called for all available Blue Max (ARA gunships) to help the Saber gunships keep the enemy off the men on the ground. The Cobras came and from then on one or more were almost constantly on-station to provide extremely close aerial rocket support to the troops.

"Fortunately, I had my artillery FO on board. He did a beautiful job of calling in and coordinating massive artillery. But as the commander there was nothing else I could do. If those pinned Blues, 5th Cav grunts, and aircrews were to be rescued, it would be up to individuals to take the initiative and do what American soldiers do when it becomes necessary. 'White-Six just let down and brought out two wounded,' radioed O'Grady. It was starting to happen."

It was happening on the ground too. While Murphy coordinated and worked the radio, four of the remaining Blues on the ground fought off the NVA and provided cover fire for the men pinned beneath the chopper. The other two Blues each grabbed a fire extinguisher from the downed chopper, threw themselves to the ground by their buddy who was pinned beneath it, and lay in the open ready to protect him if fire broke out. No doubt those two Blues knew that those fire extinguishers would be of little use if the fuel in the depression caught fire. They knew if this happened they would likely die with their trapped buddy in the resulting explosion. But that guy beneath the chopper, immersed in fuel, needed support—and he got it, despite the risks involved to those who gave it.

Captain Lou Niles carefully lowered his LOH over the bomb craters, down among the limbless trees, to hover motionless a few feet above the ground while wounded troopers were loaded on.

Niles explained. "I used my rotor blades to widen the hole for the chopper [by chopping branches and leaves off the trees that surrounded the clearing] and then hovered a few feet above the ground because there was no place to set down.

"Niles balanced one skid on a log and had his front seat gunner hold it steady," said O'Grady.

Niles continues, "The pilot of the slick ship leaped over a log with his arm above his head as he ran toward me. There was nothing I could do as I watched my rotor blades chop off his fingers. After the wounded were loaded on, I called over to Blue Six, 'What do you need?'

"'Chain saw and hydraulic jack,' Lieutenant Murphy called back."

Mike Hanlon, Niles' crew chief, stayed on the ground after helping load the wounded. Then he added his machine gun and a lot of ammunition to the defense of those in the small clearing. O'Grady said Niles left both crewmembers behind to join with the infantry in the clearing.

After lifting out of the clearing, Niles dropped the wounded at the 15th Med at Quan Loi. "Then I picked up the chain saw and hydraulic jack—part of a packet I had prepared for situations like this—and returned. Meanwhile, all the Cobras had expended their rockets, leaving a temporary lull in the danger close air support while they rearmed at LZ Buttons. You guys were the only ones with any rockets left. Pete made several very effective runs to keep the NVA off the downed crews, Blues, and Charlie 2-12 grunts until the Cobras returned. He literally pinned an NVA to a tree with one of his flechette rounds," said Niles.

From my position behind and between pilot and copilot, I watched the action and followed it over my helmet headset. Booth made several diving runs, each time placing flechette rounds where we hoped they would do some good without injuring our own. During one attack dive, I distinctly saw the rapid muzzle flashes of a heavy machine gun and several small arms that were firing at us. Mr. Danner -, the copilot, let go with a roaring, ripping burst of mini-gun fire a moment after I saw the flashes. The trajectory of the mini-gun's red tracer bullets showed that he was right on target. Booth, having failed to see the muzzle flashes and rising tracers, sharply rebuked Danner - for firing so close to American troops without a clear target. I keyed my microphone and assured him that we'd been receiving heavy fire, which took the heat off Danner -. That Booth never saw the muzzle flashes was understandable; he was fixated on the target he'd selected for our rockets while at the same time flying the chopper and avoiding hitting friendlies or becoming part of the target.

Meanwhile, Niles braved heavy NVA fire to reenter the clearing and deliver the chainsaw and hydraulic jack to the Blues. "On the ground some Blues and crewmembers started cutting down trees to expand the LZ while others attempted to free the two troopers by jacking up the chopper. The jack did not work, so they took one of the trees that had just been cut down and, using the jack as a fulcrum, they lifted the chopper high enough to pull out the fuel-soaked trooper," Niles said.

Next, while other ships extracted the 2-5 Cav and crews from the larger clearing, three Charlie Troop liftships took turns entering the slightly enlarged, hot LZ to lift out the Blues and downed liftship crew. It turned pitch dark as Warrant Officer Smith piloted the last bird up and out of the LZ. This story shows that when the commander has done all he can and can't figure out what else to do, some soldier will stand up and save the day," said Booth. It also shows that a tremendous amount of action can be squeezed into the few short minutes between when the sun touches the western horizon and full darkness. Heroics on and near the ground reversed a situation that had looked hopeless a few minutes before. Booth praised everyone who took part, especially Captain Lou Niles who saw what had to be done and did it, at extreme risk to his own survival.

According to O'Grady another Saber LOH was downed several hundred meters away and Niles also helped rescue that crew, still flying a helicopter that should have remained grounded in Maintenance.

Afterward Booth highly praised Major O'Grady for the way he handled the multi-faceted situation. O'Grady extolled the contributions of his artillery FO and Lou Niles. He considered recommending Niles for the Medal of Honor for his deeds that day. However, my sources said twenty-year-old Niles prevailed on O'Grady not to make the recommmendation because that would have meant the end of his time as Saber White—the scout platoon leader. Niles understood that 1st Cav policy required the removal from combat of anyone who was recommended for that award. General Shoemaker presented Niles with an impact award of the Silver Star instead. Everyone extolled the courage and conduct of Lieutenant Murphy and his Blues.

While the efforts of Niles and others saved the day for the 1-9 Cav, seven of the 2-5 Cav men died when that first chopper was shot down and during the subsequent fighting. All the 1-9 Cav aircrews and Blues survived, including the one who had been pinned beneath the liftship, though some were wounded.

Again we aborted our mission to visit the hospitals and returned to Phuoc Vinh, it being too late to continue on. That evening, a group of troopers and I listened to religious tapes that Helga had sent me. Attention shifts very rapidly for those who fight and serve from rear areas.

During a discussion of the events of October 10, 1969, Booth described Captain Niles as a fantastically daring and effective helicopter scout/fighter. Niles describes himself as a smart scout leader who applied good sense and tactics to survive and keep his men alive. "I detested the *kill* mentality that led to tactics that cost the lives of many young scout crewmembers. So, I established a school for scout pilots that candidates had to pass before they flew scouts in Saber Troop. None who completed the course were killed during my time as their leader—quite a change for you, Chaplain. No more weekly memorial services for Bravo Troop."

Though I wouldn't learn of it for another three days, Ted Pierce of Delta 1-5 had been dying nearby in the jungle while I was over our downed aircraft and casualties. Another trooper I knew, PFC Robert L. Lazarus of Honolulu, Hawaii, was among the dead troopers on the first Huey that went down in the larger clearing, I believe.

On October 11, I visited and conducted a worship service for Charlie 2-8 Cav, one of my old units. There were no familiar faces from 1966-67. Again, Booth and I were unable to visit the hospital, so I scheduled another tape-listening session. We finally reached the hospitals at Long Binh and Saigon on October 12.

At the Third Field Hospital in Saigon, I found Sergeant Elvin Jackson of Alpha 1-5. He was recovering from shrapnel wound to the right arm and malaria and soon would return to combat. Later, the wound would cripple him for life. No problem! The Veterans Administration would magnanimously grant Jackson a 10 percent disability, with the promise of an increase "when they cut the damn thing off."

That evening, following a worship service back at Phuoc Vinh, I filled two cassettes with words of wisdom for Helga and the children on a new cassette player/recorder.

October 15 brought reminders of the inherent dangers of helicopters, which some "experts" insist can't fly. "Because of combat losses, there will be no flights to Tay Ninh tomorrow," I was warned the night before. A ride came though, and I flew west about midmorning.

We were moving along nicely at about three or four thousand feet elevation, somewhere between Lai Khe and the Michelin Rubber Plantation. Suddenly the chopper went into an ear- popping, spiraling, almost vertical dive. That was scary enough, but inside my flight helmet and on the crew's faces, I heard and saw concern sufficient to create extra anxiety in me—a critical fire warning light glared on the instrument panel.

At the right moment, the pilot skillfully pulled the chopper out of the dive and into auto-rotation mode, and the skids thumped safely on the ground. We needed security fast. The regular door gunner was not aboard, so while the crew chief dashed off a hundred feet to the east with one M-60 machine gun, I went west with the other one.

Air cover and aircraft technicians soon arrived and diagnosed the problem. A relatively harmless short-circuit had necessitated the emergency landing. The trip to Tay Ninh would have to wait for another day. The hour forced us to return to Phuoc Vinh, where I wrote a message for inclusion in the *Cavalair*, the 1st Cav's newspaper. Then I turned my attention to administrative stuff. That's when I found Ted Pierce and Robert Lazarus listed as KIA s on a five-day-old casualty report.

According to Banks, Bowen, - and some other troopers in Delta 1-5, Ted Pierce was humping a radio on one of countless recon missions when the point element called a halt to check out some suspicious sign ahead, the first fresh NVA sign all day. Trouble was, the troopers with Pierce didn't receive word of the fresh enemy sign.

Pierce left his PRC-25 radio and stepped behind some underbrush a few feet away from the column. Moments later, he was attending to personal matters when an NVA soldier initiated a B-40 rocket attack on the flanks of the column. The first incoming rocket blew off both of Pierce's legs as he squatted in the underbrush. He might have lived, had he not lain where he fell, un-missed by his buddies during the precious minutes it took for much of his blood to drain away. In the heat of the surprise attack and ensuing fight it was some time before Pierce's buddies got to him.

Pierce was conscious when they found him and complained of terrible pain in his legs, one of which dangled in view high in a nearby tree. His last words before losing consciousness were an avowal of love for his wife. Banks and Bowen - provided religious administrations to Pierce. He died about an hour and fifteen minutes after being wounded, still waiting for the Medevac chopper, which might have saved his life.

Ted Pierce missed *making it* by just a few hours. He'd been selected to leave the field later in the day to fill the coveted and relatively safe rear-area position of company mail clerk.

Some days later, Elder Marion D. Hanks contacted Mrs. Pierce and conveyed to her Ted Pierce's dying declaration of love for her. I missed Ted Pierce's unit memorial service on October 1. It occurred while I was on the way to LZ Vivian to attend it. The next day the LDS men at Phuoc Vinh held a service for both Pierce and Lazarus.

That was also the day—October 15—that I was awarded the Combat Infantry Badge (CIB). Unknown to me, Captain Copley of Bravo 1-5 recommended me for the award. Rasmussen told me the award went through only with the help of influence in high places, and over the division chaplain's dutiful objections because "chaplains are neither infantrymen nor combatants."

The rest of the story I got in early 1977. I was en route to Modesto and Fresno to notify a father and mother of the death of their son in Germany. At the beginning of the trip I stopped at a convenience story in Marina, California. There, the attendant pointed to my CIB and said in effect, "I helped get you that. Everybody insisted a chaplain could not receive the CIB, but with Lieutenant Colonel Rasmussen's permission, I took the matter to General Casey. The general overrode all objections and ordered that the CIB be approved for you." This man was the former sergeant major for the 1-5 Cav.

It is even more amazing that when the orders arrived in Washington, personnel in the Office of the Army Chief of Chaplains allowed the award to be entered in my records without objection. At least, if anyone objected I never heard about it. So for the next twenty-four years on active duty I wore the CIB with reverence, respect and gratitude.

According to reliable sources and my best knowledge, the CIB was awarded only twice to chaplains for periods of combat in which they served as chaplains. The first CIB went to Holland Hope who, upon finding himself the last officer alive, took charge and successfully led an infantry unit through a furious battle during the Korean War. The other CIB was awarded to me, not for any single action, so far as I know—though I had led an ARVN band on a combat operation back in '67.

On October 16 an incident occurred which reminded me of March 13. That was the time that ARVN Sergeant Van Nie with Bravo 1-5 shouted "beau coup GI!" when lots of NVA were sneaking up on the CP group that had taken cover in a bomb crater. This time, a Blue trooper died when a Kit Carson scout didn't understand that "Friendlies coming in" which meant "Don't shoot, the next people you see are on our side."

The Blues, like other troopers, seemed at times to be losing their aggressive spirit, to be yielding to the changing *climate*. Still, I was surprised on October 20 when during a search for an NVA communications source, a Blue Platoon leader "missed" obvious sign of recent enemy presence in a bunker complex and then led the platoon over clean, freshly laid strands of enemy communications wire as if it wasn't there. The lieutenant was embarrassed when I pointed out and explained the sign to him. Looking back, I believe the lieutenant ignored the commo lines in order to avoid getting more troopers killed in exchange for intelligence of dubious value in a no-win war.

Back at Phuoc Vinh for the night, I sulked because I'd not received mail from home for days. My recent mail consisted only of a letter from my good friend, Dallas Murdoch, which contained something that impressed me. He suggested I write a book. That suggestion might have been the seed which bloomed (or festered) into my first book as well as this one. The next day at Ton San Nhut, Chaplain Robert Christiansen nourished the seed by making an identical suggestion.

A letter from home focused my thoughts and energy on October 22 and 23. Helga wrote of Jeannie being lured into an oath of secrecy regarding criminal activities by a classmate. My concerns became a taped message discussing an error in logic that is common among law-abiding people, an error that fits in well with criminal designs upon them. My message was that, contrary to the flawed logic, we have a civic duty to act on knowledge of criminal intent and action, and it is wise for us to be very careful in the promises we give.

The next day, October 24, Lieutenant Colonel Booth flew and worked the western part of War Zone C, between the Fishhook and the area between the Black Virgin Mountain and Katum, near Cambodia. We were flying northward near flooded LZ Becky when we heard the muscle-tightening, relatively slow *chunk-chunk-chunking* of incoming—upward-coming—51-caliber machine-gun bullets. We could easily hear the burst, despite the muffling effects of flight helmets. "What is that?" a crewmember asked.

"Fifty-one caliber," I answered. In retaliation, we shot a few rockets and some mini-gun bursts at spots from which the enemy fire may have come.

Having spent the previous night at Tay Ninh, I spent much of October 27 trying to accompany the Apache Blues on a mission, only to remain behind because the choppers were overcrowded. So I returned to Phuoc Vinh, only to turn around and go back to Tay Ninh for no other reason than that I felt impressed that I should do so.

Back with Apache Troop at Tay Ninh, I found two pilots who wanted to discuss theology, which we did until quite late in the evening. Then I turned in for the night on the cot of a pilot who'd invited me to use it any time it was unoccupied. I lay awake for a long time, wondering about the impression that brought me back and if the theological discussion with the two aviators was the reason for it. *No, I don't think so,* I concluded before finally falling to sleep.

The next day the Apache Blues assaulted into an NVA-infested area near LZ Jess. A new man, the platoon medic, struck up a whispered conversation during a pause in the sweep through the area. He looked at me curiously and inquired, "Where are you from, sir?"

"Ogden, Utah, and you?"

He said his name was Steve Blake. "I'm from Salt Lake City and I served as a missionary before getting drafted. You're LDS, aren't you?" I nodded.

"I knew it! I really need to talk with you, Chaplain Newby."

Back at Tay Ninh, Blake and I visited until late into the night. He had recently transferred from the only 82nd Airborne brigade that was serving in Vietnam, which had been designated to be one of the first combat units to withdraw from Vietnam. Blake wasn't *short* enough to return to the States with it.

"Yesterday, I prayed hard for someone to talk to about spiritual matters, about this environment and the concerns it causes me," Blake said.

242 CLAUDE D. NEWBY

After Blake explained his concerns, I thought I knew why I'd been prompted to return to Tay Ninh. He needed to talk with me now, not at some convenient date in the future.

On October 29 I came across Daniel Lang's *The New Yorker* magazine article, "Casualties of War," an extensive recounting of the Mao incident in 1966 and the subsequent actions related to the case. This magazine piece and subsequent book formed the basis of an underground movie titled, *Mao*, circa 1970. The producers of *Mao* were sued in world court for violation of movie rights. The incident was portrayed in a late-1980s Hollywood movie titled *Casualties of War,* starring Michael J. Fox. The magazine piece was accurate on every point where I have personal knowledge, except that I have brown hair, not blond, and I was a police officer in Ogden, not Salt Lake City, Utah. The story is told from my perspective in *It Took Heroes*.

Chapter Eighteen

QRFs and Crocodiles

October 30 began quietly enough, but ended on the loud side. At 0730 hours Lieutenant Dave Jenkins's Charlie Troop Blues flew to LZ Jamie to stand by as a quick-reaction force in support of Charlie Troop pink teams that were operating in the area. On the way we made what became my last visit to LZ Grant, a ghost base compared to when the 2-12 Cav had been there.

At LZ Jamie a bunker was placed at our disposal to provide us minimum shelter from sun and rain. We took advantage of the temporary quiet there to hold a worship service, after which I became better acquainted with members of the platoon, including SP4 Eugene Carroll, a squad leader. Then I visited with Captain Norman Childs, commander of Delta 2-7. We knew each other from Fort Bragg. Childs's company was also on standby as a quick-reaction force (QRF) in case the Blues got into something that was too big for us to handle. We would need the whole Delta 2-7 QRF before the day was over.

We scrambled onto choppers at 1030 hours and headed for the Cambodian border near the Fishhook. Our mission was to circle the area while a pink team conducted a BDA (battle-damage assessment) of an arclight (B-52 bomber strike). The strike, according to the plan, was to have been right on the border with Cambodia, and supposedly had occurred a few minutes before we arrived.

We'd been on-station a few minutes, circling lazily about five hundred feet above the jungle and wondering where the pink team was, when suddenly the chopper lurched right into a steep dive to gain speed. I was sitting cross-legged directly behind the left pilot's seat. The violent maneuver caught me off guard. I remained in the aircraft only by catching hold of the doorframe and with the help of the troopers deeper inside who reflexively grabbed onto my LBE (pistol belt and suspenders).

Meanwhile, whole trees leaped into the air as a quarter-mile-wide line of explosions marched straight across the area we'd just vacated; it looked as though some trees were coming right at us.

With my balance reestablished and my seat secured, I took out my camera to record the scene, but, alas, the camera was broken. The previous day, I'd forgotten my LBE in the Apache Troop latrine and had to go back for it. Someone had stolen the film and returned the camera to the ammo pouch, broken beyond repair. It was my misfortune to discover the theft and damage at the very moment when some fantastic, never to be repeated camera shots could have been taken.

We survived the arclight, thanks to the timely arrival and keen eyesight of an Air Force FAC pilot. The FAC had arrived on-station after we did and began circling several thousand feet above us. From that height he spotted our slow-moving, camouflaged chopper against the jungle background. The higher-flying B-52 bombers had already released their bombs when the FAC warned us to get out of the way. That was the warning that prompted our chopper pilot's violent and evasive maneuvering. Thanks to the chopper pilot's skills, we got clear of the target area, barely in time to avoid being knocked from the sky by the falling bombs or the subsequent concussion and air turbulence. As it was, the last of the bombs seemed to pass almost beneath us in their angled descent. Now, all this might make little sense to experts on bomb trajectories, but it's what we saw.

We returned to the area after the bombs stopped falling and stayed at about two thousand feet altitude until the pink team arrived and completed the bomb damage assessment. We arrived back on LZ Jamie at noon, ready for a hot meal.

The Blues scrambled again at 1215 hours, this time to rescue an LRRP team, call sign Talon 4-3. Hot lunch would have to wait. Sergeant Henry Morris' team of five rangers was pinned down and surrounded by NVA a few klicks from LZ Jamie. Other members of the

LRRP team were Charlie Steel, assistant team leader; Howard Shute; Julius Zaporozec of New Jersey; and Kregg P. J. Jorgenson.

Our combat assault ended unopposed in a clearing southeast of Jamie, where we arrived five minutes after we took off. From the clearing, we humped southward for fifty-five minutes, moving with relative ease through sparse undergrowth. The NVA were giving every indication of breaking contact and withdrawing by the time we reached the ranger/LRRP team. Linkup was established with the rangers without anyone getting shot at, by friendlies or NVA.

The LRRPs were in a tight defensive position about a hundred meters to the west of the swamps along the Saigon River. An almost circular clearing a little smaller than the top of a five hundred pound bomb crater, maybe twenty to thirty feet across, lay ten yards north of them. Jungle hugged the clearing on the south and east and brush encircled the rest of it, except for a four- or five-foot opening in the brush on the northwest side. A smaller clearing just beyond the opening in the brush joined a much larger clearing about thirty feet beyond us. A water-filled foxhole just inside the first clearing bore evidence of American presence before today.

After the successful linkup, Lieutenant Jenkins and Sergeant Morris conferred and then radioed their respective higher commands to report. It appeared that the NVA had withdrawn in the face of reinforcements, but Morris didn't think so, according to Ranger Kregg Jorgenson. We received prompt orders to sweep southwestward and see what it was that the NVA were hiding in the area that made them so touchy. Having not heard the new orders, I took a seat in the southeast clearing and leaned back against a bank on the north side. The clearing was in a depression, bordered on three sides by the embankment.

I'd barely sat down when thirty feet away Sergeant Morris disappeared from the clearing followed by Carroll and part of his squad. About twenty feet into the jungle, Morris rejoined the other four LRRP rangers at the place they had earlier fought off the NVA.

SP4 Carroll, who had fallen in behind the rangers, was the only Blue trooper not wearing a steel helmet, an issue I'd talked to his lieutenant about earlier. Carroll turned his head or body to the left, apparently, soon after he disappeared from view, which may have caused an

NVA machine gunner to conclude that Carroll had spotted him. A burst of 30-caliber machine-gun fire cut Carroll down from a distance of seven to ten meters. Carroll fell mortally wounded, his head laid open by an upward-angled gash from just below the left eye to above and back of the left ear.

Instantly, the rangers and Blues hit the ground and scrambled for meager cover behind the rangers' massive packs. In response to the yell, "Medic!" I dashed across the clearing and dropped to my knees against the embankment, beside the Blue platoon leader and his RTO. Carroll lay in plain view some fifteen feet into the jungle, his face to the sky and his brain clearly visible through the gash in his skull.

Already, the Blues and rangers were blasting away in response to the distinct cracks of NVA machine-gun bullets, mingled with a heavy volume of AK-47 bullets that were distinguishable for their sharper cracks and faster firing rate. Heavy fire followed immediately on the machine-gun burst. Everyone to the front had his hands full. I went over the embankment, slithered to Carroll, grasped him by his shirt collar, and started dragging him toward the clearing. The platoon medic joined me and helped get Carroll into the clearing. From there, two Blues helped the medic and me carry Carroll back the way we had come to where a small opening in the brush led to the smaller middle clearing. There the medic and I fought death for forty-five minutes while the RTO pleaded for Medevac to hurry.

Meanwhile, the LRRP s and Blues pulled back across the depression and established a defensive line in the bushes about ten feet from us. My assistant Harold Lewis voluntarily joined a Blue in the water-filled foxhole and spent the rest of the afternoon firing at the enemy. He got shrapnel in his back and neck for his troubles, but was not seriously wounded. Earlier Lewis had begged to come along today to "see what it's like on the ground." Now he knew, sort of.

We continued working on Carroll, holding onto the illogical hope that the wound would not be fatal if he reached a doctor soon enough. Carroll's heart stopped beating even as I gave him mouth-to-mouth resuscitation. Medevac was canceled before it ever arrived. A call went out for a re-supply of ammunition.

Soon Major Robert Treadway, Charlie Troop Commander, call sign Cavalier 6, slipped his Charlie-Charlie chopper in from the northwest and hovered in the air about thirty feet above the ground while the crew chief and door gunner kicked out boxes of ammunition. Delivery of the ammo had hardly begun when NVA fire raked the chopper, driving metal fragments from the aircraft into Treadway's arm. The chopper beat a hasty retreat with a lot of the much-needed ammo still aboard.

Meanwhile the ammo boxes had fallen some fifty feet away from us in the exposed larger clearing to our north-northeast. None showed any inclination to risk death to retrieve it. After quickly considering the risks—death or capture—involved in running completely out of ammo, I stooped low, ran into the field and returned lugging a box of ammo. On the way back to cover I passed several Blues who were headed out to retrieve the other boxes. Soon our return fire increased in volume, only now firing discipline was more obvious.

Once more, I intervened in tactical matters by urging Lieutenant Jenkins to call aerial rocket fire into the trees beyond a big clearing to our east and rear. We had received no NVA fire from that direction, but I figured if I were the NVA, I'd be setting up mortars there. After repeated urging on my part, a cobra fired a few rockets where I wanted them, but the pilot didn't do it without questioning Blue Six's sense and reasoning. I don't know whether those rockets were necessary. We were not mortared, which was exactly the result that I hoped for.

About 1700 hours, a platoon-size QRF from Captain Childs' Delta 2-7 Cav linked up with us, having combat assaulted in somewhere near and humped to our position. Blue Six conferred a moment with the QRF platoon leader and immediately instructed the Blues to pull out and leave the situation to the Gerry Owen troopers—Gerry Owen was a nickname for the 7th Cav dating back to America's western frontier days. The Gerry Owen QRF platoon leader objected angrily, so Jenkins agreed to stay until the rest of Delta 2-7 arrived.

While we waited, the men fashioned a makeshift stretcher for Carroll by running two green poles through the buttoned-up jungle fatigue shirts of the lieutenant and another man. Captain Childs and the rest of the QRF company arrived a half hour before twilight, and the

Blues pulled back and headed for a designated PZ several hundred meters off through the swampy river bottom.

This hasty withdrawal so bothered me that I was tempted to stay behind with Delta 2-7. It seemed we were abandoning the very troopers that had come to our rescue. Rationally, though, I knew the Blues were not equipped to stay long in the field. As it turned out, our hasty departure made no difference. We were in for a miserable overnighter.

Heavy, damp darkness descended on us before we'd gone a hundred meters through the swamp. We kept slipping, splashing and slurping over and under logs and other slimy, barely seen things. By 1930 hours we still hadn't reached the PZ. The rain was coming down hard. Because of the worsening weather, the liftships could wait for us no longer. "We'll see you at first light," the flight leader radioed.

We stopped in place about fifteen minutes later, strung out in a column. To prepare for the night, I backed up to a thick bush beside the trail we had broken, stood still until I stopped sinking into the muck, which came above my knees, and leaned back into the bush until its resistance created a very uncomfortable cradle.

The cold, miserable rain stopped about 2300 hours, but by then there was no drying out or warming to be had. Reluctantly, I proffered my shirt to the platoon leader at 0110 hours. It was much colder after that. The lieutenant's shirt was still under Carroll's body.

At 0200 hours, an artillery battery began walking artillery toward us. Individual shells were exploding successively in a line. The first shell exploded several hundred meters to our east-northeast, the next a little closer, the third one closer still, and so forth. First calmly, then with growing urgency, Lieutenant Jenkins worked the radio to stop the barrage. With nothing else to do, I estimated how many shells would fall before one exploded in our midst. Soon a 105mm shell burst about seventy-five meters from us, in water from the sound of it. We held our collective breath waiting for the next shell to hit us. It didn't come.

After the barrage, to escape the cold and to ignore the slow creep of the second hand on my watch, I focused heart, mind, and soul on considerations of life's stages and Christ's atonement for this miserable world. I considered the close calls and escapes, and whiled away some of the night in grateful appreciation for life, hope, and the strength to carry on.

Though the dawn arrived on schedule, it seemed like it came many hours after it should have. The lieutenant returned my shirt. We pried our feet and bodies from the mire, picked up Carroll's litter, and moved toward where we thought a PZ might be. Shortly the friendly clap-clap of Huey rotor blades were overhead. The blues popped smoke. The pilot confirmed that the smoke was ours by its color and said, "Be advised. You are surrounded by crocodiles!" Then he stayed close overhead to better see the big, dangerous amphibians as he guided us around and through them to a PZ.

Carroll's blood and the occasional shrapnel wound on our bodies had probably attracted the crocodiles to us. Perhaps the crocodiles left us alone during the night, postponing their meal so to speak, until the warmer dawn because they were even colder than we were.

According to the *Stars and Stripes*, more than thirty NVA soldiers died in the engagement of October 30. The body count figures must have come from the folks in the air, for the Blues and rangers saw very few dead NVA that day.

Kregg P. J. Jorgenson, one of the rangers we rescued, would become the author of *Acceptable Loss*, *MIA Rescue,* and other books. Jorgenson, who received his baptism of fire this day, described the engagement a little differently that how I remember it, which is to be expected given our different perspectives and levels of experience at the time. For example, Jorgenson thought Carroll would die almost instantly. "While I knew there was little hope for the wounded machine gunner, I was moved that the chaplain never gave up trying to save him—all the while under enemy fire. This was the heartbreaking reality of war and was true and genuine courage. God bless Chaplain Newby," Jorgenson wrote. Jorgenson had good reason for his conclusions because parts of Carroll's body sprayed over his body and soaked into his trousers as he lay there fighting off the NVA.

I appreciate Jorgenson's perspective. I owe him for providing the names of the other rangers on his team, and for his account of what transpired before the Blues arrived on the scene.

Quite a few valorous awards were given for this action, including Silver Stars and Distinguished Flying Crosses. The medic and I each received the same type of award for getting Carroll out from under direct fire. I received my third Purple Heart for minor shrapnel wounds and for bleeding from both ears, caused by the concussion of numerous explosions. In my journal for that day I wrote, "One day we might need heroes again. Who will be able to tell them [true heroes] apart from the ones who received awards for minor wounds like mine?"

Two days later I wrote, "One day I'm in the swamps surrounded by crocodiles, and the next day I'm sitting here at the feet of a great spiritual leader and theologian, miles away and worlds apart."

The day after the action with the Blues and rangers, November 1, I stopped at Tan San Nhut long enough to arrange for a bus the next day to transport 1st Cav troopers from the airfield to a religious conference site. Then I flew to Cam Ranh Bay and attended a meeting under the direction of Elder Bruce R. McConkie, noted ecclesiastical leader, author, and father of an Air Force chaplain who had recently served in Vietnam.

The next day, following a conference session at 0630 hours, I hitched a ride on the flight that took Elder McConkie to Saigon. At his urging I sat beside him and told war stories, including the action among the crocodiles two days previously. Apparently Elder McConkie was impressed for that evening he introduced me to someone as "one of the great men of the church." I could have temporarily let my helmet band out an inch.

Chapter Notes:

30 October 1969, 1-9 Cav Journal, 1035: "Fr 1-9-G2 TN X415885. C/1-9 1000 hrs; BDA of A/L [B-52 strike]."

1140: "TM 43 [LRRPs] has singing and talking about 500m to their south. Going to try an ambush if possible."

1155: "TM 43 in contact at this time at XT491677."

1345: "Medevac bird requested for TM 43, either Blue or 1-Talon member wounded in contact with unknown number of indivs…1 member of the Blues is KIA.

1430: "Heavy Bones QRF [quick reaction force, a platoon of Delta 2-7] in on the ground with Blues."

1605: "Cav 6 A/C down at "Jamie" has to be slung out. No injuries."

Closing Summary: "H. 43…were engaged by 2 indiv while setting ambush. No cas, radio antenna shot off, commo went through 2-7 …At 1315 Blues linked up with 43, came into contact with USEF, resulting in 1 US KIA…C Troop at XT491677 UH-1H recd S/A fire, hovering 60 ft while resupplying Blues with smoke and ammo, no inj., hit A/C no fly at LZ Jamie…Blues, H43 and D/2-7 neg sitrep, will be extracted when weather breaks. Total killed for 30 Oct 69-A Trp, 5; B Trp 5, C Trp Pink Team 12; C Trp Blues 10; H-43 3…We had a good day, looking for a better one tomorrow. Good Night, signed by Captain James A. Price."

30 October 1969, 1/9 Cav S-3 Log Item 1, 1140 hrs.: TM-43 has singing and talking about 500m to their south. Going to try to ambush…1155 hrs, TM-43 in contact. Cav [Charlie Troop, call sign Cavalier] en route…Blue Max in route…1220, Cav Blues inserted. 1345 hrs, Medevac requested for TM-43 either Blues or 1 Talon member wounded in contact with unknown number…1 member of blues is KIA. 1420 hrs, Heavy bones QRF is on the ground with Cav. Blues. 1605, Cav [Cavalier] 6 A/C down at "Jamie," has to be slung out. No injuries.

31 October 1969, 1-9 Cav Journal, 0810: "C Trp Blues extracted…TM 43 extracted w/C Trp Blues. PZ green.

Chapter Nineteen

THE VAGARIES

It was time to keep a promise. On November 4 I left Phuoc Vinh intent on returning to the 1-5 Cav so Chaplain Thompson could take a few days in the rear to recuperate and attend to personal affairs. En route I visited Kurt Ruth of Alpha 1-5 at Quan Loi and spent the night in the 1-5 Cav field trains area.

It took three hours the next morning to get a flight to LZ Vivian, the 1-5 Cav's new firebase north of Quan Loi. To maintain my excuse for being there, I checked in with Chaplain Thompson and sent him to the rear. Then, after several futile attempts to reach one of the companies in the field, the Division Artillery (Divarty) Chaplain Charles H. Hosutt and I conducted a joint service on LZ Vivian. Then I spent the afternoon with LTC Ronald Rasmussen on his C&C chopper.

First we flew north several kilometers to the Bu Dop Special Forces Camp, adjacent to the Vietnamese district headquarters town of Bo Duc and about five to seven kilometers from Cambodia. We'd flown there so Rasmussen could coordinate with the Special Forces commander. However, our landing was delayed because two separate battles were raging, one around the camp and the other near an ARVN camp at Bo Duc. Just ahead of us, an Air Force CV-2 Caribou sustained more than one hundred hits from automatic weapons while trying to land. Rasmussen kept his C&C on-station above the battles and directed artillery for several hours.

Lieutenant Colonel Rasmussen spent the afternoon in anticipation of orders to combat assault the 1-5 Cav into the Bu Dop area. The orders never came. Instead General George Casey, the Assistant Division Commander, called him to a high-level strategy meeting at LZ Vivian, where it was decided to let ARVN forces respond to the threat to Bu Dop and Bo Duc. The generals were concerned about putting American infantry into the area again, partly because mortars and rockets out of Cambodia had mauled a company of 7th Cav troopers near Bu Dop. As it turned out, American forces became heavily involved in the Bu Dop buildup and fighting during November, with the 1-5 Cav and my Bravo Troop scouts in the forefront.

At 0800, November 6, I held a worship service for Alpha 1-5 on LZ Vivian. Again unable to reach a company in the field, I flew with Rasmussen. This time we made it into the Bu Dop Special Forces Camp for another strategy meeting.

To avoid ground fire during our approach into Bu Dop, Rasmussen's C&C chopper pilot flew in fast at treetop level, skimmed over the Bu Dop camp, flared, and hovered just long enough for Rasmussen, the 1-5 Cav Operations Officer, and me to jump to the ground. Then the chopper sped off to wait for us out of range of the enemy's guns which were in Cambodia and around the camp.

Moving quickly off the exposed chopper pad, we hurried north up a slight incline to a wooden structure. Waiting inside was the Special Forces Camp Commander and his operations officer. General Casey joined us moments later, having arrived unhurt in the same manner we had. The two Green Beret officers shared a familiar *under siege* appearance—drawn faces beneath heavy tans, and staring and shifting eyes that belied the calm of their professional voices. These men had been through a lot, and they knew it wasn't over yet.

General Casey acknowledged everyone who was present. He expressed only mild surprise at the unexpected presence of the 1-9 Cav Chaplain in his Bu Dop strategy meeting. At 1140 hours, two minutes into the meeting, heavy mortar shells and rockets began exploding on Bu Dop and Bo Duc. The Green Beret commander calmly recommended to General Casey that we move the meeting to his TOC in the command bunker, which we did—walking, not running.

The command bunker was impressive in its size and construction. It was protected by yards of overhead cover. Inside, the bunker was well laid out and compartmentalized. Obviously this was no temporary TOC such as those on infantry firebases.

After a few minutes, I excused myself from the meeting and went to assist with wounded civilians who were being brought into the bunker, victims of the latest shelling. Among the victims were a baby with a gaping shrapnel wound over its right eye, a little girl, two women, and an elderly man. The little girl died there in the bunker while being treated, despite excellent care by the Special Forces medics. One medic said this was the second child he'd lost in two days, the previous loss being a four-year-old girl the day before. The NVA, he said, systematically and regularly targeted the civilian sectors of Bo Duc.

The wounded attended to and the strategy meeting over, we started to depart. A new barrage of incoming mortars, on us this time, prompted a delay. A row of sand-filled fifty-gallon steel drums sat just outside the inclined ramp that led from the bunker. The drums sat back from the entrance enough to allow people to easily walk around them, but were close enough to shield the entrance ramp from all but direct hits by heavy rockets or artillery.

General Casey, Rasmussen, their entourages, and I waited out the barrage standing halfway up the ramp. General Casey's demeanor was impressive. He remained calm, even when a shell exploded just a few feet beyond the barrels at the entrance. Three civilians dived over the barrels just ahead of the near miss. The civilians were a CBS news crew, one of whom was killed there the next day, I was told. According to J. D. Coleman's book *Incursion*, the special forces commander at Bu Dop refused the media admission to his camp, but November 6 was an apparent exception.

After the incoming rockets and mortars let up, General Casey's and Rasmussen's groups headed one at a time to the chopper pad. On the pad, we waited in trenches for our respective choppers to swoop in for us. All got off from Bu Dop unhurt. Unknown to me, my nephew Earl Dyer was also on the receiving end of the frequent barrages being thrown at Bu Dop. He ran the refueling (POL) point there.

Our casualties during the barrage at Bu Dop included one American soldier killed and one wounded, eight CSF wounded, two

CSF dependents wounded, and one CSF dependent killed—the little girl. Two CBS reporters were also wounded

Back at LZ Vivian, a strategy meeting continued past midnight. American infantry was going in after all. The ARVN units could handle Bu Dop and Bo Duc alone, General Casey believed, provided we reopened an old firebase to provide a conduit through which ARVN forces could be channeled.

Early the next morning on November 7, Captain William Vowell and his Charlie 1-5 Cav prepared to combat assault into LZ Jerri—the abandoned firebase situated two klicks south of Bu Dop. He and a lieutenant colonel arrived on Vivian to coordinate the assault. The lieutenant colonel would lead and command the liftships in support of the assault.

The flight leader attended a worship service I held at 0800 hours, as did SP4 Charles N. Harris, a former Alpha 1-5 trooper who was serving as a photographer/reporter for the battalion. Both the aviation commander and Harris were rapidly approaching the end of their time in combat, though neither of them knew it.

The combat assault began as soon as the worship service ended, with the flight commander in the lead of the first gaggle of choppers and Charlie 1-5 troopers. They got on the ground without taking casualties. As soon as the troopers jumped from the chopper, the flight leader took off from Jerri in a rapid climb to the west and quickly banked left toward LZ Eagle Two. An enemy 51-caliber machine gun opened up about halfway through the turn, and the chopper went down in flames. The flight leader or copilot skillfully skimmed the flaming helicopter across the treetops to a controlled crash in an open field. During the descent, the forward speed of the chopper blew the flames away from the pilots onto the crew chief and door gunner behind them. To escape the flames, both enlisted men jumped into the trees from about three hundred feet in the air. The flight leader and copilot survived.

Even as the combat assault into Jerri continued, my Bravo Troop Blues arrived to search for the crew chief and door gunner. Other units joined the search later, but the search turned up no immediate trace of the two men or of their remains. They may still be listed as missing in action.

We flew past the downed and burning chopper moments after it crashed, en route to LZ Jerri to reinforce the Charlie 1-5 sky troopers. Sporadic AK-47 fire contested our arrival on the LZ. It was 0910 hours.

Jerri had a long way to go before being reborn. A large, topless pit near the center of the perimeter marked the spot for a once and future TOC. Overhead cover was not to be found, except under the trunks of some giant trees which lay along parts of the perimeter, especially on the west side.

Soon the intensity of incoming bullets increased, and Captain Vowel 1 led part of Charlie 1-5 into the jungle to suppress it. The NVA withdrew just enough to keep thirty to fifty feet from us as we pressed forward. It was during this suppressive effort that four American snipers, who were attached to Charlie 1-5 from Division, discovered a Chinese detonator switch or Klacker in the tree line. Wires from the Klacker led across the cleared fire zone to the west perimeter berm and attached to a concealed mine that looked like it was intended to take out an M-60 tank. The claymore was well concealed and had been set facing toward the center of LZ Jerri. It was at least two feet in diameter and very nasty looking.

Safely back inside the perimeter, with less NVA lead cracking around us, we labored all day and into the night to dig holes, harden positions, and prepare for a bad night. These preparations took shape under the direction of the battalion executive officer, Robin Mangum, whom I recall as a major, though records a month later give his rank as lieutenant colonel.

Reinforcements arrived while we worked, including an artillery battery with its guns slung beneath Chinook helicopters. Most welcome among the new arrivals was Special Forces Captain Robert C. Beckman and his *Mike Force*, the 2nd Battalion, 3rd Mobile Strike Force of about five hundred Cambodian mercenaries. Also welcome was the 36th ARVN Ranger Battalion that arrived in the evening, though I don't think the latter came onto LZ Jerri.

Beckman was very impressive. Standing about six feet, six inches or more as I recall, he towered trunk, shoulders, and head above his command—an obvious, enticing target for snipers. I wondered how he could survive, standing out as he did.

After consulting with Mangum and Captain Vowel l, Beckman settled his Mike Force down inside the perimeter to rest until dark. After dark, the mercenaries sneaked from the perimeter and dug in under the trees to the west of the LZ.

Earlier, while we pushed the NVA deeper into the jungle on the west, General Casey had arrived on LZ Jerri and remained there with his aide and some hangers-on while his chopper returned to Quan Loi to refuel. Someone said General Casey was very impressive and inspiring as he walked about the LZ, not even flinching when bullets cracked about him. This is believable, based on his calm behavior the previous day at Bu Dop.

Long after dark, I joined Mangum and a couple of his CP group under a partially-sandbagged half culvert. Mangum insisted I keep his .45-caliber pistol for him "just in case." The first action of the night came at 2355 hours, when probing NVA soldiers bumped into some mercenaries and quickly retreated.

The anticipated attack began at 0220 on November 8 with a stand-off barrage of about eighty rockets and mortars, followed by a ground assault from the west. I waited out the barrage under our half culvert, and for the first and only time in combat my legs trembled uncontrollably. On occasions I'd felt greater fear than this, but this time the incoming artillery got to my knees.

Most of the grunts endured the barrage without benefit of overhead protection. Ronaldo Rodriguez was one of those. Someone on LZ Jerri that night said that at the first *bloop* of NVA mortar shells leaving tubes, Rodriguez dashed with his team from meager shelter into a hastily- prepared mortar pit, a three-quarter circle of sandbags. The same person said Rodriguez's team got two rounds into the air before NVA shells began exploding on LZ Jerri, the first or second of which exploded in their mortar pit, wounding all the team.

It happened differently according to Staff Sergeant Ray Easton. "I was Sad Sack's platoon leader," said Easton. "The day before when we landed...I told everyone...to get the sandbags filled and put on the half culverts because we would probably get hit that night. Sad Sack and his partner for whatever reason did not get their bunker protected, and decided to sleep in the mortar pit because it at least had a sandbag wall.

"I was laying in my bunker half asleep when the incoming started. It woke me up and as I raised to put on my flack jacket, the round that Claude said exploded in Sad Sack's mortar pit actually exploded in my bunker. My radio operator who was sitting closest to the blast sustained the most damage, mainly in the head area. I was hit in my left side and back. Another person in my bunker received slight damage.

"After collecting myself, I crawled out to get help for my radio operator and to check on my men and try to get a gun firing. That's when I found Sad Sack and his buddy. I went to Sad Sack first and talked to him and turned on a small flashlight so that I could look him over...the enemy outside the perimeter fired a rocket at the light. Thankfully it was about five feet too high. 'Where are you hurt?' I asked Sad Sack.

"'Sarge, I'm okay. I just have a little metal in my leg, but get help for [his buddy]. His guts are on the ground.'

"I looked over and sure enough they were. I yelled for a medic and soon one came...we decided to get Sad Sack's buddy out first, because he appeared worse off. As it turns out his buddy survived. I was told afterwards that Sad Sack died on the helicopter, with a sucking chest wound that no one was aware he had," ended Sergeant Easton.

Rodriguez and his buddy would have been no better off by staying under cover in their culvert, because an 82mm mortar shell exploded just inside the open west end of it.

Meanwhile, in the jungle on the west side of the LZ, a massive NVA assault came up short against the Mike Force. The Mike Force sustained one killed and nine or ten wounded during the fierce hand-to-hand fight that followed. We could offer little help to Beckman and his

Cambodian strikers because our mortar was knocked out and the artillery battery had failed to move its munitions from the helipad to the gun positions.

Within minutes of the last exploding shells inside our perimeter, we had gathered the wounded Americans and mercenaries inside the top-less TOC. Of the six American casualties, Rodriguez was now obviously the one most seriously wounded.

"Hang in there Sad Sack. You've got it made, Sad Sack! You're going home, Sad Sack," his buddies encouraged.

Rodriguez appeared unconscious as the medics fought to save his life. Yes, it was Ronaldo Rodriguez, whom I'd refused to call Sad Sack, the private whose leader hadn't trusted him with important tasks six months earlier.

Kneeling with Rodriguez's head cradled in the crook of my right arm, I asked softly, "Ron, can you hear me?" A faint smile or grimace flickered across his lips and his eyes opened briefly to the sound of his true name. The nurses who attended Ron said he died the next day without regaining consciousness, at the Third Field Hospital in Saigon.

The Special Forces-led Mike Forces counterattacked at dawn on November 8. Those tough little warriors killed four NVA soldiers and captured a first sergeant. At 0800 hours a chopper landed. Chaplain Thompson alighted and said, "Get aboard the chopper. I'm here to relieve you."

It was hard to leave while LZ Jerri was under siege, but I did so because I suspected someone higher up had ordered it. The battalion photographer/reporter Chuck Harris waved goodbye to me from the helipad as I flew off.

At LZ Vivian, I transferred to a Chinook. The Chinook dropped me off at Quan Loi, on- loaded some supplies and passengers, and took off, only to be shot down during its final re-approach to LZ Vivian. The Chinook crashed about thirty feet outside the perimeter, where a whirling rear rotor blade beheaded a 1-5 Cav trooper as he and the other passengers and crew scurried out of the burning aircraft. Sergeant

Elvin Jackson, who had just returned from the hospital, witnessed this horrible death of a great trooper and close friend. "He was a fine young man. We'd visit for hours every time we came on the LZ. He was married, and lived in Florida, I believe. I wish I could remember his name. Watching his head fly off was probably the worst thing I witnessed while in Vietnam," Jackson said. No doubt this experience would contribute significantly to Jackson's postwar suffering.

LTC Robin Mangum died violently on December 6, killed by the same pistol he'd lent to me a month earlier during the first NVA attack on LZ Jerri. The four snipers who found the Chinese Klacker died on LZ Jerri early in the morning on November 11. Chuck Harris, the combination photographer and reporter, lost a shoulder and the sight out of both of his eyes in the same barrage. Captain Robert C. Beckman, the Green Beret leader, was killed in sight of LZ Jerri on November 10 or 11, along with another American and five MSF soldiers.

In the early morning hours of 11 November a heavy barrage of rockets and mortars hit LZ Jerri. Harris and the snipers were in positions on the northwest side of the perimeter, and probably felt fairly secure there beneath several giant tree trunks, any one of which would deflect the biggest rocket in the NVA arsenal. Again the vagaries of war came into play.

According to one source, a 120mm rocket hit at just the right angle to pass between the logs and get to the four snipers, one of whom was reported to be PFC Charles Joseph Keitt of New York. Another grunt who was nearby at the moment said, "A 122mm rocket hit among the logs and made a partial opening. A second 122mm came in on the exact same trajectory as the first one—like lightning striking twice in the same place—blasted the rest of the way through the logs and killed five troopers, including the four snipers."

Another trooper, Larry Touchstone, recalls that the four snipers were not all killed by the same rocket. "One other thing I will never forget—two of the snipers you talked about were in the bunker next to mine....Their bunker took a direct hit....It was a sad experience putting them into a poncho. One was black and one white, which is the only way we could separate the pieces, to tell which body parts belonged in which poncho."

Harris the photographer was hit in the same barrage. Again, my original source said he was hit by a 90-recoilless while standing on the helipad where I last saw him and that he lost both his eyes.

The rest of the story came out a few months before the thirtieth anniversary of this action. We passed each other in a Holiday Inn hallway during a 5th Cavalry Regiment reunion in Peoria, Illinois. It was May 1999. "You look familiar. Where did we know each other?" I asked.

We established only that I had been his chaplain when he served with Alpha 1-5 in 1969. We parted, then I turned and called to him. "In early November 1969 at LZ Jerri, there was an enlisted battalion photographer...."

"That was me!" he blurted.

Couldn't be. "The man I was remember was blinded in both eyes a couple of days after I last saw him."

"Yes. I was blind for a long time, until a world-renowned ophthalmologist took me on as a special case and restored the sight in one of my eyes. I am Chuck Harris," he said as he extended his hand again. A name for a face after all these years!

As other Alpha 1-5 veterans gathered about us, Harris explained what happened in the early morning darkness on 11 November 1969. "A heavy barrage of 122mm rockets hit us at 0240 hours. One came in right on top of the other. The first rocket blew an opening in the overhead cover and the second rocket went right through the opening and killed five men inside their perimeter bunker. I was in a bunker nearby. Another 122 rocket hit near me and ruined my shoulder and blinded me in both eyes." Chuck showed us the shrapnel-damaged lens of the camera he was using that night. He also showed us x-rays of his upper body. An artificial shoulder was quite easy to see as were scores of white spots that indicated shrapnel, gravel, and other debris that was blown into his body,

The First Air Cavalry History Book, 1965-1969, contains a picture that was retrieved from Harris's damaged camera after he was evacuated. It is an excellent shot of a Medevac operation that took place out in the jungle the previous day. Perhaps the casualty in the picture was Captain Beckman.

SP4 Clark Robert Douglas received the Distinguished Service Cross for his actions during the attack on LZ Jerri that night, posthumously. He gave his life trying to reach the wounded whose buddies cried out "Medic!" at the height of the enemy barrage.

On the previous day, November 10, Green Beret Captain Beckman, standing almost head and belt buckle above his Mike Force troops, had assaulted uphill against the NVA on Hill 153. The attack lasted all afternoon and ended about 2400 hours, after the Special Forces-led Mike Force was reinforced by an element of the 11th Armored Cavalry Regiment. The attack was a tactical success, though Beckman gave his life in the effort, as did another American and five Mike Force strikers.

Later that same day at a hospital something of a miracle occurred, and my appreciation of God's love and blessings increased. I visited the pilot of a pink team LOH that was shot down the day before near LZ Vivian. Today he lay in the hospital in very bad shape, delirious and writhing in agony despite being heavily sedated with morphine. After praying for him, I yielded to spiritual guidance and placed my hands on his head to bless him. He stopped writhing and fell into a deep, peaceful sleep the instant my hands touched his head.

Soon after the action at LZ Jerri, three 1-5 Cav troopers were brought to Quan Loi to await transfer to LBJ for court martial for refusing to do their combat duty. At Quan Loi they went about spouting black-power slogans and tossing black-power salutes, trying to increase racial tensions. Robin Mangum's task was to control and care for the three men until they could be incarcerated at LBJ.

Bad incidents rapidly increased in number and frequency as soon as the three *mutineers* arrived at Quan Loi, including threats and fragging attempts against Mangum, the battalion sergeant major and a first sergeant.

An eighteen-year-old replacement arrived in the battalion rear at Quan Loi one evening, where he remained overnight to await a flight to his new company the next morning. A generous first sergeant gave his bunk to the replacement for the night. During the night a fragmentation hand grenade exploded under the wooden floor, directly beneath the First Sergeant's bunk. The blast completely blew off the young soldier's genitals and seriously wounded him in other ways.

At the 2nd Surgical Hospital that day, the young trooper declared to me that he was a virgin and born-again Christian. He appeared to be free of any ill feeling toward whoever had robbed him of ever having a normal marital relationship, of ever siring children of his own. That the young man lost so much to a fellow soldier or soldiers rather than to the enemy didn't seem to matter to him.

LTC Robin Mangum was found dead in his hooch on December 6, 1969, gut shot by his government-issue .45-caliber pistol. Officially, Mangum died of an accidental self-inflicted gunshot wound in consequence of a defective seer pin in the weapon, according to Lieutenant Colonel Rasmussen. That pistol had functioned quite well four weeks earlier, when Mangum lent it to me on LZ Jerri.

For days Bravo Troop scouts had been reporting the smell of elephants in the area northeast of LZ Buttons. The Third Brigade commander, Colonel John P. Barker, under whom I'd served at Fort Bragg, opined that the scouts were showing off and bragging—that they couldn't possibly smell elephants while whipping over the jungle in choppers. Apparently Colonel Barker hadn't seen the LOH choppers hover and buzz around and under the trees the way they often did, nor did he know Captain Lou Niles. "I tracked elephants by smell…never smoked, which gave me an advantage. I could smell elephant urine. I'd go out at lunch and dinnertime and fly sideways, upwind until I picked up the scent of food. Then I would continue until I could smell it no more. That's where the enemy would be. I found hospitals the same way, by the odor of alcohol," said Niles.

Anyhow, during a daily briefing, Colonel Barker lashed into Major George O'Grady, Bravo Troop Commander: "I'm tired of hearing reports about scouts smelling elephants from the air, and I'd better not hear another such report unless you bring me some fresh elephant [manure]."

"I was in that briefing. The reports about elephants were getting to George O'Grady, my troop commander, too," said Niles.

Two days later, the scouts found and killed twenty-seven elephants. The beasts were being used by the NVA to haul war supplies down the new, yet to be discovered trail, a partially bamboo-paved route that skirted the 1st Cav AO on the east, toward Saigon. There were those in high places that designated the newly discovered trail as the Surges Jungle Highway. The 1-9 Cav people preferred to call it the Jolly Jungle Highway. This was in honor of Major Jolly, who had replaced George O'Grady as Bravo Troop Commander, and whose scouts found the trail.

On November 18, I visited Steve Blake at Tay Ninh and also conducted a memorial service for the rangers. A LRRP team in support of Apache Troop had lost two men the previous day during a very bad fight.

The mission went as follows, as Sergeant Jim McIntyre described it to me a few days later, and as it was told by Sergeant Kregg P. J. Jorgenson in his intriguing book, *Acceptable Loss*.

McIntyre and four other team members were inserted in the jungle to recon for five days in the vicinity of Song Be and LZ Buttons. Each man carried nearly a hundred pounds of supplies, ammunition and arms. As per standard operating procedure, to confuse the enemy, the liftship made some fake stops in the area before hovering above a pre-selected insertion LZ. In an instant, the LRRP s were off the skids and on the ground, driven by their heavy loads to hands and knees by the five-foot drop.

On the ground, "Mack motioned for us to move into the tree line. Torres took off first, followed by Zaporozec, McIntyre, and me. Rogers covered the rear," wrote Jorgenson.

On the third day of the operation, McIntyre moved his team to higher ground to regain radio contact. After reestablishing commo, the team took a short break to gain its breath following a hard climb. Fifteen minutes later, McIntyre, who was at the point, shot his hand into the air, fist clenched. He'd found a well-used trail. Ten minutes later, after carefully crossing and re-crossing the trail, McIntyre selected a spot between a two-foot high anthill and a fallen tree. "Barely moments after we sat down, we heard Vietnamese moving up the trail." said Jorgenson.

Ten NVA soldiers came along the trail. They passed within fifteen feet of the team members. The rangers hadn't had time to set out claymore mines and adequately camouflage their position. After the NVA passed, Jorgenson barely had time to call in the sighting before more NVA came along. "I gave up counting at thirty and prayed they'd keep on going, only God wasn't listening," Jorgenson said.

McIntyre said the NVA had approached slowly and quietly, obviously searching, not moving like a unit that was intent on covering distance. He said the NVA column stopped for a break after some soldiers had passed the rangers' hiding place. Then an NVA soldier stepped to the side of the trail, perhaps to relieve himself, and squatted to investigate something. Jorgenson wrote that the NVA soldier had spotted the red pin on one of Torres' grenades. A squadron officer who was privy to debriefing information said the NVA had relieved himself and bent down to investigate the sound of liquid splattering off Torres's uniform and equipment. Whatever his reason, the NVA soldier looked into Torres' eyes, screamed, and swung his AK-47 on target. Jorgenson wrote, "Before he could pull the trigger, Torres opened up with his M-14, killing the NVA soldier instantly."

Jorgenson said Torres suddenly sat up holding his chest where blood gushed from a bullet wound, and yelled, "Oh, Jesus! Jesus!"

Up on one knee, Zaporozec, fired away, as did the rest of the team, including the mortally wounded Torres. "I felt Zap's arm grabbing mine...a bullet had hit him above the upper lip....Rogers was screaming, too, and rolling over and over on the ground, holdings onto his left leg....'Keep firing! Keep firing!' yelled McIntyre, pulling me back to the tactical situation." said Jorgenson.

Though pink teams were en route and the Saber Blues were scrambling in response to frantic radio messages, the rangers were on their own for several minutes, and receiving fire from all sides. Returning withering fire for withering fire, the LRRP s fought off repeated NVA attempts to destroy them before help could arrive.

Quickly, pink teams arrived on-station to add their fire to that of McIntyre's team. The Blues stayed out of the fight because there was no place near enough for them to be inserted in time to affect the outcome.

It took several minutes for the combined fire of the LRRPs and Pink Teams to suppress the NVA enough for the LRRPs to try to disengage and get to a usable pickup zone. To make the move possible, someone recommended that McIntyre leave Zaporozec's body behind and attempt to escape and evade to a place where the liftships could land and extract the rest of the team. McIntyre refused to leave Zaporozec, so the decision was made to extract the LRRPs using a McGuire rig.

McGuire rigs were used as a last resort to extract LRRPs and other special operations troops from harm's way. These extractions were very exhilarating, especially at night. A 120-foot rope (or four ropes) with a D-ring attached was dropped to the ground, weighted by a sandbag or other weight when necessary to get it down through the jungle canopies. The pilot had to hold the chopper in a near-perfect hover while the rope was lowered and a passenger hooked on. Booth explained, "Our lift-helicopters did not have a pulley. They extracted by lifting straight up to raise the ranger above the treetops, and then moved forward to gain airspeed. The ranger was then flown some distance to a relatively safe area, then let down into an open area where the ranger could unhook from the D-ring and climb aboard the helicopter."

Once the decision was made to use the McGuire rig, a liftship quickly came to a hover above the jungle immediately over the LRRP team. The crew chief and door gunner dropped the rope. McIntyre sent up Zaporozec's body. Rogers, the severely wounded medic went next. The mortally wounded Torres followed Rogers up through the tree branches, and then Jorgenson. Like the fine leader he was, McIntyre was hoisted up last of all.

Following this tragic mission, Sergeant McIntyre was taken out of the LRRPs and assigned to Operations in the Apache Troop TOC at Tay Ninh. He told me he'd had enough, but that's not what Lieutenant Colonel Booth remembers: "About a month before McIntyre's last LRRP mission, I considered moving a great young pilot out of the scouts. Major Bob Hardin and Captain Paul Funk—commander and XO of Apache Troop—agreed, so I met with the pilot. After an hour of talking with him in Apache Operations, he pleaded with me to leave him in scouts. I relented. Two or three days later, this young pilot's LOH was hit and went straight into the jungle at very high speed, killing him and all aboard.

Booth said, "With this weighing on my mind, and considering how many really tough contacts he'd survived recently, I ordered McIntyre transferred out of LRRPs. Like the pilot before him, Mack objected to the transfer out of his sense of duty and obligation to his men and buddies. This time there was no talking me out of it. I told McIntyre, 'I want you to leave Vietnam standing up, to return to your family alive.' We sent him to Apache Troop to work in operations.

"I visited McIntyre in the TOC frequently when I went to Tay Ninh. During one of those visits he admitted, 'Colonel you were right. It was time for me to get out of the LRRPs.'"

McIntyre's close calls hadn't all been recent, either. During one of his first missions—perhaps the first one—McIntyre saved his team members by throwing his rucksack and himself on top of a Chicom grenade.

Jorgenson came down with malaria the day after he received an impact award of the Silver Star for this action. Like McIntyre, he transferred to the Apache Troop Blues upon his return from the hospital, where he was wounded twice more. Though I didn't know it until years later, both Jorgenson and Zaporozec had been part of the LRRP team that the Blues and I had *rescued* a couple of weeks earlier on 30 October, the day Carroll was killed.

On November 23, a soldier came to me and confessed to a recent act of immorality while he was on R&R. Though he seemed repentant, I counseled with him and advised him to discuss the matter with a chaplain or ecclesiastical leader of his own faith. Afterward I thought and wrote in my journal: "I'd rather be dead than unchaste. Must not read or willingly allow anything in mind that degrades sacred things. An unchaste mind is first step to an unchaste body." Translation: I'd rather die than face the pain that unfaithfulness on my part would cause Helga and the children. As for sinning against God and one of His daughters, regardless of her willingness or motives, I echo Joseph of old when he was tempted, "How then can I do this great wickedness and sin against God?" (Genesis 39:9)

It was about this time that Alpha Troop choppers frequently took small-arms fire from a single weapon as they arrived and departed the western perimeter at Tay Ninh. The shots came from a vast field of rice or grass growing out of water. Naturally, the chopper crews tried repeatedly to find and get rid of the NVA that was shooting at them, to no avail. So one day a patrol went out with a tracker- dog team at the point. The patrol had gone out about two or three hundred meters when a shot rang out and the last man in the patrol fell dead. The shot had come from someplace in the grass between the patrol and the perimeter. To get that shot, the NVA soldier had managed to avoid detection by the sharp eyes of the troopers *and* the extraordinary nose of the black Labrador tracker dog. A few days later a LOH swept down when the crew spotted something. A crewmember jumped out into the grass and water and captured the evasive, ghost-like shooter, a badly-wounded NVA soldier who apparently was determined to keep fighting until his infected wounds killed him—which he almost succeeded in doing.

Chapter Notes:

7 November 1969, 1-5 Battalion Journal, 0935; "15 sorties of C Co touched down LZ Jerri. Completed 0947.

1012: "LZ Jerri receiving 82mm and AK-47 at this time."

1027: "Fr GM6: Request 2 sniper teams...for FSB Jerri (Snipers reported at approx 1100 hrs)."

8 November 1969, 2nd Battalion, 3rd MSFC, Operation Shaker, 0220 Hrs...LZ Jerri...5 kilometers south of Bu Dop, received 20 rounds of 82mm mortar and 50 rounds of B-40 rocket fire, One MSF was killed and nine were wounded..."

8 November 1969, 1-5 Battalion Journal, 0310: "Fr GM (LZ JERRI): At 0235 hrs. reports receiving 50 B-40, some 82mm and a ground probe on the NW side of LZ Jerri...15 line 2's, 1 line 1 (little people), (06 line 2's U.S., 05 US line 2's, litter)."

0320: "Fm 3d Bde-G-2: "C/1-5, FSB Jerri 0240 H. Rec'd 30x 82mm mort, SA, B-40 rkt fire and ground probe frm N.W. (rec'd 50x B-40)...at 0420 7x US WIA were medevaced and 9x MSF were awaiting medevac. Contact broke 0319 H, 1 x MSF KIA."

11 November 1969, 2nd Battalion, 3rd MSFC, received sniper fire from an unknown number of enemy...five kilometers south of Bu Dop. One USASF and five MSF were killed, and one USASF and 11 MSF were wounded."

12 June 1970, 1st Cav G-3 Op Reports-Lessons Learned for Nov - Jan 1969-70, paragraph (3)(d): FSB Jerri received 30x 82mm mortar rounds, 5 B-40 rockets and light ground probe commencing at 0240H on 8 November. Friendly casualties totaled 7 US WIA, 9 MSF WIA and 1 MSF KIA."

Paragraph (3)(f): "On 10 November, FSB Jerri received another heavy stand-off attack consisting of 15x 120mm and 15x 82mm mortar rounds and a ground probe from the southwest. Friendly losses included 5 US KIA and 7 US WIA [including the four snipers]."

Chapter Twenty

In Memoriam

About 0200 hours, November 25, someone blew up the Squadron Executive Officer's latrine, just behind my sleeping area. The XO wasn't using the latrine at the time.

For a week Warrant Officer Hodson had begged me to accompany him on a scout mission, saying he'd be shot down if I didn't. Hodson had transferred from the navigator seat of an Air Force B-52 bomber into the pilot's hot seat of an Army scout LOH, to get nearer the war. Having already flown scout missions for several months without taking a hit on his aircraft, Hodson said he believed his *numbers* must be about up. He asked me to fly a mission with him, else he would die. I agreed to fly a mission with Hodson. As observer, I'd be in the copilot seat on Hodson's left.

Mister (WO) Hodson, his torque (door gunner) and I departed from Phuoc Vinh before dawn on November 26, flying low with a Cobra trailing high and to the rear. By dawn we were north of LZ Buttons conducting *first-light* recon over thick bamboo. Hodson hadn't told me the observer was supposed to keep a smoke grenade in hand with the pin pulled, and to be ready to drop it at the first sign of enemy.

Thus, when we spotted a smokeless campfire beneath the bamboo I wasn't ready to "mark the target" for the Cobra. Though the campfire was out by the time we turned around, the Cobra put in a couple of rockets where we thought the fire had been.

At 0900 we were ordered west of LZ Buttons to scout for Charlie 2-12 Cav, which was in contact and had sustained three KIAs from NVA mortars. We arrived on-station and began circling at two hundred feet, intent on drawing fire to give the Cobras something to blast with their grenade launcher, mini-gun, and rockets. We quickly succeeded in drawing fire, and this time I had a smoke grenade ready to mark the target.

After a few minutes, the commander on the ground called for a resupply of smoke so he could continue to mark his position. Hodson headed us back to LZ Buttons where we refueled and took on extra smoke grenades while the Cobra rearmed. We were about five hundred meters from the Charlie 2-12 Cav position when a 60-caliber machine gun opened up and punctured the LOH in two places. "What's that?" asked Hodson when the machine-gun rounds began cracking around us.

"Thirty cal," I answered.

"I think," Hodson said, "this is the first time I've been shot at by anything that big."

While I knew gun sounds, Hodson and his torque knew the chopper. Because of changes in aircraft vibrations, changes well below my level of sensitivity to such things, they knew we'd taken a hit in the main rotor blade. Despite the hits, we continued the mission.

After kicking off the smoke at the feet of a squad of harried troopers, we stayed on-station another hour, doing what we could for the hard-pressed grunts. For an hour or more we flew in monotonous circles over the contact area. For the first and only time in my life, I almost became airsick.

We left the LOH at Buttons to be repaired in place or sling-loaded to Phuoc Vinh. Mr. Hodson was quite pleased, though he'd taken his first hit by enemy fire to his aircraft while I was aboard. "Your being with me kept me from being shot down and killed," he insisted.

The next day was Thanksgiving. As was expected, I blessed the Thanksgiving meal in the 1-9 Cav mess hall. General George Casey dined with us, sitting between Pete Booth and me. His comments and questions during the meal reflected a lot of interest in my religious support efforts and attitudes.

Following Thanksgiving activities with Apache Troop at Tay Ninh and Bravo Troop at Quan Loi, I returned to Phuoc Vinh and learned that an assignment in Germany would be mine following this tour. A letter from Germany arrived a couple of months later to inform me I would be assigned to Graffenwöhr, Germany, where my high school-age children would have to board away from home during the school season. *This assignment is not acceptable. I'll resign first. No need to weigh the pros and cons. There are no pros, not after spending 24 of the last 42 months away from James and Jeannie.* I so informed the necessary military and church officials and wrote to Helga to explain my position and intentions in the matter.

On 29 November two Bravo Troop pilots were killed when their Cobra, part of a pink team, was shot down north of LZ Buttons. The NVA also shot down a LOH as its crew fought to keep them away from the crash site until another pink team and the Blues arrived. The Blues inserted successfully and reached the Cobra in time to sustain casualties when it exploded.

This little blurb appeared in a 1st Cav newspaper, in an article titled, "Traveling Cav Chaplains Bring Church to Boonies," *Cavalair,* November 19, 1969:

> *One example of the chaplain's willingness to get out in the field with the grunt is Chaplain (CPT) Claude Newby.*
>
> *Chaplain Newby spent six months with a line company. Given a choice in rear area jobs, he selected the Airmobile 1st Squadron, 9th Cavalry -. His 'rear area' assignment still keeps him in the field most of the week.*

On December 1, I began my tenth month on this tour by conducting a memorial service at Quan Loi. From there I flew to Tay Ninh and spent the day and night with Apache Troop, which kept me away from Phuoc Vinh in the early hours of December 2, and out of a nasty and accurate mortar attack. Two 1-9 Cav troopers died and twenty-one were wounded during the barrage. One KIA, a member of Delta Troop, died when a mortar exploded directly over his cot. His room was about fifty feet from mine. I visited wounded troopers at Long Bien before returning to Phuoc Vinh.

One day in late November or early December, an obviously troubled lieutenant—Apache Blues—came to me following a worship service and said in essence, "Chaplain Newby, I used to believe in God, but I can't believe anymore."

"What brought you to this opinion?" I asked.

"This war, chaplain. If there were a God, he wouldn't allow horrors like this to happen."

The man's confusion seems understandable, provided one believes in a God whose mercy robs justice, a God with no more plans for His children than to use them in a gigantic harp orchestra. For more than an hour, I tried to help the lieutenant understand the principles of agency and consequences and how vital these are in the eternal scheme of things. But he departed sorrowing, his doubts apparently unresolved.

On December 7, Pearl Harbor Day, this same lieutenant and his Blues got into a nasty fight. Enemy fire cut both his legs from under him. When he fell his upper body wedged in the fork of a small tree, where he hung, barely alive, until the fight was over. I wonder what became of him and his crisis of faith.

A second Blues trooper took a stomach wound during the same fight. The next day, the trooper sat upright while I visited him as a nurse cauterized bleeding vessels in his abdomen. He looked good and his prognosis was fair. He died within 24 hours.

The Army tested my ears on December 8 or 9, declared me deaf in several high frequency ranges, and placed me on a medical profile that forbade exposure to loud noises! For a few days I honestly tried to avoid loud noises (combat), but I repented on December 16. *As long as I am in the Army, I will do what needs doing, profile or not,* I decided.

On December 10, I accompanied a Delta Troop platoon on an overnight operation southwest of Phuoc Vinh. We rode in vehicles to a site near a village. The vehicles returned to base and we set an ambush along the west side of a road, *right* where we were let off. To make matters worse, in my view, civilian children hung around until dark. I thought surely we would move to another location after dark; but no, we stayed exactly where the natives last saw us at twilight. The objections I expressed to the lieutenant served only to wear out my welcome. A few nights later, Delta Troop was attacked and the same lieutenant received the Purple Heart and.

In Apache Troop on December 21, almost two months after his twentieth birthday, SSG Christopher James Gray was shot down and died in a flaming crash; along with Thadius Yanika, the pilot of the scout LOH; and Barry Paul Kaletta of Ohio, door gunner.

I've said little about worship and memorial services in the past chapters. Suffice it to say I held worship services often, with more focus on Sunday than had been the case with infantry battalions. Memorial services, like the one for Yanika, Gray, and Kaletta, were held almost as often as regular worship services. My work in the 1-9 Cav left me feeling like a circuit-riding memorial service provider.

It was hard to objectively gauge the effects of memorial services on the troops. Most of the remarks by those who said anything at all suggested that the services helped a lot. Some appreciated that appropriate honors were provided to fallen comrades. Others insisted the services boosted flagging hope, even as close buddies kept getting killed.

Others said the services reawakened—or gave birth to—faith to sustain them as they faced their own mortality and the high odds that they could be next.

I was concerned, however, that memorial services on an almost weekly schedule, with the same men standing in the same formation—each man intensely aware of who was missing—might lose their effect and even become counterproductive.

Kregg Jorgenson describes one of the memorial services I conducted. "The mounted bayonet held the M-16 rifle in place in the hard-packed, orange soil. The helmet rested on the upturned butt of the rifle's stock, while a pair of polished jungle boots stood beside the rifle, forming a quiet monument, an outdoor altar.

"The battalion chaplain was reciting a final prayer.... When he finished, he looked into the faces of the soldiers who stood in formation before the memorial; somber faces, some still with adolescent acne. But their eyes made them different, they had the cold, hard stares of people who'd seen too much in too short a time.... The memorial service was more for us than it was for the fallen soldiers.

"'Take solace in that Thaddeus, Chris Gray, and Barry Kletta—'

" 'His name was Kaletta!' someone yelled from the rear of the formation as heads turned. An officer scowled at the soldier who'd interrupted the service.

"'And Barry Kaletta,' the chaplain said, carefully pronouncing the name. 'To those of you who knew them, they were special people, performing a special mission. Though I didn't know them, I don't intend to let their memory die without pausing to think of the personal sacrifice they endured—'

"'In a bull sh— cause!' someone else said.

"The ceremonies were never easy, and usually very emotional. Though the senior NCOs and officers would yell, 'At ease!' they knew they could do little to quell the feelings that arose.

"'This war is more than politics, more than duty. It is a commitment to friendship between you and those who have died. Yours is a personal war with personal tragedies and extraordinary sacrifices for that friendship. I urge you to not let those friendships or memories die in this war. Remember Tad Yanika, Chris Gray, and Barry, and remember their names and their sacrifices for you, rather than to a cause or political purpose. Speak their names and share your stories about their friendship.

"'I…I wish you safety and peace in your lives as well as in the war, and I pray to God to this end. I know that God understands and loves him who lays down his life for a friend. These men's sacrifices of life and of future on earth will weigh heavily on the side of mercy when they stand before their Creator to give an account of their lives.'

"The chaplain walked off toward the command post. His was an awkward, uncomfortable gait."

The service Jorgenson describes stands out in my memory precisely because the trooper corrected my pronunciation of Barry Kaletta's name. Though I don't recall the other interruption, I understand it very well. The word was out. American forces were pulling out of Vietnam, leaving the job undone. It is no wonder that soldiers had a hard time seeing any meaning in their own or their buddies' deaths and sacrifices.

This description reinforces my concerns that memorial services held too frequently for the same small group might become counterproductive. Imagine a family that had to endure almost weekly funerals for one of their own. How would they handle it? How would it affect their relationship with the officiator? How would the officiator handle it? Not well, I expect.

Now-retired Lieutenant General Paul Funk, who replaced Bob Hardin as Apache Troop Commander, told Colonel Booth that he lost thirty-eight men during the four months he commanded Apache Troop, compared to seven out of a whole division in Desert Storm.

The services continued in the First of the Ninth in a seemingly never-ending sequence. They had to, regardless of the difficulties involved, for the troopers and leaders wanted—needed—the chance to pay final tribute to their friends. We owed our comrades and their families that—and those soldiers were accustomed to hard things.

By the way, Jorgenson nailed me on one point. The "awkward, uncomfortable gait" he described was the result of a combat-assault injury back in January 1967. Sometimes the awkward gait became quite pronounced when things weighed heavy on my soul.

December 25, Christmas day! I spent the morning providing worship services at Phuoc Vinh, Quan Loi and Tay Ninh. In the afternoon I visited hospitals at Long Binh and Saigon. In the evening I returned to Tay Ninh because of spiritual distress I'd detected earlier in SP4 Blake.

My impression proved correct. Blake really needed to talk. He'd slumped into deep melancholy, a combination of Christmastime homesickness and remorse over how some around him observed Christ's birthday. From my journal: "Encouraged him to realize that our duty is to continue because honest people seek the light. Increased darkness will…make our light more noticeable…. Well, the muddy river [world] is now more like a cesspool. All the more reason to cast out to those who call for help." I needed my own advice. All around me were young men who daily laid their lives on the line, who honored their heritage, and who needed all the support they could get. I was so thankful at this Christmas season to be privileged to serve them as a chaplain, and to help them remember the good things they knew before the war.

In my first post-Christmas mail from home, Helga related how on Christmas she had answered the door and found Elder Marion D. Hanks and Keith Garner (former head of the Southeast Asia LDS Mission) singing Christmas carols on her doorstep. Hanks and Garner took the children shopping for clothing and gifts, including *Skittle*. The skittle game, which we still have, is a favorite of three generations of the Newby family, and a reunion tradition.

Happy thirty-third birthday to me! Happy birthday, Helga ! I celebrated my birthday on December 27th and Helga's on the 30th. *I'm now old enough to mourn, rather than celebrate birthdays.* But I still felt young and didn't dread aging. *I'll be pleasantly surprised if I have the privilege,* I sometimes thought.

While I relaxed briefly on my birthday and dreamed of wife and home, Apache Troop lost four choppers and sustained two KIAs in the Tay Ninh area. Because of the intense fighting, it took a while to find the bodies of two crewmembers. We thought they'd been captured.

That was the day a mysterious fixed-wing aircraft flying out of Cambodia fired on an Air Force plane. American fighters forced it down. I heard nothing more about it.

I celebrated the end of 1969 at Phuoc Vinh, in company with troopers David Van Outen, Harold Lewis, Russell Rinehart, Wandler, McDill and three others. We gobbled hamburgers and sodas and pretended we were ten thousand miles away. All around the base camp, troopers fired weapons into the air to welcome in the new year, the year that every one of them was due to rotate home. A few soldiers on perimeter guard even fired on an ARA gunships as it patrolled the perimeter. The shooting stopped quickly, however, when the ARA pilot radioed, "Be advised. I am receiving fire and will roll hot on its source if it doesn't cease immediately." A staff officer became very excited at the pilot for threatening to return fire. My sympathies were with the pilot.

At 2230 hours, January 3, the NVA attacked the 1-9 Cav at Phuoc Vinh with rockets, recoilless rifles, and mortars. When the attack began, I rolled under my cot and watched through the open door as rockets and recoilless shells exploded among the revetments and choppers of Charlie and Headquarters Troops. Meanwhile, several 82mm mortar shells landed squarely on and among the troops' living areas. Four rounds burst directly behind my room. Delta Troop sustained direct hits on three sleeping areas. In a December attack a mortar had crashed through a roof, killing a trooper. This time, in the exact same spot, another man was killed in the same spot as he took cover beneath his mattress. We sustained one killed and eight wounded in the attack.

The NVA shot down three 1-9 Cav choppers on January 9 and also hit the 1-9 Cav area at Phuoc Vinh. We sustained no casualties this time, though eighteen choppers were damaged on the ground. The next day I flew with LTC Clark Burnett, the new 1-9 Cav Commander. After patrolling all morning north of LZ Buttons, we ate lunch there during a rocket attack. After lunch we joined up with some pink teams and made several rocket and mini-gun dives against NVA forces that were attacking an ARVN convoy. Then, being low on everything, we headed for LZ Buttons to refuel and rearm, only to be waved off because the base was under attack. So we refueled at Duc Phong and made it back to Phuoc Vinh in time for a religious meeting at 1900 hours.

Chapter Twenty-One

A St. Valentine's
Day Massacre

About February 20, Major Hefner, the division psychiatrist, sent an LDS trooper to me for counseling. A few weeks earlier PFC Jerry Clayton had transferred out of the rangers to Charlie 2-8—part of my battalion during the 1966-67 tour. The account of what brought Clayton to me is reconstructed from his recollections and from official and unofficial documents.

On Valentine's Day, February 14, Charlie 2-8, commanded by Captain Joseph Gasker, was working with a unit of the 11th Armored Cavalry Regiment. They were operating a few klicks north of the Black Virgin Mountain. That area in Tay Ninh Province consists of large open areas pockmarked with large, irregular-shaped clumps of jungle and bamboo.

On this day, the tanks and APCs stopped in a clear area so a platoon of infantry could dismount and move through a stretch of jungle, one of several that jutted finger-like into the clearing. While the infantry moved into the first stretch of bamboo, the tanks and APCs skirted wide around it and passed beyond yet another protruding stretch of jungle. Suddenly the tanks and APCs spun around and headed the other way. The infantry platoon they'd just dropped off was in heavy contact and taking casualties.

The tanks and APCs came under small-arms and rocket fire as they approached the near side of the first stretch of jungle, opposite from where they had dropped off the platoon earlier. Quickly the ACR commander and Captain Gasker decided to reach the beleaguered platoon by charging straight through the bamboo rather than circle around the end of it again. The infantry dismounted, and the tracked vehicles charged into the jungle in two columns; knocking down everything in their path.

Apparently, in anticipation of the armored reaction, the NVA hunkered down in well-hidden bunkers and spider holes and waited for the tracked vehicles to pass over them. The charge ground to a quick halt when, within moments, the NVA knocked out a tank and two APCs, while the infantrymen lumbered over downed vegetation and struggled to keep up.

The shooting on the near side of the bamboo thicket slacked off after the charge halted, allowing the platoon that PFC Jerry Clayton was in to catch up. Soon, the point man moved cautiously forward, passing to the right of the disabled tank. He probably noted that the right front of the tank was stopped atop a bunker. A few feet past the tank, the point man came passed around a termite hill. About ten meters beyond the mound, he discovered a trail and commo wire running across his direction of advance. Platoon leader Lieutenant Gregory C. Schoper moved forward in response to a whispered message from the point. The NVA resumed firing and Schoper and two troopers fell dead even as they were examining the commo wire.

From farther back in the platoon, a trooper ahead of Clayton was hit by gunfire. Clayton reacted by running forward. "I saw the tank on my left and an APC on my right as I ran forward and went over the termite hill—not a very smart way to get past it under the circumstances. In front of the mound, I found a wounded machine gunner fighting off the NVA alone, surrounded by the bodies of the lieutenant and the two troopers," Clayton said.

After dragging the wounded machine gunner back around the mound and pushing him into waiting arms, Clayton went forward again and manned the machine gun. He was determined to hold the NVA off his buddies and the NVA seemed just as determined to take out the American and machine gun that blocked their advance. Though he now has no idea long he stood off the NVA, Clayton kept firing for what seemed like an eternity, pausing only to ram in fresh belts of ammunition that his buddies scavenged from the disabled vehicles to his rear. Clayton didn't realize he was being attacked from the rear too. The grunts back behind the termite hill saw a Chicom grenade hurtle in Clayton's direction from the partially collapsed bunker beneath the tank. They ended that threat by tossing a grenade of their own into the bunker, but not before Clayton sustained wounds to his right side and arm.

Sometime during the standoff, "[a] very brave medic crawled up to me and was tending wounds on my arm when a burst of enemy fire split open his head, killing him instantly, and spraying me with his blood. I became very scared after the medic was killed, not of dying but of dying alone. I prayed. Something, almost a voice, answered, 'You are not alone.' All fear left me then, and I kept firing because I realized that the NVA fired at me only when I paused to reload. Though the NVA and I were very close to each other, I couldn't see them or even the trail. Apparently they thought I was shooting from behind the protection of the termite hill, for their fire was high, which probably saved my life.

"That machine gun and I were one. It was as if there were nothing else in the world—just me, the gun, and the NVA," explained Clayton.

The machine gun became so hot that it burned him wherever he touched it, but, "I was oblivious to pain and everything else," Clayton recalls. He stopped shooting only when the machine gun blew up in his face. Only then did Clayton realize that he was the only grunt still alive anywhere near the termite hill and destroyed vehicles. "I *lost it* and fled wildly to the rear, with green tracers cracking all around me, my buddies told me later," Clayton said.

His wild flight ended when he broke into a clearing and came upon his surviving comrades as the last of them scrambled aboard armored vehicles to get out of the area ahead of an air strike. Clayton's buddies may have presumed him dead when the machine gun fell silent, or may have written him off. The citation for the award he would receive read, "When a platoon came under intense fire, he moved forward to lay down a heavy base of fire, enabling the platoon to move back to safety." Before withdrawing with the 11th ACR, Clayton's buddies doused him with five gallons of water to combat heat exhaustion and ease the pain of his burns. Clayton says eight Americans gave their lives in the fight. The Army Casualty Information System names

Lieutenant Schoper, eight enlisted infantrymen (MOS 11B), and two with infantry MOS 11D as KIAs on Valentine's Day.

Of this action the *Cavalair* wrote, "The firefight began on the afternoon of Feb. 14. Charlie Company, 2nd Battalion, 8th Cavalry, conducting a joint operation with 11th Armored Cavalry Regiment tanks and APC's came upon enemy bunkers 13 miles north of Tay Ninh City at 2:45....Twenty minutes later, said SP4 Ralph Branzalli, 'The tanks kept moving up....when RPG's started flying at the tanks." At the same time, the skytroopers were caught in a crossfire....The two forces maneuvered for advantage....The battle flared sporadically until 6:40, when contact finally broke. By then, 31 North Vietnamese had been killed."

For his part in the fight, SP4 Jerry Clayton was recommended for the Medal of Honor (MOH). Following medical and psychological treatment, Clayton returned to the 2-8 Cav for about a week, then became the 3rd Brigade Commander's driver; this was to keep him out of the field pending the outcome of the MOH recommendation. After the MOH was downgraded to a Silver Star, Clayton extended his tour in Vietnam six months to became a door gunner on a brigade scout chopper. He finished his tour back in the 1-9 Cav as a door gunner on a scout LOH.

In June 1970 Clayton had been selected to star in an Army documentary, but his movie career was cut short when he sustained second- and third-degree burns over most of his body. Clayton recovered and served in the Army and National Guard for twenty-five years. He resides with his wife the former Kimberley Belt at their home in Sandy, Utah.

I recall three tragic incidents that never made it into my journal. The first incident occurred back in June and the other two toward the end of my tour. In the ranger billets at Phuoc Vinh a team of LRRP rangers prepared for a mission. At least one of the rangers placed a detonator in a claymore mine—each team member carried a claymore and they always armed them before hitting the ground at the beginning of a mission, the better to set up rapid defenses, if necessary. The rangers deemed the advantages of being prepared to outweigh the dangers inherent in this risky practice. But this time the negative vagaries of war won out. There in the barracks, one or more claymore mines exploded in a rucksack and, "Three rangers died," recalls Pete Booth.

Natural human tendencies during those moments toward the *end*— the end of patrols, the last hours of the night, the end of a war—aid and bet the negative side of the vagaries of war. Around the same time that the claymore killed the rangers in their billets, a motorized Delta Troop element returned to base camp from patrolling around Phuoc Vinh. The lead vehicle mounted a 106mm recoilless rifle. The gun, a breech loader, should have been cleared before the patrol reached the gate. But with a flechette round still in the chamber, the vehicle stopped at the south gate with the gun pointed slightly off to the right, toward a quadrangle or parade field of sorts. The gunner, instead of opening the breach of the recoilless rifle from above and forward, stood directly behind it. The gun fired accidentally, spraying the division chapel and chaplain's offices with steel arrows. The back-blast blew the gunner in half and wounded the platoon leader and a sergeant who were in the jeep right behind the recoilless rifle.

From experience and such memories, I maintain that anything one can imagine happening in war will happen.

One afternoon an element of the 11th Armored Cavalry Regiment pulled a tank up to the south-gate of Quan Loi, near the south end of the airstrip. At that point the tank cannon accidentally fired a flechette round. *Down range*, to the west or left of the airstrip, about eight shirtless grunts were soaking up sunshine atop a bunker. Those men quietly fell over dead with their bodies covered on one side by small, almost bloodless wounds, entry points of hundreds of steel darts.

I conclude my chronicle of the actions, heroics, and vagaries of the war in Vietnam by recounting a tragedy that occurred in one of my former companies two years after I left the field for the last time.

By May 10, 1972, the 1st Cavalry had essentially stood down from the war. That same day, Captain Kenneth Rosenberg and his Delta 2-8 Cav troopers lifted out of the field for the last time. Rosenberg boarded a Chinook with his First Platoon (former call sign, White Skull), thirty soldiers in all, to fly to the in-country R&R center at the beachfront city of Vung Tau. The Chinook crashed en route, killing all aboard. Thus on its last day on the field of battle, Delta 2-8 lost more men than it had during the past two years of combat. The remainder of Delta Company returned to the United States a month later along with the rest of the battalion.

Chapter Notes:

26 November 1969, 1-9 Cav Journal, Summary: "A OH6A rec'd fire at 50 ft and 80 knots...took two hits and no-fly at LZ Carolyn...C Trp OH6A rec'd fire at 40 ft and 50 knots, 1 hit, no-fly at P.V.... C Trp OH6A rec fire at 50 ft and 40 knots, neg hits. Also B trp UH1C rec fire at 1500 ft and 80 knots, 11 hits, no fly at Bu Dop. A Trp had OH6a rec fire at 60 knots and 30 ft, no hits....

February 14, 1970, Army Casualty Information System, KIAs: 1LT Gregory C. Schoper ; SP4s William L. Cline, Rivera Ernesto Cuevas, Harold P. Fesperman, and Wayne D. McRay; PFCs Jerold B. Day, Joseph H. Duncan, Gary Smith, Ferdinand J. Sochurek III, Earl C. E. Tidwell Jr., and James H. Wilbanks.

May 10, 1972, from the Honor Roll, Angry Skipper web site, roster of Delta 2-8 Cav troopers who were killed in a Chinook crash on the last day of that company on the field of battle in Vietnam: Sgt. Mike John Aguilar of Compton, California; SP4 Oscar Aguilar of Fairfield, California; Sgt. William Arvel Boatright of Abbott, Arkansas; PFC Steven Edward Bowersock of Lima, Ohio; Sgt. Edward Denzel Burnett of Jay, Oklahoma; PFC Clint Edwin Carr of Alexandria, Louisiana; SP4 Dennis Guyman Dunning of Raymond, Mississippi; SP4 David Cruz Flores of Agana, Guam; Sgt. Deiter Kuno Freitag of Ft. Dix, New Jersey; Pvt. James Douglas Groves of Marysville, Kentucky; PFC Dale Lamont Hayes of Detroit, Michigan; SP4 William Frederic Henaghan of Bethpage, New York; SP4 Frank Theodore Henson of Massapequa, New York; SP4 Donald Edward Howell of Los Angeles, California; SP4 Freddie Jackson of Cocoa, Florida; SP4 Thomas Allen Lahner of Eau Claire, Wisconsin; Captain Kenneth Rosenberg of New York, New York; PFC David Allen Lydic of Johnstown, Pennsylvania; SP4 Gary Robert Monteleone of Saugus, California; PFC Dean Anthony Phillips of Tiro, Ohio; Sgt. James Christian Jensen of

Elsinore, Utah; Pvt. Jackie Ray of Jackson, Mississippi; SP4 Richard Ridgeway of Bloomington, Illinois; Pvt. Errain Rivera-Agosta of Sabana Grande, Puerto Rico; PFC John Tenerio Sablan of Agana, Guam; SP4 Clarence L. Saulsberry Jr. of Chicago, Illinois; SP4 Raymond Joseph Shiko of Kingston, Pennsylvania; Sp4 David Wesley Sulser of Galion, Ohio; and PFC Thomas Eugene Wood of Tacoma, Washington.

Chapter Twenty-Two

PEACE WITHOUT HONOR

It was my last day with the 1st Air Cavalry Division. General Casey's jeep stopped near where I was saying goodbye to Division Chaplain (LTC) Charles F. Powers, his staff and several others. On impulse, and perhaps contrary to protocol, I jogged over to General Casey, saluted, and informed him of my admiration for his demonstrated leadership and care for the troops.

General Casey graciously accepted my compliments, said he regretted I was leaving so soon, and promised he'd be watching my great future in the Army. He and all aboard his C&C helicopter gave their lives a few months later. He went down in the Central Highland mountains during a trip to Cam Ranh Bay to visit his troops in the hospital.

⚔

SP4 Bill Ellis, a trooper in Bravo Company 1-5 Cav during 1968-69, composed ballads about the grunt's life. Jim Miller, Public Information Officer for the Third Brigade, *discovered* Ellis as the latter was singing and strumming a guitar during one of the company's rare breaks at a "VIP" Center like the one at Quan Loi. Before he knew it, Ellis was pulled away from his buddies to sing for all the troopers in the 1st Cav AO. Probably, Ellis' most popular ballad was about the civilian charter airplane that took veterans home. "Freedom Bird," he called the ballad. Ellis cut a record of his ballads for the 1st Cavalry Division, on condition that each sky trooper then serving in the division would get a free copy. My copy is a choice treasure to my wife, children, and me.

On March 2, 1970, I boarded a *freedom bird* and left Vietnam for the last time—a day late, sad, and tired but without personal regrets for the way I served. My first tour had started slowly and ended with a bang. This tour began with a series of gigantic bangs and petered out during the last couple of weeks. In 1967 I had returned to an America where patriotism was still somewhat in vogue. Now, in 1970, I returned to an America where both patriotism and America's heroic young soldiers were increasingly held in disdain. Where in 1966-67 and early 1969 infantrymen were infantrymen without regard to race or color, by 1970 even they showed evidence of succumbing to civilian and rear-area trends, of dividing into *us* and *them*.

Leaving the 1st Cav for the last time was difficult. Staying would have been harder. It was especially hard to leave while the grunts and aircrews continued to die, for nothing anymore but one another, betrayed by their civilian leaders. Gone was much of the unit cohesion and esprit of 1966-67, with the exception, perhaps, of the 1-9 Cav— and esprit was suffering there. Staying longer would have been torture because I couldn't bear to watch this slow *death*, at least not without a break.

In September 1967 my colonel had *thrown* me out of the field to go home. The men, the war, everything had pulled at me. Only as I drew nearer to home could I let go for a little while. Now, in 1970, I just went home, hurting for those I left behind, dead and alive, but having to go.

Psychologists speak of combat veterans and others suffering from survivor's guilt, feelings of having let their fallen buddies down. Well, for a long time I thought I had escaped survivor's guilt. I knew about *survivor's surprise* and *survivor's gratitude*, but felt no guilt, or so I believed. I was wrong. In part, this work and its predecessor, *It Took Heroes*, are products of that guilt, my way of apologizing in a sense to men who died while I lived.

This might seem strange coming from a former chaplain, but I cringe when I hear someone boastfully attribute his survival to God's recognition of his prayers and those of his family, as above the prayers of another family. I know that men fell in battle whose families, present or future, needed them as much as mine needed me. I know that men fell whose hopes were buttressed by the prayers of loved ones as faithful and righteous as mine. Yet I laid my life on the line as a sacrificial offer and lived to pick it up again, while others laid their mortal lives down for keeps. Why them and not me?

Of this I am certain: God in His loving and incomprehensible way can and sometimes does intervene to deflect bullets. He always answers prayers, and always from His higher perspective.

In His great love and wisdom, our God understands that though many heroes survived Vietnam, few of them can escape. So perhaps I survived precisely because of my ability to remember. Perhaps God allowed me to come home to pay tribute to the heroes, to help others understand the horrors of war, and to chronicle the unsung heroism of so many of America's best and brightest of the era who stepped forward when their country called. Perhaps I lived to provide a bit of healing balm to the veterans whose inescapable suffering would increase with the passing of decades, and to the loved ones of some that never returned.

Fortunately I was, and am, keenly aware of the advantages and privileges of coming home when so many others didn't. I'm very blessed to be physically whole when so many are maimed and mangled, to be mentally and emotionally functional, and to have my faith in God intact. So many became emotional and spiritual basket cases—others just as deserving and capable as me. I'm grateful I could return and father a seventh child, Daniel Bryan, who in turn has fathered two grandchildren for me thus far. So many young men gave their all, leaving not even posterity behind to remember them and carry on their name or their line. I'm left feeling eternally grateful to God, to my family, and to those heroes that paid so much more than I did.

That I came home was consolation in years to come after chaplains replaced line officers in the efficiency rating scheme and career advancement slowed. How could I complain? I came home from the *wars* at least.

Only after many years and the writing of these books did I fully awaken and realize that I returned from Vietnam an alienated man in many respects. I was alienated from the Army for policies, like six-month commands in combat that all too often deprived soldiers of experienced officers. I was alienated from civilian leaders who sent us off to war with our hands tied and later welcomed home the draft dodgers before expressing thanks to the faithful who served. I was alienated from the American people who participated in or tolerated public abuse of its faithful sons and daughters, and from the whole system for pursuing "business as usual" while heroes suffered faithfully, and died. I was alienated from myself for feeling relieved to be going home while so many grunts, medics, scouts, pilots, dog handlers, rangers, green berets, artillery men, and others remained behind. But *I'd* be okay, though the images, smells and feelings of wars in Vietnam would linger, perhaps forever.

For me, perhaps the most difficult adjustment to peacetime life had to do with the pace of events. Life in *the world* was agonizingly slow after two years of living on the fine edge between mortality and eternity. Time in *real life* seemed to stand still after two years of repeatedly living lifetimes in minutes. Civilian life was surely just as different for the former infantryman coming home, cut off from his buddies, both living and dead. He was disdained by peers and constrained by *rules of life* that hadn't applied in combat. He had to endure each day, perhaps in a boring job or no job, facing and dealing with people who didn't—couldn't—understand. Many of these people judged him and refused him work because of his *employment history* the past year. Undoubtedly returning from war was easier for me than for the infantryman. But I never escaped without scars.

There was a lot to adjust to besides the maddeningly slow pace of postwar life and tales of returning soldiers being spat upon and called baby killers. Some of the events most difficult for me to adjust to included the pardoning and welcoming home of draft dodgers in 1974; the fall of South Vietnam in 1975; and the deployment in 1990 of the First Cavalry Division to Desert Shield and Desert Storm— without me. I had a hard time, too, on most of those occasions when protocol forced me to mingle in social gatherings.

Eventually I volunteered for a third tour in Vietnam, in an attempt to assuage my mixed feelings. "Request denied."

Colonel Rasmussen would call in 1973 and ask me to join his staff at the US Army Sergeant Majors Academy. That did not work out because the people in the Office of the Chief of Chaplains had other plans for me. He called again in August 1974 from Fort Carson, Colorado. I was at Fort Ord, California. "One-Niner? This is Motors [short for General Motors] Six." He wanted me to be his brigade chaplain. Again, the chaplain branch didn't cooperate. The next to last call came from his brigade chaplain, a Catholic priest. He said in essence, "Please come to Fort Carson as soon as you can. Colonel Rasmussen has suffered a severe heart attack, and Mrs. Rasmussen would like you at his side."

I took leave and hurried to Colorado, only to find Ron conducting a brigade staff meeting from his bed in the cardiac intensive care unit. In counseling with Ron's wife, I discovered in her the source of much of Ron's greatness.

The last call came the day after I left Colorado. "The colonel suffered another heart attack and did not survive. Mrs. Rasmussen and the commanding general of Fort Carson request that you return and deliver the funeral sermon," said his brigade chaplain, as I recall. The funeral and that very difficult duty, willingly performed, occurred in the Fort Carson Post Chapel on October 4, 1974.

At the conclusion of the funeral service, a strikingly attractive woman introduced herself to me. The lady was one of those heroic souls that waited for the man that never came home—the widow of General George Casey.

Helga and I were at a conference in early April 1975 when the South Vietnam forces crumbled and the NVA and Vietcong stormed into Saigon. The news was full of pictures of Vietnamese clamoring to board departing American helicopters, of choppers being pushed into the sea to make room on American ships for "withdrawing" forces and refugees. Sensing, sharing, the turmoil I was experiencing, Marion D. Hanks greeted Helga and me. "I thought you'd be swimming to Saigon." He seemed to understood what I was going through.

Another tragic image was on our minds, that of a USAF C-5 transport aircraft that crashed soon after lifting off from Saigon with a load of Vietnamese children. "We might try to adopt some Vietnamese orphans," we said to Chaplain Robert Cordner and his wife Karen at dinner that evening.

Hearing this remark, Elder Boyd K. Packer, a high ecclesiastical official, said, "No, you don't want to do that. That part of your life is behind you, and it is time for other things." We heeded his counsel.

The events I describe in *It Took Heroes* and this book involved America's best and brightest as they served in great units. Mine were but five of scores of combat battalions. The heroics and actions I describe were occurring—and would continue to occur—to greater or lesser degrees at any given time across Vietnam and throughout the war. I was but one of hundreds of chaplains serving and witnessing these faithful, heroic Americans as they answered the call of their friends and neighbors, even when those neighbors seemed to turn on them.

I'm sustained by memories of great men, and strengthened by the belief that they appreciated my service to them. I'm glad I went to serve the draftee soldier who in most cases, knowing what he knows now, would go again. He would go because someone would have to take his place if dodged his lawful duty—even to die in his stead. He could neither value his doubts—which were as real as those of the protestors and politicians—above the life of another, nor his own life above personal responsibility. I served the regular-Army soldier who went to Vietnam again and again because he'd vowed to obey lawful orders, and that was his duty, as he saw it. I believe many of us at ground and air level went to Vietnam in part for altruistic reasons. I don't accept that the results disproved the domino theory that was in vogue then in some circles. For example, communists nearly took over in Indonesia. Instead the non-communists prevailed—in great part because American forces were in the area. Perhaps historians will someday realize the Vietnam War marked the high-water mark for communism's expansionist plans to bury America and dominate the world—that things would have turned out very differently for the world, had American blood not been sacrificed with honor in the jungles, rice paddies, deltas, and mountains of Vietnam.

At the conclusion of the *peace* talks in Paris, an American military officer said to his North Vietnamese counterpart, "American forces won every time on the battlefield."

"That is irrelevant. We won the war," said the NVA officer.

The American officer was correct and the NVA officer only partly so. Communist forces didn't win victory in the war. Rather, America grew tired of the infringement of the war and its protestors on their consciences via the nightly news. Her civilian leaders ceded an unearned victory to North Vietnam in the pursuit of a so-called *peace with honor* that was neither.

Chapter Twenty-Three

Invisible Heroes

Look around you, children of the World War II and Great Depression generation. Search carefully and you will find three kinds of true, almost invisible heroes walking in your midst.

You will not be able to see the first type of hero, except as he is reflected in the eyes and demeanor of the other two. He is the hero who never returned from the terrible wars of the twentieth century, or who came home in a metal box. He is very real, but invisible to all but a very select few—family members who grieve still and buddies who accompanied him through the carnage. The memories of him dim each time a loved one or former comrade-in-arms passes from the mortal stage. Those who keep track of such things say that some twelve hundred World War II veterans die each day, taking their stories and memories with them.

The second type of hero is visible to all, but seen by very few. He goes successfully about the daily pursuits of life as farmer, janitor, banker, and clergyman. He is the retired person fishing along a river bank. This hero survived the war but cannot escape it. He can't forget the carnage or erase the ethereal presence of buddies who fell around him. He suffers quietly as he re-experiences things that none should have to endure. Frequently he flashes back to those anguished last moments when death entered the face of a buddy by his side, or in his arms, or in his place.

Mostly this hero succeeded in taking up his life where he left off when he responded to his friends' and neighbors' call and marched away to war. Though we all see him moving in our midst, few recognize him for the true hero that he is.

Although the actual percentage is small, far too many combat veterans, especially those of the Vietnam War, find the memories unbearable. Some remain trapped in a 1960s stunted growth stage booby trapped with drugs and alcohol, and littered with shattered relationships. You'll find many of these sad heroes on the streets and in our prisons. Others of them, often the most heroic in combat, escape into seclusion or suicide.

This second hero, almost to a man if he saw combat in Vietnam, yearns to understand: "Why do I feel guilty for doing what you selected me to do on your behalf? Or if I'm not guilty, why did you take so long to begrudgingly welcome me home? To assuage this hero's longing—need—to feel welcome at home, he often greets a fellow Vietnam veteran with "Welcome home!" and a firm handshake and probably a hug.

Freddie Owens of Knoxville, Tennessee, is a good representative of these invisible heroes. Freddie, a friendly, outgoing former sergeant, has been deeply involved in the leadership of the 5th Cavalry Regiment Association since its inception in the early 1990s. But his memories and grief overcame him after thirty-five functional and successful years. On August 6, 2000, he wrote me: "The battles in Nam…will not escape your mind, but I had to bring those memories back to start my life all over. Ia Drang and Bong Son were hellholes as those of us who were there can attest. I [just] spent six long weeks in therapy trying to put some of those memories in perspective, and have finally gotten some inner peace. I never had the opportunity to say 'good-bye' to some of my dearest friends who lost their lives alongside of me in battle, but I finally did. …Cannot make the reunion at Fayetteville because the doc says it's too early to converge with the crowds."

The third type of hero, certainly making up the largest and probably the bravest group, includes the families of those who served. Their lot was hardest because while their loved one served, they wondered and worried, seldom knowing just what he endured. Even when their soldier had a chance to relax, they couldn't because they had no way of knowing. Because it took time for the word to reach them, these heroes often continued to pray for the safety of a son, husband, or father for days after he fell dead or wounded. Many of these heroes on the home front endured the brunt of anti-war protests and disdain with nowhere to escape.

Barbara Conrad and her children and grandchildren represent these heroes. Barbara, the widow of SP5 (Doc) Andrew Conrad, resettled her family in Flint, Michigan, following his death. None welcomed her there. "My neighbors resented me because my husband was killed in Vietnam. Our daughter, Cynthia (Cindy), the oldest of three children and ten at the time, still suffers from being taunted at school because, 'Your Daddy was stupid enough to get his head blown off in Vietnam.' Andrew did volunteer for Vietnam. We were stationed in Japan in 1967, where he tended the steady stream of wounded guys pouring into the Army's 249th Station Hospital. Often, Andy brought guys home with him, those who were recuperating and getting ready to return to combat. Andy volunteered for combat duty in Vietnam because of these experiences, over the objections of loved ones. Then he gave his life trying to reach wounded soldiers on a terrible *hell*-top called LZ Pat. Stupid? No! Noble and extremely heroic? Yes," avowed Barbara Conrad. Barbara wrote the following poem the day she received notification that her husband had been killed in action (used with her permission):

You've gone ahead before us,
To well earned rest,
Having given to this life
Your very best.

There's a private place, Darling,
Where you'll never depart.
And there you're very much alive—
It's a special corner of my heart.

You volunteered for combat,
Leaving the children and me,
You went to help the battle
To keep other people free.

I know, could we turn back the years,
You would do it all again,
In your quiet gentle manner
You died helping your fellow man.

You won't go down in history books
Or ever remain immortal.
But I know God said: "Well done,
My son," when you entered Heaven's portal.

So in my own way, Darling,
I've written this remembrance to you—
No one here can know how much
I miss you—
But I somehow feel you do.
I love you,

—Babbie

You will do well, America, to seek out the heroes among you. Find them, especially those among your own kin, and sincerely welcome them home. Help them to feel what they probably know but haven't heard very clearly—that the guilt of a nation and its politicians, if such there is, belongs not on their once-young and faithful shoulders. In his book, Tom Brokaw called your great-grandparents—those who endured the Great Depression and shouldered the burdens of World War II—the *Greatest Generation*. Most of the unsung veterans of Korea and Vietnam are true sons of the greatest. They are America's sons, who honored the legacy left them.

Chapter Twenty-Four

A BENEDICTION FOR HEROES

My first objective in writing *It Took Heroes* and *It Took Heroes, Part II*, was to pay tribute to heroes in the field and on the home front. Second, I wanted to help others understand what they called you to do, what sacrifices were demanded of you, and how faithfully you performed your duty. I wanted your fathers and grandfathers, veterans of other wars, to know that you always fought to the end and never surrendered as a unit, no matter the overwhelming odds against you. Naturally I also desired to preserve our mutual history for my posterity and yours.

In appreciation for your efforts, I hoped to provide aids in these books to help you find answers to your questions. What happened after you or a buddy or both of you fell, or disappeared into the medical evacuation system. I wanted to help you, the gold-star mother, to identify others involved in the action that your son gave his life in, to help you find solace and answer questions that next-of-kin telegrams and official reports did not always address to your satisfaction. To these ends, these books contain the best descriptions that I could manage, along with chapter notes and an extensive index of names. Veteran, these tools may help you find a buddy when all you recall is his face, nickname, shared experiences, and how important you once were to each other.

As your former chaplain, I desire to bless you one last time. I want you to know that I know that, no matter your faith or lack thereof, there is a God in Heaven who loves you and knows what you endure. As a son or daughter of the "Greatest Generation," you inherited a mantle of responsibility and a sense of duty to country, which values prompted you to swim against the growing tide of public opinion and to fight rather than to flee.

I'm certain that a loving and just God smiles very favorably upon you for making an honorable, value-based choice to go and do service that required you to "lay down [your] life for a friend." That same loving God understands the great courage and sacrifice involved when a parent, spouse, or child surrenders a loved one to the sacrificial altar of service. If it were possible, I would wipe pain and irrational guilt away with a word. I can't do that, but I assure you, as one who knows, that you have paid the price long enough.

Fellow veterans and families, heroes, we've endured the darkest hours, the worst of the vagaries of war and the aftermath. We don't have to stay "down there" forever. Former Captain Lou Niles reminded me that, "To every thing there is a season, and a time for every purpose under the heaven...a time to kill, and a time to heal; a time to break down, and a time to build up...a time of war, and a time of peace" (Ecclesiastes 3:1-8). You fought when you had to. You returned home and helped build. Now it is time to heal and to let yourselves be healed. To this end, I offer these words of prayer and sacred hymn by Jeremiah E. Rankin (1828-1904):

"God be with you till we meet again; by his counsels guide, uphold you; With his sheep securely fold you. God be with you till we meet again...When life's perils thick confound you, Put [God's] arms unfailing round you, God be with you till we meet again...Keep love's banner floating o'er you, smite death's threatening wave before you. God be with you till we meet again."

To each of you, whichever type of hero you are, "The Lord bless thee, and keep thee. The Lord make his face shine upon thee, and be gracious unto thee. The Lord lift up his countenance upon thee, and give thee peace" (Numbers 6:24-26). Amen.

GLOSSARY

A/C	Air Craft, also Air-craft Commander
Air Cav:	Air Cavalry; 1st Cavalry Division, Airmobile
AK-47:	Letter A in Army phonetic alphabet, as in Alpha (A) Company
Alpha 2-8:	Thus used, *Alpha* refers to company, the numbers to the battalion and regiment the company belongs to
AO:	Area of Operations
APC:	Armored personnel carrier, light skinned, tracked vehicle used as mount for various weapons and to transport troops
ARA:	Aerial Rocket Artillery
Area Support:	Army principle whereby certain assets are provided across unit lines, for example legal services and religious-denominational assets
Arclight:	B-52 strategic bomber strike (raid); carpet bombing of an area one-quarter- mile wide by one-mile long; often ineffective because enemy had advance warning—USAF registered B-52 flights with international agencies favorable to Hanoi
Arty:	Abbreviation for Artillery
ARVN :	Army of the Republic of Vietnam
AWOL	Absent without official leave
B-40:	Rocket propelled grenade. A nasty weapon used by the NVA and VC against armor and personnel
Barrier:	Primary base defenses; used at the An Khe Base Camp, 1965-68
Battery:	Basic unit of Artillery, persons, guns and equipment; comparable to a Company in non- artillery organizations
Beehive:	An artillery round containing steel flechettes, or tiny steel arrows; see Flechette round
Berm:	Earth barrier around defensive perimeters and bunkers
BF Goodrich:	Footwear cut from car tires and worn frequently by NVA and VC soldiers; also called Ho Chi Minh sandals
Bird:	A helicopter; see chopper, LOH, Cobra, snake and Gunship
Bubble:	OH-13, a light observation helicopter; a deathtrap that was replaced by the LOH
Blues:	Infantry rifle platoon, one-each in each Air Cav Troop in the 1st Squadron, 9th Cavalry - ; member of Blues
Bravo:	Letter B in Army phonetic alphabet

C-Ration:	Individual Combat rations
C-47:	Fixed wing cargo air craft, see Chinook Helicopter
C-130:	Air Force Hercules Transport Aircraft, see also C-133 and Caribou
CA:	Combat Assault; also *Charlie Alpha*
Cav:	(1) The 1st Cavalry Division (The Cav); (2) Troopers of the division; 3) Infantry battalions in the division; 4) First Squadron, 9th Cavalry (the "real" Cav, as its members referred to the unit)
C and C:	Command and Control; also, *Charlie-Charlie*, the Commander's command and control helicopter
Call Sign:	Radio call sign name for units in the field; also identified commanders, leaders and staff at each echelon when followed by a number, as in Fence Post (Charlie Company 1-5 Cav) and Fence Post-6 (Company Commander)
Canister:	Rounds containing steel ball bearings for tank and artillery cannon, and the M-79 grenade launcher,
CG:	Commanding General
Caribou:	CV-2, a light cargo aircraft, capacity about 32 persons
Charlie:	Letter C in Army phonetic alphabet; short for Viet Cong
Charlie Model:	Huey chopper used primarily as gunship, replaced by Cobra
CONUS:	Continental United States
Chieu Hoi:	Vietnamese for "Open arms," a program to entice enemy soldiers to change sides in the war
Chinook:	CH-47 tandem-rotor transport helicopter; also, *Hook*
CIDG:	Civilian Irregular Defense Group; home guard; Natives recruited to serve with US Special Forces
Chopper:	Helicopter; see Huey, LOH, Cobra, Snake, Gunship and *bird*
Claymore:	Anti-personnel mine. American, spews our hundred of steel balls in a fan-shaped arc, lethal at fifty meters
Close Air Support:	Airforce operations in support of ground forces (see also Danger Close Support)
Clover Leaf:	Pattern utilized to keep friendly patrols from accidentally engaging each other in combat
CO:	Commanding Officer, also Conscientious Objector
Cobra:	Nickname for the AG-1G helicopter Gunship; also, *Snake*
Combat Trains:	Battalion forward support site, usually on a firebase during the Vietnam war; see Field Trains
Company:	Basic unit of Infantry and other non-Artillery, persons, weapons and equipment; usually with between one and two hundred men—Infantry companies, about one hundred and forty
CP:	Command Post

CS:	Tear gas
Daisy Cutter:	Ten thousand-pound bomb used by USAF to cut instant landing zones in thick jungle
Danger Close:	Fire support against enemy positions that creates a serious risk of danger for nearby friendly forces. Danger-close support is any fire is delivered by friendly land and sea-based aircraft, and by land and sea-based artillery. By it's nature, Danger-close requires special procedures and care
Delta:	Letter D
Det-cord:	Explosive fuse-like cord used to explode multiple charges simultaneously
DivArty:	Division Artillery, may mean headquarters or all artillery organic to the Division
Division:	The major maneuver element of the Army, ranging in strength (during Vietnam era) from eighteen to twenty-four thousand personnel
Door Gunner:	Machine gun operator on a helicopter
Echo:	Letter E
EM:	Enlisted man (men); later, EP for enlisted persons
EPW:	Official designation for captured enemy prisoners, more commonly called POWs
FAC:	Forward Air Controller; an officer who direct air strikes while flying in his own aircraft
Field Trains:	Rear-support area, usually located at a major base camp; see Combat Trains
FIX:	To entrap or confine an enemy so he can be destroyed
Flagpole:	Jargon for a position under the direct influence and/or sight of a commander, at echelons above companies
Flare:	Illumination device (noun); or the landing attitude of an aircraft (verb)
Flechette:	Small steel arrows or darts in canister or beehive shells
FO:	Forward Observer. Usually artillery officers attached to infantry companies to call and adjust artillery fire; also an individual members of mortar platoons in support of rifle platoons
FOB:	Forward operating base for an infantry company, often used interchangeably with NDP (night defensive position) earlier in the war
Fougasse:	"Home-made napalm used for defense around American fire-bases
Frag:	Fragmentation grenade (noun); part of an operational order or *frago* (verb); criminal act of attacking one's own leaders in a war zone, usually by hand grenade, but the term expanded to

	include other attacks against one's own leaders during the Vietnam War
Friendly Casualties:	American and allied persons that become killed, wounded, or captured. By enemy or friendly action
Friendly Fire:	Munitions of all types fired by American and allied forces, having nothing to do with relational qualities
FSB:	Fire Support Base; usually a battalion-size operational base which included the battalion combat trains, TOC and a battery of howitzers; also, officially called an LZ prior to mid-1969, and unofficially after that
Full Metal Jacket:	Standard, copper small-arms bullet, intended to wound and kill without messing up the body the way as soft-nose munitions do
GI:	Term for American soldier, carried over from World War II
Gook:	Derogatory word some American soldiers used to refer to the enemy. It is used in this book only in direct quotations, and then only when necessary to the action being described
Greenline:	The generic term for the outer defensive ring of bunkers, wire, towers, etc., at most base camps
Grunt:	American Infantryman; popularly believed to have arisen from the infantryman's grunting as he hoisted his heavy rucksack
GSW:	Gun shot wound
Hotel:	The Letter H
HE:	High Explosive ammunition
Hoi Chanh:	VC or NVA soldier that joins South Vietnamese; see Chieu Hoi
HQ:	Headquarters
Huey:	UH-1 utility helicopter. Also, *HUEY*
Hump (verb):	*Maneuver by* foot, tactical march or patrol by dismounted soldiers. May have derived the large, heavy rucksacks that infantry and LRRPs carried, reminiscent of a camel's hump
H-13:	Light observation helicopter, a two-seat bubble with fuel tank right over the crew's head, a firetrap; replaced by the LOH
In-country:	Military phrase (jargon) meaning physically present in Vietnam
In-process *(verb):*	Military phrase meaning to process into a new unit or onto a military installation
IO:	Information Officer; also PIO (Public Information Officer)
KIA:	Killed in Action
Kit Carson Scout:	Former VC or NVA who served as scout for American units in the field
Klick:	Kilometer, slang
Leg:	A non-airborne infantryman; also called a *straight leg*
LNO:	Liaison Officer

LOH:	Light Observation Helicopter, used primarily as a scout bird
LP:	Listening Post, usually two men placed in front of friendly forces to listen for approaching enemy under cover of darkness. See OP
LRRP:	Long-range Reconnaissance Patrol member or team, Member of ranger company such as H Co. 75th Rangers that was attached to 1-9 Cav, 1st Cav Division; also called LRRP
LZ:	Landing Zone; any place used for aircraft to land, once or more times. See also PZ and FSB
MARS:	Pre-internet/e-mail system by which soldiers call loved ones
M-1:	Clip fed, semi-automatic rifle, WW II and Korean vintage
M-14:	U.S. Caliber 7.62-mm, predecessor to M-16, and in use in Vietnam
M-16:	U.S. Caliber 5.56-mm, the basic US forces assault rifle
M-60:	U.S. Caliber 7.62-mm machine gun; platoon and company weapon, also used on Hueys and Armored Personnel Carriers (APCs)
M-72:	LAW (Light Anti-tank) weapon. HE round fired from a throw-away tube; used in Vietnam to attack bunkers
M-79:	40-mm grenade launcher, breech-loaded, shoulder-fired
Machine gun:	Crew-served automatic weapon
MACV:	Military Assistance Command, Vietnam; commanded advisors, special operations, etc.
MG	(1) Machine gun; (2) Major General, two stars
Medevac:	Aerial medical evacuation, 1st Cavalry term
Medic:	Medical Aid man; also, affectionately called *Doc* by many troopers
Mike force:	Mercenary strike forces, frequently Cambodians, led by American Special Forces; also called MSF and *strikers*
Mini-gun:	Multi-barreled machine gun with firing rates of 2,000 and 4,000 rounds per minute, every fourth round a tracer
NDP:	Night Defensive Position, used interchangeable with FOB or forward operations base, especially in 1969
Net:	Short for radio network. All tactical radios operated within a defined network on a designated frequency
OER:	Officer Efficiency Report
OP:	Observation Post; usually one or two men posted in front of friendly forces to watch for approaching enemy during the daylight; see LP
OPCON:	Operational Control
Pace man:	Individual designated to keep track of a unit's location in the trackless, featureless jungle
Palace Guard:	Relatively safe duty protecting base camp from attacks

Picket Line:	The defensive area several kilometers beyond a base camp barrier line or perimeter; also, Rocket Belt
Pink Team:	Two-helicopter team, Cobra Gunship and LOH scout helicopter
Point:	Person or element in the lead during movement, also called point man
Police *(Verb):*	To clean up or search an area
PX:	Post Exchange, on base store for military people
Popular Forces	Local Vietnamese Force (PF)
POW:	Prisoner of War
PRC-25:	FM radio, back-packed; basic communications for nearly every level of command within the division
Prep:	Short for preparation of an LZ by artillery, ARA and, occasionally, by air strikes
Prone Shelter:	One-man position; shallow, body-length trench used frequently early in the war in place of foxhole
PSP:	Perforated sheets of steel that joined together to provide a runway for fixed-wing aircraft; also used to reinforce overhead cover on bunkers
Punji Stake:	A small sliver of bamboo, stuck in the ground and in punji pits to impale "enemy" forces; sometimes tipped with feces and other matter to cause the wound to fester; Used by VC forces
PZ:	Pickup zone, temporary site where choppers pick up soldiers, as opposed to a place to drop them off (LZ)
Rocket Belt:	The area around a target from which rockets can effectively be fired at it
QRF:	Quick Reaction Force, usually a platoon or company, sometimes a larger unit which might be designated a reserve force
Quad:	Four guns, M-60 machine guns, 40-mm launchers, etc., configured to fire together
R&R:	Rest and Relaxation leave
Recoilless:	Called a rifle, but more like shoulder of vehicle mounted and fired artillery, recoilless because a dangerous back blast when fired equalized forward blast to prevent *kicking*
Recon:	Reconnaissance
Reconstitution:	Operations to rebuild a fighting unit, to reconstitute its numbers, material, readiness, stamina, morale and spiritual, etc.
Roger:	Formerly, the letter R, and radio language for "yes" or "affirmative." Grunts often shortened it to "Rog" or "That's a Rog"
Rome Plow:	A standard D7E tractor, equipped with a heavy-duty protective cab and tree-cutting blade. Rome-plowing was carried out to deny the enemy sanctuary by removing jungle and to enhance base defense by clearing around bases

RPD:	Soviet 7.62-mm machine gun (NVA)
RPG:	Soviet 82-mm rocket-propelled antitank grenade; used by NVA as an antipersonnel weapon; see B-40
RTO:	Radio Telephone Operator
RVN:	Republic of Vietnam
S/A	Small arms or small-arms fire
Sandwich:	One who wore patch of 1st Cavalry Division on both shoulders, signifying a being in combat with unit previously to current tour
Sapper	Soldier (originally an engineer) who attacks fortifications. VC and NVA used sappers extensively and effectively
Satchel	Explosive package fitted with a handle for ease of handling Charge and throwing; favorite weapon of the NVA sapper
Sitrep:	Situation report
SIS:	Soviet carbine
Spider Hole:	Small, easily concealed NVA and VC foxholes
TOC:	Tactical Operations Center
Torque:	Crew chief/door gunner on a scout LOH, credited with being one of the most combat- effective positions on the Vietnam battlefield
Tracer	Bullet that burns as it moved from a weapon toward impact, leaving a *trace* of fire in its wake. Our tracers burned red, NVA tracers burned green
Tube Arty:	Tube artillery. Also, field artillery and Naval guns
USAF:	US Air Force
USARV:	US Army Vietnam
Vagaries:	Unpredictable manifestation , action, or outcome
VC:	Viet Cong, also Vietcong, Victor Charlie or Charlie
WIA:	Wounded in Action
XO:	Executive Officer, "first officer" at echelons below division
37-mm:	Soviet anti aircraft weapon, electronically aimed and fired
40-mm:	Projectiles or rounds for the M-79, for a four-barrel launcher, and launchers on gunships
51-Cal MG:	Heavy machine gun favored by NVA forces
82-mm:	Medium size mortar favored by Communist forces in Vietnam
90-mm:	Recoilless rifle, shoulder-fired *artillery*
105-mm:	Field artillery piece and/or shell
107-mm:	Recoilless rifle, often jeep mounted; Also, rocket used by the NVA for stand-off attacks
122-MM:	Heavy "artillery" of the NVA forces

311

INDEX